The National Curriculum and
the Early Years

I

2

154720

/

The National Curriculum and the Early Years:
Challenges and Opportunities

Edited by

Theo Cox

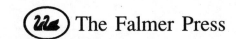 The Falmer Press

(A member of the Taylor & Francis Group)
London • Washington, D.C.

UK   The Falmer Press, 1 Gunpowder Square, London, EC4A 3DE
USA   The Falmer Press, Taylor & Francis Inc., 1900 Frost Road, Suite 101, Bristol, PA 19007

First published in 1996

A catalogue record for this book is available from the British Library

Library of Congress Cataloging-in-Publication Data are available on request

ISBN 0 7507 0601 5 paper

Jacket design by Caroline Archer

Typeset in 10/12pt Times by
Graphicraft Typesetters Ltd., Hong Kong.

Printed in Great Britain by Biddles Ltd, Guildford and King's Lynn on paper which has a specified pH value on final paper manufacture of not less than 7.5 and is therefore 'acid free'.

Contents

Contents

Acknowledgments

The University of Wales Swansea Study entitled 'The Impact of the National Curriculum on the Teaching of 5-Year-Olds', findings from which are reported in Chapters 2, 6 and 8, was funded by the University of Wales Faculty of Education. The author of these chapters, Theo Cox, would like to thank the Director of the LEA in which the study was carried out for his permission to carry out the study. Special thanks are due to the head teachers and Year 1 class teachers of the participating schools for their cooperation with the research at a time when they were fully occupied in meeting the demands of the National Curriculum and other changes stemming from the 1988 Education Reform Act.

In addition Theo Cox would like to thank the staff at the University of Wales Swansea Education Library for their unfailing helpfulness in locating and obtaining various publications. He also wishes to record his appreciation of the encouragement, support and patience of his wife, Angela, throughout the preparation of this book.

List of Tables

1   Introduction and Overview

Theo Cox

The National Curriculum

The passing of the Education Reform Act (ERA) in 1988 marked a strikingly inter-
ventionist phase in government policy compared with the post-war decades, characterized by central control of the content of the curriculum across the 5 to 16 age
range in state-maintained schools. This was coupled with a deliberate weakening of
the power of local government in educational matters through the enforced delega-
tion of responsibility for management and budgeting to the schools themselves. The
political agenda driving this legislation seemed to be based upon a belief, at least
in part, in the power of market forces to drive up educational standards and a
distrust of the influence of the educational establishment as 'trendy theorists', and of
LEAs in the practice of education in schools (see Chitty, 1992 and Carr and Hartnett,
1995 for analyses of this political context).

The National Curriculum was introduced in September 1989 to the nation's
5-year-olds at the beginning of Key Stage 1 after a barely notional period of prior
consultation with teachers and others. The core foundation subjects of English,
mathematics and science (and Welsh in Welsh medium schools in Wales) were
introduced at first, soon to be followed by the non-core foundation subjects[1] of
design and technology, information technology, history, geography, art, and music
and physical education, during the following four years. Thus the brunt of the first
phase of the new National Curriculum programme was borne by early years teachers. The pressures imposed on these teachers by the speed of implementation of
such a complex curriculum structure and its associated assessment requirements
were compounded by a series of ongoing changes to the curriculum or its assessment just as teachers were getting used to them (see Barber *et al.*, 1996 for a critical
account of the government's handling of the construction and implementation of
the National Curriculum). The bewildering and demoralizing effect on Key Stage
1 teachers of this heavily overprescriptive curriculum and the rapid subsequent
changes to it have now been well documented (see for example, Pollard *et al.*, 1994
and Cox and Sanders, 1994).

The accumulated and overwhelming evidence for the sheer unmanageability
of the National Curriculum in the form that it was introduced at Key Stages 1 and 2
(see for example, OFSTED, 1993), led the government to commission a wholesale
review of it in 1993, led by Sir Ron Dearing, with the aim of streamlining and
simplifying it. Sir Ron consulted widely in the course of this review and produced

an interim report in 1993 and a final report in 1994. In these he recommended a slimming down of the National Curriculum, especially in the non-core subjects, so reducing its prescriptiveness, and a reduction and simplification of the programme for national assessment. His recommendations were accepted by the government and led to a review of all National Curriculum subjects by the newly established curriculum and assessment body for England, the School Curriculum and Assessment Authority (SCAA), and the Curriculum and Assessment Authority for Wales (ACAC) respectively. In the words of a DFE publication (undated) the aim of this curriculum subject review was to focus the curriculum requirements on the core essentials for each subject, to improve their manageability, and to give primary school teachers more time to concentrate on the basics. A further aim was to set higher standards for the National Curriculum particularly in the basics of English, maths and science.

This subject by subject review was carried out in the Spring term 1994 with the support of advisory groups of teachers and others representing the various subjects and also groups representing each key stage and children's special educational needs. The proposed new subject orders were then put out for wide ranging consultation in England and Wales during the Summer of 1994 and, following these, the final recommendations of the two curriculum bodies were made toward the end of the year. The government accepted these and the orders for the revised National Curriculum came into force on 1 August 1995 for Key Stages 1 to 3. Also, in keeping with Sir Ron Dearing's recommendations, a five-year moratorium on any further major change to the National Curriculum was declared with the aim of ensuring that teachers should enjoy a period of stability in which to implement it.

Whether the revised National Curriculum and its assessment will achieve the government's main objectives of reducing teacher workload, enabling primary teachers to concentrate more on teaching 'the basics', and freeing up to 20 per cent of school teaching time for discretionary uses remains to be seen. The responses so far received to a follow-up written questionnaire sent in 1996 to the head teachers and Year 1 teachers in the Swansea University Impact Study described in Chapter 2 indicate that they had not noticed any significant reduction in teacher workload following the revision of the National Curriculum. Some of them commented that even the revised curriculum was still too prescriptive and overloaded in content, making it difficult to teach the basic skills in the necessary depth.

The Early Years

There is a good deal of variation in usage of the term 'early years'. At its broadest it covers the years 0 to 8 years, for example in the context of primary initial teacher training courses (DES, 1990). In other contexts however the term is confined to the years 0 to 5, the so-called 'pre-school years', although these have now been re-named the 'pre-compulsory school years' to avoid the confusion caused by the fact that a high proportion of 4-year-olds in England and Wales attend reception or mixed age infant classes in LEA maintained schools (SCAA, 1996). The usage in this book is the widest, i.e., 0 to 8 years although some contributors focus on particular age groups within this range.

Underlying these differences in usage of the term is the issue of whether it makes educational or psychological sense to think of the years 0 to 7 or 8 as a single broad phase as the Early Years Curriculum Group (EYCG, 1989) and the Early Childhood Education Forum (see Chapters 10 and 12) advocate, or whether it should be restricted to the years 0 to 5 or 6. The starting age for compulsory schooling is not a very reliable guide in this respect for the Plowden Report (Central Advisory Council (England) 1967) states that the choice of 5 as the starting age for compulsory schooling in England and Wales was made almost by chance in 1870,[2] and in most other European countries the starting age is 6 or sometimes 7 years. The Plowden Report recommended that compulsory education should begin for children in the September following their fifth birthday (which would mean a median starting age of $5\frac{1}{2}$ years), to be followed by three full years of education in a 'first school' and transfer to a 'middle school' at an average age of $8\frac{1}{2}$ years (Central Advisory Council for Education (England), 1967, Para 386). Prior to compulsory school entry children should receive part time nursery education if their parents wished it. These recommendations were never implemented nationally although a number of first and middle schools were created in England.

Two researchers at London University Institute of Education, Moss and Penn (1996) argue that, to avoid undue pressures from the National Curriculum upon 5-year-olds, the age of compulsory education should be postponed to 6, with the ages 0 to 6 being regarded as the first stage of education. Similarly Gillian Pugh, Director of the Early Childhood Unit at the National Children's Bureau urges that there should be an overall national policy for the care and education of children from birth to 6 years (Pugh, 1996).

Despite these differing views regarding the span of the early years there is much to be said for the view adopted in this book that the broad principles of early childhood education (see in particular Part 3 of this book) should apply to the full 0 to 8 range, even though compulsory schooling in England and Wales, and now the National Curriculum, start at age 5. However, *within* this broad span, it also makes sense to focus upon the distinctive educational, social and care needs of particular age groups of children, notably 0 to 3, 3 to 5 and 5 to 7 which are the age phase groups of the Quality in Diversity project described in Chapter 12. For example the Early Childhood Unit of the National Bureau is currently conducting a research and development project on the learning needs of children under 3 with the aim of exploring staff development and training models. The age range 3 to 5 years has traditionally been thought of as the nursery school stage in Britain, with its own distinctive curriculum and strongly play-based approach to learning but now, in the context of the government's nursery voucher initiative, the focus is upon the educational needs of this age group across the full range of educational and care settings to be found in Britain (see Chapters 10 and 12). The years 5 to 7/8 have not only constituted the traditional infant stage of British education but now, of course, cover Key Stage 1 of the National Curriculum.

In fact the introduction of children *under* 5 to Key Stage 1 of the National

Curriculum appears to be officially sanctioned in a recent guide to curriculum planning at Key Stages 1 and 2 published by SCAA (1995) and written with the help of primary teachers. This states that, while the revised National Curriculum at Key Stage 1 has been designed to be taught and assessed within a period of six terms (i.e., 5 to 7 years), schools may choose to spread their teaching of this curriculum over a longer period and thus cover aspects of the National Curriculum with reception classes *if they judge this appropriate to the needs and stage of development of the children* (my emphasis). The guide goes on to say that there should be continuity between the curriculum for under-5s, and the Key Stage 1 curriculum. The possible dangers of a premature introduction of the more formal subject knowledge and skill requirements of the National Curriculum to such children, and the nature of the continuity between the National Curriculum and the curriculum for under-5s are discussed in the present book.

The Impact of the National Curriculum in the Early Years

The National Curriculum and its apparatus of national assessment has been perceived by many early years practitioners as threatening to some of their fundamental professional values, beliefs and practices. Anning (1995) describes how, prior to its introduction, certain right wing politicians and educationists attacked and even derided what they perceived as the weaknesses of child centred education, in particular the play-based approach to learning. As she says the value systems which underpinned the ERA, such as quality assurance, value for money, preparation for employment and, one might add, competition between providers, clashed with the value systems of early years practitioners which:

> ... emphasised the value of play as a powerful vehicle of learning, the importance of the social and emotional needs of the child, the significance of physicality and first hand experiences, the need to develop literacy and numeracy as tools for learning and the importance of fun and enjoyment in motivating young children to want to learn. (Anning, 1995, p. 4)

Anning goes on to outline some ways in which the ERA reforms have affected three interrelated aspects of education at Key Stage 1, namely curriculum, assessment and pedagogy and these headings are adopted in the following discussion of the impact of the National Curriculum in the early years.

Curriculum

As pointed out in an earlier publication (Cox and Sanders, 1994) the specific subject orientation of the National Curriculum contrasts with the view in the Plowden Report that for young children only the broadest divisions of the curriculum are suitable and even older primary school children should not be exposed to 'rigidly defined subjects' (para 538). Plowden's suggested broad divisions were however broken down further in a curriculum model for children aged 5 to 16 put forward by HMI (DES, 1985). This proposed the following 'areas of learning and experience':

- aesthetic and creative;
- human and social;
- linguistic and literary;
- mathematical;
- moral;
- physical;
- scientific;
- spiritual; and
- technological. (DES, 1985, para 33)

These areas were not suggested as discrete elements to be taught separately in isolation from one another and were not equated with particular subjects, although it was acknowledged that some subjects would contribute more to some areas than others. Many would support this focus upon areas of learning experience in planning the early years curriculum rather than the separate subjects traditionally associated with the secondary curriculum. Indeed it is the approach adopted by SCAA in its recent (1996) publication on desirable outcomes for children's learning on entering compulsory education. While only six areas of learning are listed (see Chapter 10) these can easily be mapped onto the HMI classification outlined above.

The National Curriculum not only imposed a subject specific model upon primary schools traditionally geared to broader areas of experience but its prescriptive subject knowledge requirements posed a very strong challenge to the cross curricular integrated approach to curriculum planning through project or topic work which prevailed in them. It should be acknowledged however that the areas of mathematics, English (reading) and physical education were often taught in a more subject specific fashion in primary schools long before the National Curriculum was introduced. Under this pressure there at first appeared to be a shift towards more subject focused topic work at Key Stage 1 (Cox and Sanders, 1994) and towards more subject specific teaching (Pollard *et al.*, 1994). However more recent evidence indicates that the cross curricular topic work approach still prevails in primary schools at this stage (see Chapters 2 and 5 and OFSTED Chief Inspectors' annual report for 1994–5, OFSTED, 1996a).

The National Curriculum subject requirements also exposed weaknesses in primary teachers' own subject knowledge and expertise, particularly in those areas such as science, technology and aspects of history and geography which had not previously been taught, or at least not taught with any depth or rigour. The latest OFSTED inspection evidence (OFSTED, 1996b) indicates that in 1994–5, the inadequate level of teachers' subject knowledge constituted a serious problem in one school in eleven at Key Stage 1 and in only one school in five at this key stage were there no serious weaknesses in this respect. The report comments that, partly because of the small size of many primary schools, and because of the imbalance in the subject background of the teachers, only a minority of schools are staffed by teachers who, between them, have the subject expertise necessary to cover all the subjects in the basic curriculum when such expertise is defined in terms of the teachers' main subjects or first degree qualifications. Other studies highlighting some primary teachers' limitations in their understanding of certain subject knowledge are reported in Chapters 3 and 5.

On the question of subject balance across the curriculum there is good evidence that primary schools, including reception and infant classes, have traditionally tended to place a heavy emphasis upon the teaching of the basic skills of literacy and numeracy (Cox and Sanders, 1994; Pollard *et al.*, 1994). The reduction in curriculum content in the revised orders for the non-core foundation subjects and the increased emphasis in the revised National Curriculum upon the teaching of the basic skills might well have the effect of exacerbating this traditional curricular imbalance. Indeed the OFSTED reports for 1994–5 (OFSTED, 1996, a and b) describe an over concentration upon core subjects and skills in some primary schools at the expense of giving sufficient time to the non-core foundation subjects (see Chapter 8 for a further discussion of this question in relation to children with special educational needs).

Assessment

Although the National Curriculum assessment system originally proposed by the Task Group on Assessment and Testing (TGAT) (DES, 1988) put its emphasis upon formative assessment in which the results would provide teachers with a basis for decisions about pupils' further learning needs (see Shorrocks *et al.*, 1993), the system now in place puts far more emphasis upon summative or 'snapshot' assessment which takes place at the end of each key stage. The results from these assessments will provide the basis for the publication of the highly controversial Key Stage 2 performance tables announced by the government, commencing with the 1996 (Key Stage 2) test results in England and the 1997 (Key Stage 2) test results in Wales. As described in Chapter 6 the Standard Assessment Tasks (SATs) which were intended by the TGAT group to act as calibrating devices to ensure common standards of judgment among teachers and, also to act as training devices to help teachers to develop their professional assessment skills, are now being replaced by more formal pencil and paper tests which more readily provide 'hard data' for public reporting and accountability purposes.

At the same time the government is now turning its attention to the possibilities of systematically assessing the attainments of 5-year-olds on entry to compulsory education in connection with its new nursery voucher scheme. The DFEE (1996) document entitled *The Next Steps* states explicitly that the government considers that SCAA's (1996) desirable outcomes provide a suitable basis for developing baseline assessment at the start of compulsory education and has commissioned SCAA to carry out a survey of current practice in, and views on, such assessment which will feed into a formal consultation exercise to be mounted later in 1996.

(See Gill Harper Jones' discussion of baseline assessment in Chapter 7.) A strong possibility is that the data yielded by such assessments will be used either by the government and/or by primary schools themselves for the purpose of carrying out 'value added' analyses of their educational input, especially if the assessment results come from some form of standardized testing.

Such a development could threaten the character of early years education as one of the dangers of conducting value added analyses is that summative assessment takes on a 'high stakes' character and may threaten to narrow the curriculum as teachers focus more sharply upon the curricular content sampled in the tests. In her study of the impact of National Curriculum assessment at Key Stage 1 (see Chapter 6) Gipps *et al.* (1995) found that in 1992–3 there was more attention in schools to the basics of spelling, handwriting and mental arithmetic, which could be attributed, at least in part, to the influence of the end of key stage tests/tasks. More recent evidence in support of this prediction comes in the latest OFSTED inspection evidence (OFSTED, 1996b). The report for 1994–5 states that the implementation of tasks and tests for statutory teacher assessment at Key Stages 1 and 2 is beginning to affect curricular planning and teaching in a significant number of schools. Some of the effects are beneficial, i.e., causing schools to give greater thought to the curriculum and how it can be taught (especially in science), but, on the negative side there was some narrowing of the curriculum content in those schools and a concentration on core subjects at the expense of the non-core foundation subjects. Clearly children's entitlement to the full National Curriculum is under real threat where teachers feel impelled to concentrate even more on the basic skills of the core subjects.

Pedagogy

The basic principles of early childhood education put forward by the EYCG (1989) include an emphasis upon the value of intrinsic motivation leading to child initiated learning and the importance of learning through first-hand experience. Although play as such is not specifically mentioned in these principles other documents give it some prominence, including the Rumbold report on the quality of education offered to 3- and 4-year-olds (DES, 1990) and, more recently, the consultation document published on desirable outcomes by the Curriculum and Assessment Authority for Wales (ACAC) in 1996. The latter not only sets out a set of principles for the education of nursery aged children but also endorses the importance of play in children's learning and of adult involvement in it.

Research carried out to date on the impact of the National Curriculum upon pedagogy in the infant classroom has found that teaching has become more firmly teacher directed, with some reduction in children's free play opportunities, and less flexibility in curriculum planning to take advantage of children's spontaneous interests (see Cox and Sanders, 1994, Pollard *et al.*, 1994). Evidence regarding its impact upon the learning experiences of children under 5 is less substantial although there was some indication from the Swansea University Impact Study of a reduction of play and activity based teaching for these children, in some schools at least, under the formalizing influence of the National Curriculum (see Cox and Sanders, 1994 and Chapter 2 in the present volume). Also in the present volume Gill Harper Jones (Chapter 7) and Tricia David (Chapter 11) warn of the pressures to formalize the broad curriculum for under-5s that could stem from recent government initiatives such has the proposed baseline assessment at age 5 and their heavy current stress upon the direct teaching of the basic skills.

In a survey of educational practice in a sample of local authority nursery centres Sylva *et al.* (1992) found that most of the nursery workers believed that many of the attainment targets specified in the National Curriculum could be reached by some of their children. More worrying was the fact that even targets which the authors judged to be incompatible with good nursery practice because they required formal teaching were viewed by at least one or more of the respondents as compatible with their practice. Despite this the authors concluded that, although well aware of the potential threat to the traditional nursery curriculum posed by the National Curriculum, most of the staff felt that they had taken from it what was compatible with their customary practice and avoided aspects which they felt were inappropriate for young children.

Reports based upon HMI or OFSTED inspections of educational provision for under-5s do not provide any conclusive evidence regarding the impact of the National Curriculum upon the quality of teaching and learning experiences of these children. An HMI report on under-5s in the infant classroom carried out in 1990–1 (DES, 1992) states that fears that the introduction of the National Curriculum would result in the 'force feeding of under-5s with inappropriate work' had proved unfounded. It expressed the view that early years teachers now had more certain knowledge of what would be taught at Key Stage 1 and were better able to plan a balanced programme for under-5s. Against this the findings of an HMI survey of provision for under-5s in Wales during 1994–5 gave some indication of possibly adverse knock-on effects on the teaching and provision for these children in some schools or classes, particularly reception and mixed age infant classes (Office of HM Chief Inspector for Wales (OHMCI) 1995).

The report stated that there was a growing concern among the early years teachers to prepare children appropriately for the National Curriculum, for example through assessing their progress in specific areas of the National Curriculum core subjects. In some cases this concern led to children being offered experiences which were unsuited to their stage of development and for which they had not been prepared adequately. The report also commented that in around one fifth of schools, mainly those where under-5s were taught in classes containing school aged children, there was not enough close observation of 3- and 4-year-olds during their play and other practical activities, with the result that the teachers lacked the information necessary to enable them to set appropriate targets and provide effective teaching for them. The assessments carried out by these teachers tended to be narrowly focused upon skills linked to the National Curriculum requirements.

On the other hand some of the head teachers and class teachers in the Swansea University Impact study reported in Chapter 2 clearly felt that children under 5 who were developmentally and educationally ready for it benefited from the intellectual challenge of working alongside older children following the National Curriculum in small mixed age classes.

The OHCMI report just cited also found that the general quality of teaching and provision for children aged 4 to 5 tended to be poorer in mixed age infant and in infant reception classes than in nursery schools and classes, which is very much in line with earlier inspection and research findings (see Cox and Sanders, 1994 for a brief review of these). About one fifth of the teachers in the units surveyed, especially in reception and mixed age infant classes, needed to update their professional skills to help them to cater more effectively for the children's developmental needs and capabilities. In about one quarter of such classes a distinction tended to be made between play and work, with children being allowed to 'play' as a reward for finishing their 'work', which consisted of table based activities in language and mathematics. In these classes resources for play and other practical activities were not effectively integrated into the daily routines and not enough use was made of them to enrich and extend the children's learning. In fairness the report also points out that the adult–child ratios and resources available were more favourable in nursery schools and classes than in the reception and mixed age infant classes.

In his annual report for 1994–5 (OFSTED, 1996a) the Chief Inspector for England, Chris Woodhead comments that teachers should expect more of their pupils in all key stages but his main criticisms of teachers' methodology seem to be aimed particularly at Key Stages 2 and 3. Features of better teaching which he identifies include the effective use of exposition, instruction and direct teaching and the sensitive use of questioning to involve pupils and deepen their thinking. He also advocates an appropriate balance between whole class, small group and individual work in the classroom and the use of ability grouping to help achieve a match between pupils and tasks, as well as the use of other adults in the classroom.

While some of the elements of teaching method advocated by Woodhead should be perfectly acceptable to early years practitioners the thrust of his comments is toward that of very firm teacher direction and control of children's learning environments. For example, while acknowledging the high priority given in nursery schools to the development of pupils' personal and social skills and the attention given to early literacy and numeracy, he states that there is scope for more direct teaching of reading and number in such schools. In contrast the report of HMI on under-5s provision in Wales referred to earlier (OHMCI, 1995) adopts a more open-ended stance as regards the relationship between the teacher and the pupil. Best teaching practice for this age group, observed in around 50 per cent of classes is described as follows:

> . . . teachers give as much attention to children's play and other practical experiences as they do to the direct teaching of key skills and concepts during more formal activities. All aspects of work are carefully planned and prepared for, and efficient use is made of space, materials and equipment to support teaching. Almost all of the teacher's time is spent directly with individuals or small groups of children. (OHMCI, 1995, p. 10)

The contrast between the two models of teaching described above underlines the challenge facing early years teachers working within the context of the National Curriculum. It is also reflected in the different perceptions of the nature and purpose of the curriculum for under-5s that emerged between some head teachers in the Swansea University Impact Study (Chapter 2). Teachers have to strike the right balance in curriculum planning to ensure both breadth and an adequate grounding in the basic skills, and an appropriate balance between the provision of child centred learning opportunities and the use of more firmly structured and directed approaches, taking full account of the ages and developmental status of the children they teach. Further, through the careful and sensitive use of formative assessment and recording they must try to achieve a good match between the teaching/learning tasks set and the child's learning needs at the time. In the case of Year 1 and 2 teachers these records will contribute toward the children's end of key stage assessments (see Chapter 6).

At Key Stage 1 teachers must also strike the right balance between subject specific and cross curricular forms of teaching and learning. The advice offered in the curriculum planning document for Key Stages 1 and 2 mentioned earlier (SCAA, 1995) seems sound on this question. It states that schools will need to decide which aspects of the curriculum are best suited to single subject teaching and which should be combined. Such decisions should not be based upon a 'general, unchallenged adherence to a single approach' but should take account of a range of considerations, including the nature of the various aspects of the curriculum, the teaching techniques and classroom organization used, teachers' subject knowledge and expertise and the resources avalable. The guide is neutral on the question of the merits or deficiencies of the different approaches to the organization of the primary curriculum. Important pedagogical and other issues concerning subject specific teaching are discussed in Chapters 3 (Maynard) and 4 (Sanders) of this book.

Challenges and Opportunities

The position of the authors of this book is that the demands of the National Curriculum and the ERA and the potential threats they pose to traditional early years educational philosophy and practice present a strong challenge to the professionalism and flexibility of practitioners, particularly those working with children in the 3 to 8 year age range. The main demands of the National Curriculum at Key Stage 1 can be summarized as follows:

1   Teaching a broad entitlement curriculum spanning ten subjects (eleven in Wales), plus religious education, which emphasizes children's cognitive understanding, knowledge and skills relevant to those subjects;
2   Teaching the basic skills of literacy, oracy and numeracy with the expectation that most children will reach at least Level 2 in the key aspects of those skills assessed at age 7;

3 The management and administration of an assessment and record keeping system which tracks children's progress in learning the core subjects during this stage and culminates in the summative assessment of the children's attainments in these areas at age 7;
4 Identifying and meeting the educational needs of children with special educational needs within the framework of the Code of Practice and the National Curriculum in ways which honour their legal entitlement to a broad and balanced curriculum;
5 Where relevant, ensuring that children under compulsory school age who are being taught alongside children at Key Stage 1 experience a curriculum appropriate to their age and developmental level.

At the same time the National Curriculum also provides them with an unprecedented opportunity and stimulus to focus and explicate their thinking, and to raise the standards of their teaching to the benefit of their children. Two of the major gains from the introduction of the National Curriculum have been the provision of a curriculum planning framework for the age range 5 to 7 and a shift in the context in which teachers work in primary schools from one of relative independence and isolation to one of collegiality, collaboration and shared responsibility, often spanning the whole age range from the nursery years to age 11 (see Chapter 2). These developments should help early years educators to achieve some continuity in curriculum planning for the 3 to 7/8 age group in a way which preserves their educational principles and avoids the dangers of formalizing and narrowing that curriculum.

In this volume our authors have put forward some positive suggestions and strategies and frameworks to help early years teachers and practitioners to achieve this continuity. In their positive spirit these contributions are in keeping with the views of some of the teachers in the Swansea University Impact study who felt that, after teaching the National Curriculum for over five years, they now felt confident enough to meet its requirements in ways which preserved their fundamental educational values and practices, especially with regard to the teaching of children under 5.

The book is presented in three parts. In Part 1 we present the views of primary teachers and parents about key aspects of the National Curriculum and discuss how the changes recorded might affect future educational practice. Theo Cox outlines the findings of the Swansea University study of the impact of the National Curriculum at Key Stage 1 as judged by teachers themselves. Trisha Maynard describes how a small group of primary teachers gradually changed their attitudes towards subject knowledge and found ways of reconciling subject centred and child centred approaches to teaching. The chapter by Felicity Wikeley discusses issues raised by parents in response to the National Curriculum in the context of a research study of their views. This revealed their desire to be involved in their children's education in active collaboration with teachers.

Part 2 of the book explores selected pedagogical, curricular and assessment issues. Susan Sanders discusses the extent to which teachers of early years pupils have moved from the traditional cross-curricular approach toward more subject focused teaching and explores ways in which the current tensions for early years teachers between the subject knowledge requirements of the National Curriculum and their traditional beliefs and practices might be resolved. Drawing upon research and other findings, including the Swansea University Impact Study, Theo Cox outlines the main developments in National Curriculum assessment and record keeping and the impact that these have had upon teachers' thinking and professional practice. Key questions about the future forms of assessment are discussed in the light of the recent revision of the curriculum. Gill Harper Jones provides an overview of recent developments in the baseline assessment of children at age 4 to 5 and the political and educational context of these developments. She discusses the important issues raised by this controversial topic. Theo Cox discusses the impact of the National Curriculum and its assessment upon the teaching of children with mild or moderate special educational needs in ordinary primary schools, within the context of the new Code of Practice. This draws upon research and inspection findings, including the Swansea University Impact Study.

Part 3 of the book contains four chapters which explore ways in which high quality education can be achieved for children within the full early years range (0 to 8) in ways which accept the statutory demands of the National Curriculum but attempt to reconcile them with the principles of early childhood education held by the authors. Drawing upon international early years practice Mary Jane Drummond argues that early years teachers must place a proper value upon play and learn to communicate this effectively to others. Christine Pascal discusses the requirements of a high quality curriculum for 3 to 5 year olds within the wider context of the National Curriculum and describes how the Effective Early Learning Project, of which she is the Director, is designed to help to achieve such a curriculum within a wide variety of pre-compulsory school settings. Writing from an international perspective Tricia David considers the impact of the National Curriculum and other related government initiatives upon provision for the under-5s, raising the issues of the purposes of early childhood education and the education and training needed by early years educators if they are to achieve these. Finally Vicky Hurst, Director of the Quality in Diversity Project, discusses how this project aims to improve and develop educational provision for children throughout the 0 to 8 age range by providing a conceptual framework through which all early years practitioners can work. Based upon developmental principles this framework can accomodate the National Curriculum but gives full weight to children's emotional and social needs and to their distinctive ways of learning.

Notes

1 Strictly speaking these subjects are described in the Act as 'non-core' subjects since all of the National Curriculum subjects, including the core subjects are foundation subjects. Usage throughout this book will vary between 'non-core subjects' and the widely popular use of the term 'foundation subjects'.

2   For a fascinating account of how the Parliament of the day came to reach this decision see Szreter (1964).

References

ANNING, A. (Ed) (1995) *A National Curriculum for the Early Years*, Buckingham, Open University Press.

BARBER, M., WOODHEAD, C. and DAINTON, S. (1996) *The National Curriculum: A Study in Policy*, Keele, Keele University Press.

CARR, W. and HARTNETT, A. (1995) *Education and the Struggle for Democracy*, Buckingham, Open University Press.

CENTRAL ADVISORY COUNCIL FOR EDUCATION (ENGLAND) (1967) *Children and their Primary Schools: Vol. 1: The Plowden Report*, London, HMSO.

CHITTY, C. (1992) *The Education System Transformed: A Guide to the School Reforms*, Manchester, Baseline Books.

COX, T. and SANDERS, S. (1994) *The Impact of the National Curriculum on the Teaching of Five Year Olds*, London, Falmer Press.

CURRICULUM AND ASSESSMENT AUTHORITY FOR WALES (ACAC) (1996) *Desirable Outcomes for Children's Learning before Compulsory School Age: A Consultation Document*, Cardiff, ACAC.

DEPARTMENT FOR EDUCATION (DFE) (undated) *Final Report on the National Curriculum and its Assessment: The Government's Response*, London, DFE.

DEPARTMENT FOR EDUCATION AND EMPLOYMENT (DFEE) (1996) *Nursery Education Scheme: The Next Steps*, London, DFEE.

DEPARTMENT OF EDUCATION AND SCIENCE (DES) (1985) *The Curriculum 5 to 16*, London, HMSO.

DEPARTMENT OF EDUCATION AND SCIENCE (DES) (1988) *National Curriculum Task Group on Assessment and Testing: A Report (The TGAT Report)*, London, HMSO.

DEPARTMENT OF EDUCATION AND SCIENCE (DES) (1990) *The Report of the Committee into the Quality of the Educational Experience Offered to 3 and 4-Year-Olds: Chaired by Mrs Angela Rumbold, CBE, MP (The Rumbold Report)*, London, HMSO.

DEPARTMENT OF EDUCATION AND SCIENCE (DES) (1992) *Education in England 1990–1: The Annual Report of HM Senior Chief Inspector of Schools*, London, DES.

EARLY YEARS CURRICULUM GROUP (EYCG) (1989) *The Early Years and the National Curriculum*, Stoke on Trent, Trentham Books Ltd.

GIPPS, C., BROWN, M., McCALLUM, B. and McALISTER, S. (1995) *Intuition or Evidence? Teachers and National Assessment of Seven-Year-Olds*, Buckingham, Open University Press.

MOSS, P. and PENN, H. (1996) *Transforming Nursery Education*, London, Paul Chapman.

OFFICE FOR STANDARDS IN EDUCATION (OFSTED) (1993) *Curriculum Organisation and Classroom Practice in Primary Schools: A Follow-up Report*, London, DFE Publications Centre.

OFFICE FOR STANDARDS IN EDUCATION (OFSTED) (1996a) *The Annual Report of Her Majesty's Chief Inspector of Schools: Standards and Quality in Education 1994–5*, London, HMSO.

OFFICE FOR STANDARDS IN EDUCATION (OFSTED) (1996b) *Subjects and Standards: Issues for School Development arising from OFSTED Inspection Findings 1994–5: Key Stages*

1 and 2: A Report from the Office of Her Majesty's Chief Inspector of Schools, London, HMSO.

OFFICE OF HER MAJESY'S CHIEF INSPECTOR FOR WALES (OHMCI) (1995) *Report by Her Majesty's Inspectors: A Survey of provision for Under-Fives in the Playgroup and Maintained Sectors in Wales (1994–5)*, Cardiff, OHMCI.

POLLARD, A., BROADFOOT, P., CROLL, P., OSBORN, M. and ABBOT, D. (1994) *Changing English Primary Schools?: The Impact of the ERA at Key Stage One*, London, Cassell.

PUGH, G. (1996) 'Teething troubles', *Times Educational Supplement*, 17 May, p. 10.

SCHOOL CURRICULUM AND ASSESSMENT AUTHORITY (SCAA) (1995) *Planning the Curriculum at Key Stages 1 and 2*, London, SCAA.

SCHOOL CURRICULUM AND ASSESSMENT AUTHORITY (SCAA) (1996) *Nursery Education: Desirable Outcomes for Children's Learning on Entering Compulsory Education*, London, SCAA.

SHORROCKS, D., FROBISHER, L., NELSON, N., TURNER, L. and WATERSON, A. (1993) *Implementing National Curriculum Assessment in the Primary School*, London, Hodder and Stoughton.

SYLVA, K., SIRAJ-BLATCHFORD, I. and JOHNSON, S. (1992) 'The impact of the UK National Curriculum on pre-school children's practice, some "top–down" processes at work, *International Journal of Early Childhood*, **24**, pp. 41–51.

SZRETER, R. (1964) 'The origins of full-time compulsory attendance at five', *British Journal of Educational Studies*, **13**, pp. 16–28.

Part 1

Teachers' and Parents' Views

2 Teachers' Views on the National Curriculum

Theo Cox

This chapter presents the findings of the Swansea University Impact Study on the views of head teachers and Year 1 class teachers concerning various aspects of the National Curriculum. The study was carried out in 1994, just prior to the major review of the National Curriculum. The findings are related to those from other research studies and consultations. Some conclusions are drawn and some educational issues raised.

Introduction

Since teachers are the key agents in the implementation of the National Curriculum it is important to discover their collective views about it and to keep track of these over time. It is true that, in the course of making revisions to the National Curriculum, the government, through its curriculum agencies, the School Curriculum and Assessment Agency (SCAA) and the Curriculum and Assessment Agency for Wales (ACAC), has consulted teachers and others, from time to time, most recently in connection with the major revision of the National Curriculum in 1994. However the resulting publication of the results of these consultations is done in a summary fashion and the samples of teachers and others responding are not necessarily representative. For this purpose independent research studies are necessary. This chapter presents selected findings from a longitudinal study of the views of a sample of teachers drawn from a particular LEA in South Wales about the impact of the National Curriculum on the teaching of 5-year-olds and these are related to other findings.

The Swansea University Impact Study

The study, carried out in the Spring and Summer terms 1994, was a follow-up phase to an original study of the impact of the National Curriculum on the teaching of 5-year-olds carried out from 1989 to 1991, i.e., during the initial stage of the introduction of the National Curriculum into primary schools. Both the initial and follow-up phases of the study were funded by the University of Wales and carried out in the Department of Education at University of Wales Swansea. The findings of the original study were published in 1994 (Cox and Sanders, 1994). For convenience the study, in both phases, will be referred to as the 'Swansea University Impact Study'.

The Original Study (1989–91)

This was based on a random sample of twenty-six primary and infant schools (approximately one school in five) drawn from an LEA in South Wales. The sample was judged to be representative of the LEA schools in terms of size, ranging from fewer than 100 pupils, and social catchment area, middle class to lower working class. The geographical area of the study was predominantly urban but included some rural areas containing well established village communities. Two of the schools were voluntary aided, with the rest being state-maintained schools. In two schools teaching was through the medium of Welsh at Key Stage 1, one of them being an officially designated Welsh medium school. In both of these schools Welsh was taught as a core subject, rather than a non-core (foundation) subject, as in the remaining schools.

The views of the head teachers and Year 1 class teachers, i.e., those teaching classes containing children in Year 1 of the National Curriculum (aged 5 to 6 years), were gathered by means of structured interviews carried out in the schools by the Project's research officer, an experienced primary teacher. These were based upon questionnaires, with separate versions for the head and class teachers respectively. Interviews were conducted during the Summer terms of 1989 and 1990, i.e., spanning the first year of the implementation of the National Curriculum, and the teachers in the sample were asked to complete a short written follow-up questionnaire in the Summer of 1991. In 1989 the sample comprised twenty-six head teachers and thirty-one class teachers.

Full details of the findings of this study can be found in Cox and Sanders (1994), but the main conclusions were as follows:

1 While there was a general welcome for the clear planning framework provided by the National Curriculum this was offset by their widespread concern at the overloaded curriculum, with the sheer number of attainment targets threatening the depth and quality of the children's learning;

2 Teachers of Key Stage 1 of the National Curriculum reported a significant increase in their workloads following the introduction of the new curriculum and a strong feeling of being under pressure to meet the many attainment targets relevant to their pupils. This pressure may be adversely affecting the teaching of slower learners and children under 5 because of a reduction in their opportunities for play-based, experiential learning;

3 The assessment and record keeping requirements of the National Curriculum were a major focus of the concerns of the class teachers and head teachers alike because of the demands they made upon the time and managerial skills of class teachers at the expense of their teaching time. This

deep concern was coupled with the view of the majority of teachers that the formal assessment of children's educational attainments at age 7 was educationally unsound;

4   Teachers' use of cross-curricular topic based work changed over the period of the research. Topic work became more structured to take in as much of the National Curriculum as possible. Topics also became more focused with a trend toward science led topics. There was also something of a move away from cross-curricular work even at Key Stage 1.

Follow-up Study (1994)

It was decided to carry out a follow up to the original study in 1994, five years after the introduction of the National Curriculum at Key Stage 1 in order to monitor any possible changes in the views of the teachers about the working of the new curriculum. Twenty-three of the original twenty-six schools agreed to take part, providing a sample of twenty-three head teachers and thirty Year 1 class teachers. Of the twenty-three head teachers ten had taken part in the original study but only nine of the thirty class teachers had done so. As before the teachers' views were gathered through structured interviews based upon questionnaires circulated to the schools beforehand. The interviews were carried out by the present writer.

At the time of the study the full range of eleven National Curriculum subjects was being taught in Wales, including Welsh either as a core or a non-core subject, plus religious education. During the Summer term 1994 all schools and LEAs in Wales were engaged in a consultation exercise mounted by the Curriculum and Assessment Authority for Wales (ACAC). This followed on from the Dearing review and a similar consultation was being carried out at the same time in English primary schools by the School Curriculum and Assessment Authority (SCAA). When the interviews were being conducted not all of the teachers had had the opportunity to examine or discuss the new curricular proposals, at least, not in detail.

Topics covered in the interviews were as follows:

- Current problems in implementing the National Curriculum;
- Further guidance, training and resources needed;
- The balance between cross-curricular and subject specific teaching (see Chapter 5 for a discussion of these findings);
- Assessment and record keeping (see Chapter 6 for a discussion of these findings);
- The impact of the National Curriculum on more able children, slower learners and children under 5 (see Chapter 8 for a discussion of these findings);
- Teachers' overall views of the National Curriculum; and
- Benefits and disadvantages of the National Curriculum Review in 1994.

Findings from the 1994 Study

Current Problems in Implementing the National Curriculum

The main problem identified by nearly three-quarters of the head teachers was the overloaded content of the National Curriculum which put pressure upon the teachers trying to cover it. As one head teacher put it:

> The time factor is a constant problem generally in delivering the National Curriculum. Pupils are under constant pressure to complete programmes of study. Staff feel that there is insufficient time to consolidate work completed and have to move forward immediately to maintain momentum.

The next most common problem, mentioned by just under one-third of head teachers, concerned assessment and recording which they felt to be too time consuming. Other problems mentioned were teachers' lack of expertise, especially in technology and information technology, and the number and pace of changes that had been made to date in the subject orders.

In response to the question about which of the problems mentioned were most likely to remain after the National Curriculum had been slimmed down, six head teachers anticipated that there would still be too much curriculum content so that the problems of insufficient teaching time and heavy workload would remain. Three head teachers thought that assessment and record keeping would still be a burden unless it was restructured and five head teachers thought that the lack of teaching expertise in certain subjects would remain until teachers had received sufficient training to increase their confidence in those areas.

The Year 1 class teachers were asked to identify any problems in the teaching of the various subjects of the National Curriculum. The teaching of English attracted most comment (seven teachers), with the problem of finding sufficient time for the teaching of reading and for listening to children read being mentioned in particular. Other problems mentioned were the management of practical science investigations on a whole class basis, difficulty in relating class themes or topics to particular subjects and a felt lack of subject expertise, especially in technology and music. Problems in assessment were lack of time to assess children on a one-to-one basis, and uncertainty about how to assess children's performance, especially in technology.

More generally five teachers echoed the views of the majority of head teachers that lack of time to cover the whole National Curriculum was a serious problem. For example one teacher in a school serving socially disadvantaged children referred to the problem of:

> The time element to fit these (foundation subjects) into the curriculum given the ability of the children. I am constantly pushing them to complete written work. The content is a lot even at Key Stage 1.

Table 2.1: Teachers' feelings about the National Curriculum at Key Stage 1

	Head teachers[1]		Class teachers	
very happy	0	(0)	0	(0)
fairly happy	12	(54)	20	(67)
not very happy	8	(36)	7	(23)
definitely unhappy	2	(9)	3	

Notes: [1] I head teacher did not respond to this question
[2] Numbers in brackets are percentages

On the question of which problems were likely to remain after the slimming of the National Curriculum five teachers reserved judgment by saying that it depended on the amount of slimming down, while a further six teachers thought that the revised curriculum would still be overloaded, so that lack of time to cover all subjects would still be a problem. Three teachers expressed the hope that the National Curriculum would be slimmed sufficiently to allow more time for teaching the core subjects and three more predicted continuing problems in the assessment of certain attainment targets.

Training and Resource Needs

Teacher training needs highlighted by the head teachers were for up to date training in the National Curriculum and its assessment (for head teachers) and for training in National Curriculum assessment and record keeping (for class teachers). The class teachers themselves put the latter as their highest priority.

Resource needs stressed by both head teachers and class teachers were for smaller classes or for extra support for teachers within the classroom, and for non-contact time for class teachers, especially for curriculum leaders, to enable them to function more effectively.

Teachers' Overall Views about the National Curriculum at Key Stage 1

Both head teachers and Year 1 class teachers were asked how happy they were about the introduction of the National Curriculum at Key Stage 1 and the results are shown in Table 2.1.

Table 2.1 shows that over half of the head teachers and two-thirds of the class teachers felt 'fairly happy' about the National Curriculum, with the remainder feeling 'not very happy', or, in the case of a very few teachers, 'definitely unhappy'. Although there was a higher proportion of class teachers than head teachers expressing themselves as fairly happy with the new curriculum the difference was not a statistically significant one.

In addition to responding to the above question the teachers were invited to add their own free comments about the National Curriculum and most did so. These comments were classified as either positive or negative in content but a number of teachers made comments of both kinds. For both head teachers and class teachers the number of negative or critical comments outweighed the number of positive ones by a ratio of more than 2 to 1. This perhaps suggests that, at least for those teachers making spontaneous comments, their acceptance of the National Curriculum was strongly tempered by certain reservations about it.

1 Head teachers

The bulk of the positive head teacher comments (nine) referred to the helpful planning framework provided by the National Curriculum which helped teachers to achieve continuity and progression in curriculum planning and encouraged them to work as a team.

One of the serious concerns expressed by the head teachers (seven) related to the reduced time available under the National Curriculum for the teaching of the core subjects and the basic skills of reading, writing and number in particular. For example,

> Too much emphasis has been placed on the development of foundation subjects and their related skills and concepts. This has had a detrimental effect on the basic learning and teaching strategies. We have seen a lowering of standards with the core subjects as children have gone on to Key Stage 2.

An overloaded curriculum, with a consequent increase in workload for teachers was highlighted by seven head teachers. Other adverse effects mentioned were pressures on teachers caused by the speed of introduction of the National Curriculum and the number and pace of changes subsequently made to some of the subject orders.

2 Class teachers

The aspect of the National Curriculum which the Year 1 class teachers focused on in their comments were broadly the same as those of their head teacher colleagues just reported. Seven class teachers welcomed the planning framework which it provided. For example:

> It has given us a basis on which to work, a framework. We were groping in the dark. There was too much freedom before. It has helped us in our planning. I am *pro* the National Curriculum provided it is slimmed down.

> It has improved planning and progression and highlights aims and objectives. Teachers have always known what to do and when. This has made them clear. It makes you think of continuity and progression through collaborative planning. I am more aware of what is being taught throughout the school.

Five teachers expressed concerns about the reduced time for teaching the basic skills under the National Curriculum. For example,

The National Curriculum aids planning and avoids repetition. By checking through the statements of attainment during the assessment of each child one ensures coverage of a variety of subjects. However at Key Stage 1 children need plenty of practice in the basic skills to aid understanding of fundamental concepts. Although the core subjects demand that understanding permeates our teaching, especially in maths and science, with all other Orders to consider the emphasis is on quality not quantity. The teacher needs the freedom to determine what children need next in educational terms. She should not feel pressurized to leave out valuable child initiated experiences that don't map onto the National Curriculum somewhere. I feel that the National Curriculum allows for a broad and balanced curriculum but do question its relevance at Key Stage 1 as I feel that it steals from the basic skills, especially for the less able. I cannot justify repetition of the basics if I am not on target in my coverage of the National Curriculum. (Year 1 Teacher)

Concerns about the overloaded curriculum and its associated heavy workload were expressed by six class teachers. Other concerns mentioned were to do with the speed of introduction of the National Curriculum and the number of subsequent changes to it and the loss of the teacher's former spontaneity and informality in curriculum planning. The latter concern was well expressed by a reception/Year 1 teacher of two years standing:

I feel that the amount of record keeping and paper work involved in teaching is taking away vital attention and association from the children. A sense of guilt sets in when drama, role play and singing/music encroaches on 'morning academics'. Spontaneous teaching has lessened and the pressure put on me is sometimes noticeable in the classroom. On the other hand my organizational skills have strengthened and methods of teaching have been looked at critically . . . The younger children have shown that they are capable of adapting to more structured education with enthusiasm and enjoyment.

Benefits and Disadvantages of the National Curriculum Review

Both head teachers and class teachers were asked what they thought were the advantages and disadvantages in carrying out the wholesale review of the National Curriculum which was in process at the time of the interviews. The following is a brief summary of their responses.

1   Benefits

The benefits anticipated by both groups of teachers could broadly be summarized under the headings of a reduction in pressure on teachers and children through having a more manageable curriculum, with less assessing and recording, leading to improved quality in teaching and learning. The following comments illustrate the teachers' hopes:

Obviously to allow more time for staff to concentrate on basic language and number skills. Also to allow time for staff to develop children's individual learning and scientific skills which enable them to develop as independent learners. The current overprescription of content leads to more didactic teaching in order to cover everything. (head teacher)

Both groups hoped for the return of some of the flexibility in teaching which characterized primary teaching before the introduction of the National Curriculum. A number of teachers were either sceptical about the extent of the likely reduction in National Curriculum content following the review or cautious in making predictions, due to their uncertainty about what the final changes would be. For example,

Difficult to answer. This time there has been some attempt at consultation but they are still doing it in haste because of political pressures. No real benefit. There is some genuine reduction, for example in history and geography, but the slimming of science is 'a sleight of hand' (i.e., three attainment targets condensed to one). (head teacher)

2 Disadvantages

Just under half of the head teachers (ten) and of the class teachers (fourteen) did not consider that there could be any real disadvantage in carrying out the review exercise. The main disadvantage mentioned by the remaining teachers was the fact that it meant further change in schools which had come to terms with the previous changes. For example:

Disheartening for teachers who have more or less come to terms with the documents etc. and, after the upheaval of things, have now put the National Curriculum in place. But schools will continue to review the National Curriculum even during the five-year moratorium. (Head teacher)

The only disadvantage is the thought of everything being changed, Morale is low but what is proposed is better. (Class teacher)

Teaching Children Under 5

Although the National Curriculum was designed to start at age 5 it is important to consider how its introduction might have affected children under 5, especially those in reception classes (i.e., 4–5 years of age), who are on the threshold of the National Curriculum, or those in mixed age classes in smaller schools. For this reason the study elicited teachers' views on this question.

Both head teachers and the Year 1 class teachers with such children in their classes were asked about the effect of the introduction of the National Curriculum on the teaching of children under 5 years old. They were also asked whether the curriculum, or methods of classroom organization and teaching for these children had undergone any significant change since the National Curriculum had been introduced. Only eight class teachers were eligible to respond to these questions through having under-5-year-old children in their mixed age classes so that the views now reported are predominantly those of the head teachers.

1 Effects of the National Curriculum on under-5s

Just over half (twelve) of the head teachers judged that the under-5 children had not been affected by the introduction of the National Curriculum although two of these did refer to the danger of downward pressure from Key Stage 1 on the curriculum for these children. A further two head teachers did not see the coexistence of under-5s with Year 1 children as posing any problems. For example,

> We work as we always have. Under-5s are in a class working alongside children on the National Curriculum. The work is subconsciously geared to the National Curriculum, e.g., children work on the same curricular themes. There is overlap between the work of bright reception children and Year 1 children but this mix is good because the presence of Year 1 children enhances the work with reception children. (Head teacher of small rural school)

Similarly another head teacher commented that reception children moved more quickly into the National Curriculum in a mixed reception class than if they had been in a pure reception class. Whether this was a good or a bad thing depended on the level of ability of the children in question. If they lacked the basic skills it would be difficult. In a reception class the pace is slower and there is more time for oral work.

Another head teacher raised the problem that could potentially exist in mixed age classes, especially where there was a small reception group within a class of mainly Year 1 children. She pointed out that it was easier for the teacher if the younger children were doing the same work as the older ones. During the year of the interview the particular group of reception children were relatively mature, and, after a period of 'gentle easing in from the nursery', they were being treated like their Year 1 counterparts. She added that the teachers of the reception and Year 1 classes liaised closely especially with regard to any mixed age groups.

Approximately one quarter of the head teachers (five) felt that the introduction of the National Curriculum had adversely affected the under-5s in their schools mainly because they felt that the teaching of these children had become more formal as a result of downward pressure from the National Curriculum, with a reduction in children's opportunities for free play and active experience and a greater emphasis on work structured by the teacher. For example:

> I'm a great believer in active experimental learning for under-5s. Teachers are becoming quite neurotic about levels of achievement. Children are being pushed to write but they need a lot more active experience.

This head teacher added that the pressure even extended downward to the nursery with teachers, abetted by their parents, pushing the children towards writing.

Five head teachers reported beneficial effects from the introduction of the National Curriculum for under-5s. These included the involvement of teachers of reception and nursery groups in collaborative curriculum planning with Key Stage 1 teachers, for example, with regard to curriculum themes. One of these stated that her school was working towards a more structured curriculum for under-5s which she perceived as a positive development. The benefit of such collaborative planning would be curricular continuity and progression.

The view that under-5s teachers should lay the foundation for the National Curriculum was summed up by the head teacher who judged that the effects of the National Curriculum had generally been beneficial to these children through giving structure to the development of foundation skills and concepts. She conceded that this could be the cause of pushing children too early which had been a concern to her teachers in the early stages. Now however, the teachers were much more confident regarding what early years education is supposed to be about, namely 'developing a broadly based curriculum, not driven by the National Curriculum but by what our children need'.

The head teacher and staff of a large primary school serving a socially disadvantaged area had made a conscious decision to keep the under-5 curriculum separate from the National Curriculum, at least in some important respects:

> We have made a conscious decision that the National Curriculum will *not* be introduced into the reception class. In other schools reception children receive a watered down version of the National Curriculum. We adopt an early years approach through structured play. The National Curriculum has compartmentalized things and children don't learn in this way. At first the National Curriculum challenged the confidence of teachers regarding their philosophy but now teachers are taking a more relaxed view of it.

The eight Year 1 class teachers whose classes contained under-5 children were divided in their views on how the National Curriculum had affected them, with two reporting benefits, three stating that it had not affected them and three reporting adverse effects. The benefits included a greater variety of curricular activities for the children and the provision of a planning structure to follow in collaboration with other early years teachers. The adverse effects included a trend towards more formal work with less free play and more written work and a reduction in the time spent on the basic skills because of the wider curriculum coverage.

2   Changes in the curriculum for under-5s

On the different but related question of whether the curriculum for under-5s had undergone significant change since the introduction of the National Curriculum the head teachers showed more unanimity with three-quarters of them (sixteen) judging that there had been such a change. The main changes were a broadening of the curriculum to reflect the wider scope of the National Curriculum, more focused, structured and, in some cases, more formal work for the under-5s, particularly in the basic skills, and a move toward more collaborative planning among early years teachers.

Some of the head teachers reporting increased structuring of the curriculum for under-5s clearly favoured this trend. For example the head teacher of a former Social Priority Area school described a marked difference in the curriculum at the reception stage in that the children now worked towards Level 1. In his view this resulted in far more structure and urgency in the delivery of lessons. While some of his class teachers felt that too much formal work was now being done with reception children in view of the amount of free play they needed, he disagreed, taking the view that the children needed formality and structure in the curriculum where structure was lacking at home. Another head teacher commented that maths and language activities had taken on a new urgency due to the 'spectre of SATs at Key Stage 1'.

Of the eight class teachers with under-5s children in their classes two felt unable to respond to this question due to lack of relevant National Curriculum experience but all of the remaining teachers felt that the curriculum had changed in some ways for the under-5s. The changes mentioned reflected two of those mentioned by the head teachers, namely the broadening of the curriculum and a trend toward more formal activities with an overall reduction in free play. As one reception/Year 1 teacher put it:

> The workload at Year 2 is brought down to reception . . . There is pressure on teachers to achieve a certain level by a certain age. Where children are ready to move on OK but in some cases we're moving too quickly too soon.

It is clear from the responses of some head teachers that the changes just described had even percolated down to the nursery to some extent in some schools. One head teacher referred to a 'slight formalization' of work at the nursery level for those ready to receive it. Another, who taught a class of 3–7-year-olds stated that she tried to structure the nursery education a little more in line with the National Curriculum but still through play. She regarded this development as positive in the case of nursery children able to accept the challenge of joining in with older children's activities. The inclusion of nursery teachers in the collaborative planning process with other early years teachers was welcomed by several head teachers.

3   Changes in teaching methods/classroom organization for under-5s

Head teachers were fairly evenly divided as to whether their teaching methods for under-5s had undergone change. Just under half (ten) stated that they had and just over half (twelve) felt they had not. (One head teacher failed to respond to this question.) By far the most common change reported was a reduction in the amount of free play engaged in by the children (nine head teachers). Coupled with this was a movement toward more focused and more structured play within the overall context of the National Curriculum. Some of the head teachers reporting such changes clearly welcomed them, taking the view that the educational value of 'unstructured free play', prior to the introduction of the National Curriculum was very limited. In contrast two head teachers had been instrumental in reasserting the importance and value of free play in their schools. One of these was a recently appointed head teacher to a primary school where the early years teachers had felt under pressure from the National Curriculum to produce concrete evidence of children's work. The new head teacher had encouraged the teachers to pull back from this approach and to adopt a more play and activity based approach. Similarly the head teacher of a large primary school serving a socially disadvantaged area stated that the teaching approaches for under-5s had tended to be too formal following the introduction of the National Curriculum, with free play being curtailed. Now the teachers were looking at the educational needs of these children and planning ways of providing a foundation for the National Curriculum through 'natural developmental levels of free play'.

Two of the head teachers reporting no change endorsed the value of free play. For example:

> There is still very much an accent on free play although reception teachers are aware that at Year 2 certain levels are expected. Three or four years ago they felt some pressure to work towards them. Now they realize that good early years education covers the National Curriculum — they are achieving a good basis. Reception teachers are gradually regaining their confidence. The introduction of the National Curriculum was too rushed and undermined teachers' beliefs.

Of the six class teachers responding to the question concerning changes in teaching methods four thought that there had been a reduction in the amount of free play for the children under-5 and an orientation towards the National Curriculum in respect of the choices of activity themes. One teacher commented that work with reception children was now more concentrated on books, worksheets and reading. Once they had done the work required children had opportunities for free play but she added that if they are not directed in this they don't know what to do. She wondered whether this lack of spontaneity in free play might be due to the amount of teacher direction that they were receiving.

Summary of Main Findings

1 Although a majority of head teachers and Year 1 class teachers expressed themselves as 'fairly happy' with the National Curriculum since it provided a helpful planning framework, there was strong criticism of its overloaded content and of the perceived overemphasis on assessment and record keeping which was felt to place an undue burden upon class teachers;

2 The teachers anticipated that the forthcoming revision of the National Curriculum would reduce pressure on both teachers and children since it would become more manageable and should lead to improved quality of teaching and learning. The burden of assessment and record keeping was also expected to be reduced, releasing more time for teaching the basic skills. Some doubt was expressed by a small number of teachers as to whether the content of the Revised National Curriculum had been sufficiently reduced to improve its manageability;

3 There was some disagreement among head teachers regarding the effects of the National Curriculum on children under 5. The majority judged that these children had not been noticeably affected but there was a minority view that they had been adversely affected by downward pressure from the National Curriculum which resulted in reduced opportunities for free play and the formalization and tighter teacher control of these children's learning activities. However the majority of head teachers agreed that there had been significant changes in the curriculum for the under-5s, namely, a broadening of the curriculum, with more structure, more focused work and more collaborative planning among early years teachers;

4 There was evidence for some polarization of head teachers' views about the nature of the curriculum at the reception stage in relation to the National Curriculum. On the one hand some head teachers seemed to regard it as essentially a preparation for the National Curriculum and welcomed the tighter teacher control of the curriculum and of children's learning activities. Others on the other hand were anxious to reassert the child-centred nature of the curriculum at this stage which laid the foundations for the National Curriculum but was not directly geared towards it.

Discussion

The main findings of the 1994 follow-up study largely echo those from the original study carried out during the introduction of the National Curriculum from September 1989, namely, the fact that there was a general welcome among the teachers for the clear planning framework provided by the National Curriculum, tempered by the concern about curriculum overload and the overemphasis upon assessment and record keeping. The finding that the National Curriculum appeared to have brought some curricular benefits for children under 5, but at the expense of some loss of flexibility and informality in teaching and a reduction in children's opportunities for play based experiential learning, was also in line with the earlier findings. In these respects therefore the teachers' views of the National Curriculum in the research sample schools do not appear to have changed significantly over the five years between the original and follow-up phases of the study.

It should be remembered however that our sample of primary and infant schools was drawn from just one LEA and involved only the head teachers and Year 1 class teachers in those schools. While there are good grounds for believing that the sample was fairly representative of all the primary schools in that LEA (see Cox and Sanders, 1994), it should not be assumed that they are equally representative of the views of primary and infant teachers in other schools throughout England and Wales. In order to establish this we need to look for independent evidence.

Other Studies of the Impact of the National Curriculum

The PACE Study

Regarding independent research by far the most thorough and wide ranging study of the impact of the National Curriculum (and the Education Reform Act) at Key Stages 1 and 2 is the Primary Assessment Curriculum and Experience (PACE) Project centred on the Universities of Bristol and the West of England. This longitudinal study is based upon a sample of forty-eight primary schools drawn from eight LEAs in England. For the Key Stage 1 phase of the study data were gathered from two rounds of structured interviews with forty-eight head teachers and eighty-eight Key Stage 1 class teachers, i.e., Year 1 and Year 2 class teachers, carried out in 1990 and 1992 in order to obtain their views on the working of the National Curriculum, plus written questionnaires. In addition the research team made their own direct classroom observations in a subsample of the project schools and also interviewed some of the pupils themselves. Further interviews were scheduled for subsequent years, as the original cohort of children moved through their primary schools, but the main publication produced to date (Pollard *et al.*, 1994) covers only the findings up to 1992.

The findings of this project which bear upon those of the Swansea University study reported in this chapter are as follows (see Chapter 6 for the relevant findings on teacher assessment and Chapter 5 for those concerning teaching approaches).

1   Many teachers were positive about the National Curriculum in general and appeared to regard it as a worthwhile educational development, particularly with regard to its clarification of teaching aims and the provision of an overall structure that could facilitate progression. However they expressed serious misgivings about particular aspects of the National Curriculum, especially its overloaded and overprescriptive content and inflexibility, which was felt to restrict the teachers' capacity to adapt their teaching to their children's needs;

2   Teachers experienced constraint and the options open to children to select, organize, pace and time their work were considerably reduced. In response to the pressures of the National Curriculum teachers appeared to be adapting by tightening their classroom control and by providing more direction to children's activities. Classroom observation showed the dominance of work in English and the preponderance of work in the core subjects, especially English and maths;

3   Evidence from the study of whole school changes indicated that there was

a steady move away from teachers working with their own individual curriculum planning systems toward more coordinated whole school approaches, using the structure provided by the National Curriculum.

The authors concluded that findings from the study, such as the development of more rigorous curriculum planning and acceptance of increased workloads, reflected considerable commitment and expertise among the teachers studied. Given their acceptance of the principle of the National Curriculum most teachers worked very hard to deliver it. They felt, however, that, in later phases of the study, teachers were increasingly feeling that the National Curriculum was flawed and this, combined with the associated assessment requirements, could threaten rather than help them to fulfil their basic commitments to the teaching and development of young children. Although the PACE study did not investigate the impact of the National Curriculum on the teaching of children under 5 specifically the findings at Key Stage 1 summarized above are broadly supportive of those from the Swansea University Impact Study.

Consultations on the National Curriculum Review

On the question of teachers' views about the proposals for a slimmed down National Curriculum following the Dearing review the main national evidence has come from large scale official consultations. Both the School Curriculum and Assessment Authority (SCAA) in England and the Curriculum and Assessment Authority in Wales (ACAC) published reports on the results of the consultations which they carried out with schools, LEAs and other interested bodies concerning the proposals for a revised National Curriculum.

The report on the consultations in Wales (Curriculum and Assessment Authority for Wales, 1994) states that the majority of primary school schools expressed reservations about the proposed statutory curriculum within the recommended times (80–85 per cent of weekly teaching time). The greatest reservations were expressed at Key Stage 2. At Key Stage 1 respondents identified higher expectations of children's performance in English as a particular concern which could result in a disproportionate allocation of time to the subject, thereby affecting manageability of the whole curriculum. Respondents at all key stages also expressed concern about the possible impact on manageability of any assessment requirements brought in after the curriculum had been finalized.

The results from the consultations in England were very similar to those from Wales (SCAA, 1994). While individual subjects were judged to be manageable by teachers with particular subject interests the curriculum as a whole was felt by many primary teachers to be too heavy, particularly at Key Stage 2. In addition primary teachers in England shared the concern of their colleagues in Wales that, at Key Stage 1, the high expectations of children's performance in Levels 1 to 3 in English (especially writing) would threaten the overall manageability of the revised curriculum.

It seems that the teachers responding to the curriculum consultation exercise in Wales were, in general, less optimistic about the manageability of the proposed new curriculum than the teachers in the Swansea University study. One possible reason for this might be to do with the timing of the two enquiries. Despite some overlap in time the consultation exercise took place somewhat later than the teacher interviews in the Swansea University study, which meant that the teachers taking part in the consultation were probably more familiar with the content of the new curriculum proposals. Following these consultations both curriculum bodies claim to have modified their curriculum proposals which the government accepted for implementation from September 1995 as the Revised National Curriculum. It remains to be seen whether these adjustments will improve the manageability of the Revised National Curriculum.

Conclusions

On the basis of the findings of the Swansea University Impact Study, and the other research and consultation studies summarized in this chapter the following conclusions are drawn.

1 Teachers have generally welcomed the National Curriculum at Key Stage 1 as providing a helpful planning framework which helps to achieve continuity and progression in curriculum planning. This acceptance has been tempered by strong concern about its overloaded and overprescriptive content which puts pressure on both teachers and pupils to drive forward to reach particular attainment targets and threatens the quality and depth of children's learning, particularly in the basic skills of reading, writing and number;

2 While the introduction of the National Curriculum has brought definite educational benefits for children at this key stage, including a broader, more varied curriculum, it has significantly reduced teachers' former freedom and flexibility of planning and teaching and has led to a general tightening of their control of children's learning activities. This trend towards stronger teacher direction and structuring of learning has also affected children at the reception stage and reduced their opportunities for free play. However some schools are now actively resisting this constraining of the curriculum for under-5s and are trying to safeguard the child traditional, centred character of early learning;

3 The full scale revision of the National Curriculum in 1994, prior to its introduction at Key Stages 1 to 3 in September 1995 was widely welcomed by teachers in the Swansea University study, who looked forward in particular to a reduction in the burden of assessment and record keeping and an increase in the time available to teach the basic skills. However the results of wide consultations carried out by the government's curriculum and assessment agencies indicate concern among many primary teachers

about the manageability of the Revised National Curriculum within the time allocations proposed.

The findings presented in this chapter raise several important educational issues which are taken up in other chapters as follows:

1   The curricular demands of the teaching of the basic skills in relation to those of the Key Stage 1 curriculum in general (Chapter 8);
2   The relationship between subject specific teaching and cross curricular, topic based teaching at this key stage (Chapter 5);
3   The relationship between curriculum for children under 5 and the National Curriculum (Chapters 9–12);
4   The place and functions of assessment and record keeping within the teaching process (Chapter 6).

References

Cox, T. and Sanders, S. (1994) *The Impact of the National Curriculum on the teaching of five Year Olds*, London, Falmer Press.

Curriculum and Assessment Authority for Wales (ACAC) (1994) *The National Curriculum Proposals in Wales: Report on the Consultation, Summer 1994*, Cardiff, ACAC.

Pollard, A., Broadfoot, P., Croll, P., Osborn, M. and Abbott, D. (1994) *Changing English Primary Schools?: The Impact of the ERA at Key Stage One*, London, Cassell.

School Curriculum and Assessment Authority (SCAA) (1994) *The review of the National Curriculum: A Report on the 1994 Consultation*, London, SCAA.

3   The Missing Element? Early Years Teachers' Attitudes to Subject Knowledge

Trisha Maynard

In this chapter I chart the changing attitudes of five early years teachers towards 'subject knowledge'. As part of a research project based at the University of Wales Swansea, these teachers were asked to mentor an aspect of subject knowledge to the student teachers on placement in their schools. Initially the mentors objected to focusing on subject knowledge and their comments reflected a commitment to the child-centred ideology. Over time mentors' attitudes towards subject knowledge were challenged and gradually the role and importance of this knowledge in their teaching and in pupil learning became 'visible' to them. Ultimately, mentors maintained that subject knowledge had been the 'missing element' in their practice. But mentors found that acknowledging the importance of 'subjects' did not negate the importance of their child-centred beliefs; they found ways in which to reconcile the subject-centred and child-centred approaches. It is concluded that if there is a belief that standards in primary schools would be raised through a more subject-centred approach to teaching, then it is teachers' attitudes towards subject knowledge that need to be addressed first and foremost. Even so, there is no guarantee that changing teachers' attitudes will change their classroom practice. As Cox and Sanders (1994) point out, although attitudes may predispose us to behave in certain ways, our behaviour in real life situations will be subject to other influences.

Education is defined . . . in terms of its processes rather than its content or its extrinsic 'aims and objectives'. And provision and experiences are planned in relation to, and in harmony with, the developmental level of the individual child. (Blenkin and Kelly, 1994, p. 28)

. . . while it is self evident that every individual, to an extent, constructs his/her own meanings, education is an encounter between these personal understandings and the public knowledge embodied in our cultural traditions. The teacher's key responsibility is to mediate such encounters so that the child's understanding is enriched. (Alexander, Rose and Woodhead, 1992, para 64)

Being 'Child-centred'

For nearly three decades, primary school teaching — and in particular, early years teaching — has been closely associated with the 'child-centred' ideology. This ideology is often characterized by the slogan, 'We teach children not subjects' and associated with 'progressive' teaching methods such as discovery learning and topic work. Within this ideology, the child is believed to develop and grow through carefully planned learning experiences which are consistent with the way in which the child perceives the world. To the child-centred teacher 'subjects' may therefore be seen as inappropriate: incompatible with the child's natural view of the world and providing an unnecessary constraint on the child's thinking.

But the child-centred ideology is not without its critics. Those belonging to the New Right (e.g., Lawlor, 1990; and O'Hear, 1986) and others within the profession (e.g., Alexander, 1984; McNamara, 1994) have argued that teachers should adopt a more subject-centred approach: that 'subjects' rather than 'the child' should be placed at the heart of primary teaching. These writers maintain that it is the right of children, even early years children, to be inducted into 'the discourse and disciplines of subjects' (Anning, 1995). Anning cites Alexander, Rose and Woodhead (1992) who describe subjects as 'some of the most powerful tools for making sense of the world which human beings have ever devised' (1992, 21, p. 64).

The voice of these critics has grown both stronger and more influential in the last decade and has been reflected in the implementation of a national curriculum and assessment system. Indeed, it is the National Curriculum that now seems to offer some writers a justification for the need for teachers to become more subject-centred. Alexander and his colleagues, for example, maintain that since the 'arrival' of the National Curriculum the task of the primary teacher has changed dramatically. They state, 'The resistance to subjects at the primary stage is no longer tenable. The subject is a necessary feature of the modern primary curriculum' (Alexander, Rose and Woodhead, 1992, para 3.2).

But it is not only teachers' commitment to the child-centred ideology that has been brought into question but teachers' own subject knowledge. A number of research studies in the UK (e.g., Wragg, Bennett and Carré, 1989; Bennett and Carré, 1993; Furlong and Maynard, 1995) have highlighted teachers' difficulties with subject understanding. These studies have revealed that many teachers feel insecure about their subject knowledge in several of the curriculum areas they are required to teach. This must be of crucial significance to those who see subject knowledge as closely associated with effective teaching and high standards of pupil achievement (e.g., OFSTED, 1994; OFSTED, 1995).

One way of attempting to improve teachers' subject knowledge whilst also bringing about a more subject-centred approach to primary teaching is through reforms of Initial Teacher Training (ITT). In the recent government Circular 14/93 (DFE, 1993) (Welsh Office Circular 62/93, WO, 1993) the first three stated priorities for primary ITT centre on improving teachers' subject knowledge — particularly in the core areas of the National Curriculum. As a result of this Circular, teacher training courses are required to include a minimum of 150 hours of 'directed time' for the teaching of each of these core areas. Significantly, the Circular states that 'directed time' may be spent either in schools or in higher education institutions (HEIs).

This recommendation means that from September 1996 when this Circular comes into force, it is likely that student teachers will spend some time on their school experience focusing specifically on 'subjects'. It is also likely that it will be teachers rather than Higher Education Institution (HEI) tutors who will be responsible for this work — mentoring aspects of subject knowledge to the students on placement in their schools. It is this — mentoring subject knowledge in the primary school — that became the focus of a research project based at the University of Wales Swansea (see Maynard, 1996).

One aspect of this research was an exploration of teachers' attitudes to subject knowledge. We were interested to find out, for example:

- How far were the teachers who took part in this project committed to a 'child-centred' approach to primary teaching?
- What were their attitudes towards the role of subject knowledge in their own teaching and the importance of subject knowledge in their pupils' learning?
- Would mentoring aspects of subject knowledge change these teachers attitudes in any way?

Background

Initially, schools were invited to bid for inclusion in our project, nominating a specific teacher who would take responsibility for working with students. The five schools eventually selected were chosen because of their enthusiasm and commitment to developing a whole school approach towards mentoring. Of the five nominated teachers, three had trained specifically as 'early years' teachers (teaching children of 3–8 years) although two of these teachers had extensive experience in teaching throughout the primary age range. The fourth teacher had trained to teach children aged from 3–11 years and although she was now working with older primary children, had spent a substantial amount of time as the deputy head of a nursery school. The fifth teacher involved in our project had trained to teach in the upper primary age range (7–11 years) although the vast majority of her experience had been with teaching Year 3 (Y3) children (aged 7–8 years). All the teachers maintained a commitment to the child-centred ideology and to experiential and investigative ways of teaching. As we shall see, the fact that these teachers had undergone different forms of training and had different professional experience was to prove useful in sharpening our understanding of early years teachers' attitudes towards subject knowledge.

As part of our project these teachers were asked to design and implement their own action research projects which were to be centred on mentoring an aspect of subject knowledge to the student or students on placement in their school. In order to facilitate the action research projects, mentors, together with the author acting as researcher, formed an action research team. This team met every two to three weeks in the Spring and Summer terms and group discussions were recorded, transcribed and analysed (approximately twelve hours of recordings). Mentors were also interviewed individually and recordings of these interviews were transcribed and analysed (approximately seven and a half hours of recordings.) In addition, the researcher took on the role of tutor for students in two of the participating schools and spent a day in each of these schools for every week of the students' two block teaching practices (twelve weeks). Field notes were made of observations and of discussions with students, senior mentors and other teachers.

Teachers' Subject Knowledge

If we are to explore teachers' attitudes towards subject knowledge, it is important initially to examine the nature of 'subject knowledge' and the kind of subject understandings it is claimed that teachers need. Following the work of Schwab (1978) there appears to be general agreement amongst researchers that subject knowledge can be understood as incorporating two different dimensions: substantive and syntactic knowledge. Substantive knowledge is knowledge *of* the subject and will include the facts, concepts, procedures etc. of the subject area and also a knowledge of the way in which a particular body of knowledge is structured and organized. Syntactic knowledge is knowledge *about* the subject and incorporates an understanding of the way in which a particular body of knowledge is generated and validated.

It has been suggested that if they are to be effective in their work then teachers need to have a 'flexible, thoughtful and conceptual' understanding of the subject areas that they teach (McDiarmid, Ball and Anderson, 1989). It is not enough for teachers to be 'one step ahead' of pupils in terms of their subject understanding. Teachers need to be able to 'make connections' — to know about relationships between given phenomena both inside and outside their field; how knowledge in their field is generated and validated; and about fundamental ideas and relationships that underlie interpretations of particular phenomena (McDiarmid *et al.*, 1989, p. 198). In addition, it has been argued (Sanders, 1994) that beliefs about the nature of subjects profoundly influence teachers' practice. This aspect, therefore, must also be incorporated into any discussion of teachers' personal subject knowledge.

Pedagogical Content Knowledge

But teachers' personal subject knowledge, however flexible and sound, is not enough. Teachers, it is claimed, need to find ways of transforming this knowledge in order to make it accessible to the pupils in their class. McDiarmid *et al.* (1989) maintain that in teaching for subject matter understanding, the teacher's role is to 'connect children to the communities of the disciplines' (p. 194) and that appropriate activities will 'emerge from a bifocal consideration of subject matter and pupils' (p. 194).

Teachers' subject knowledge for teaching — pedagogical content knowledge — therefore involves more than a sound personal subject understanding, it is also dependent on an understanding of children and how they best learn. Shulman (1986) maintains that this knowledge includes 'an understanding of what makes the learning of specific topics easy or difficult: the conceptions and preconceptions that (pupils) of different ages and backgrounds bring with them' (p. 9). Shulman characterizes pedagogical content knowledge as 'the most powerful analogies, illustrations, explanations and demonstrations — in a word, the ways of representing and formulating the subject that makes it comprehensible to others' (1986, p. 9).

Teachers' understanding of subject knowledge, according to many researchers, has a powerful influence on how they transform and represent this knowledge to their pupils. Hashweh (1985), for example, found that the representations of knowledgeable teachers reflected their deeper understanding of the topic — they were able to relate the specific topic to key concepts, principles and themes within the discipline. Similarly Grossman, Wilson and Shulman (1989) describe how in their research beginning teachers with graduate training in their field were more likely to stress conceptual understanding and syntactic knowledge — the 'whys' as opposed to the 'how tos'. But how did these findings relate to the mentors in this project? Indeed, what were mentors' attitudes to the role and importance of subject knowledge in early years teaching?

Initial Attitudes to Subject Knowledge: Ideological Objections

When mentors were asked to focus their activities on developing student teachers' understanding of 'subject knowledge', their initial responses were tough and uncompromising. The importance of subject knowledge was dismissed for themselves as teachers and for their pupils — particularly for younger children. In discussing their objections mentors adopted what appeared to be a 'typical' child-centred stance. They maintained, for example, that the content of their activities should not be constrained by the imposition of what they saw as 'unnatural' subject demands and subject boundaries. One mentor commented, 'I think the whole practice in early years is seeing the world as a whole. I don't think children see things in isolation.'

Mentors maintained that they were keen to give their pupils meaningful and relevant learning 'experiences' and that these often cut across several curriculum areas. They essentially appeared committed to the topic or thematic approach to teaching. For example, one mentor, criticizing her student teacher's work commented, 'She sees science as floating and sinking, she sees maths as capacity — all isolated little pockets, but they don't intermingle. She hasn't chosen something she can bring capacity into, she can bring history into . . . a natural, whole approach . . .'

It was not simply that mentors were concerned that the activities they devised should appear meaningful and relevant to their pupils. Rather, it appeared that when planning pupil activities the mentors themselves thought in terms of 'experiences' and not in terms of individual subject areas. Mentors commented, for example, 'I find it difficult to plan in separate subject areas' and, 'The HMI came in and said how many hours do you spend doing English and how many hours doing history and I said, "I can't tell you, that's impossible."'

Mentors also maintained that they saw their role as more than being concerned with pupils' intellectual development but with the development of the 'whole child' and this included their emotional and social development. For example, one mentor maintained, 'When you have them for a year you get to know them, know all their problems, family background. You're more than just a teacher . . . you are in *loco parentis* . . . you are a caring person, a social worker, you are all those things . . .'

It became apparent that, for these mentors, *what* pupils learned was ultimately regarded as less important than the *way* in which they learned and how far these approaches contributed to enabling pupils to become enthusiastic and independent learners. Mentors commented, 'Does it matter how you get there if the children are enthused?' and 'I'm not interested in them just being able to do blah, blah, blah. I want them to be independent . . .' Mentors' attitudes in this respect seemed to be based, at least in part, on their own memories of 'effective' teachers. One mentor maintained, 'I think of teachers who stick in your head, I think some of them . . . they did things all wrong. But they were still bloody good teachers that made you sit up and go "wow", and make you want to think about it. And it's something about the quality of the way that person was saying, doing or whatever.'

Effective teaching appeared, therefore, to be seen as independent of teachers' subject knowledge but relied more on who teachers were 'as people' and their ability 'to get ideas across' and to enthuse and inspire children. One mentor maintained that as early years teachers, their specialism was 'in children's learning and in making knowledge accessible': they did not see themselves as specialists in subject knowledge itself. Indeed, in order to emphasize the independence of subject knowledge and effective teaching, another mentor maintained, 'You can tell someone absolute garbage, but as long as you do it well they will listen and understand. You could be telling them absolute rubbish but if you can put it over in such a way . . . it's the *way* you do it rather than the actual knowledge.'

One further factor that may have contributed to mentors' rejection of subject knowledge was that they appeared to equate *all* subject knowledge with factual knowledge and ways of teaching that were 'more about pushing facts in'. Mentors maintained that 'Teachers of secondary pupils teach subjects to children . . . I think that's the difference. They push facts in. Well I could do that but I don't. You could teach children anything in order to pass tests, but that's not teaching. It would be more like a factory . . . you put this bit in here and that bit in there and what comes out . . . It's ignoring all the stuff that we know about, the social and the emotional . . . all that stuff.' Focusing on subject knowledge was therefore seen also to threaten one of the basic tenets of the child-centred approach: the desire to create understanding.

Political Objections

Through articulating their child-centred beliefs, mentors appeared to be expressing 'ideological' objections to focusing on subject knowledge. But mentors' attitudes towards subject knowledge appeared also to be influenced by their concerns about the demands of the National Curriculum and the impact this was having on their practice.[1] These objections could be described as 'political'.

Mentors claimed that not only did the amount of prescribed content in the National Curriculum force them to teach 'superficially' but that being structured in terms of 'subjects' rather than 'experiences' the National Curriculum was not compatible with the way they thought about their practice. One mentor was particularly concerned that this militated against her student teacher's understanding of good early years practice. She explained, 'My student thinks that in Year 2 (Y2) she's got to be on top of the National Curriculum — the National Curriculum is subjects so she's thought about subjects. She hasn't thought about the experiences the children are getting. At this stage in Y2 you *are* dominated by assessment and you *have* got gaps to fill. But you try and do a day or a few days that hang together.' Similarly, another mentor maintained that she did not want her student teacher to see geography 'as a subject'. Rather, '. . . as they are very young children . . . I want her to see the value of using . . . we've got a lovely environment, a nature reserve, woods, you name it it's there, I want the student to see the possibilities of drawing everything from that.'

In addition, mentors expressed their resentment that the National Curriculum 'dictated' what they had to teach their pupils. As one mentor commented, 'You don't have any room to cover your own interests, you've got to cover all this (the National Curriculum programmes of study). It doesn't make any difference whether you dislike teaching . . . whatever it is . . . you just have to keep on doing it.' In addition, mentors who had experience of teaching older primary children claimed that being forced to teach topics about which they had little understanding had an impact on their feelings of self-esteem and the satisfaction they derived from their work. For example, one mentor commented, 'The National Curriculum pushes people beyond the point where they are naturally enthusiastic. It pushes people into places where you can't rely on your own knowledge. And I think that's where I feel a terrible teacher, when I find myself where I don't know.' Another stated, 'I did science before the National Curriculum but I only taught science that I understood. But now I have to teach certain aspects of science that I don't understand and I can't do it. The National Curriculum is going to destroy all the good practice in the primary school.'

Mentors were also concerned that the National Curriculum might force them further down the road of subject specialism — clearly something none of them wanted. The mentors maintained that they were well aware of the criticisms made of their subject understanding by the government and the media, but felt that it was simply unfair to expect them to have a thorough understanding of all eleven National Curriculum areas (including Welsh) and of religious education. One mentor explained, 'I think in the end what I am going *against* rather than going *for* is that we can't be subject specialists in all eleven subjects. It's impossible. So instead of trying to say, 'Yes we must strive towards this', we have to say, 'We don't need to strive towards this.'

Personal Objections?

Mentors may also have had other, more 'personal' objections to focusing on subject knowledge. Indeed, those mentors who had experience of teaching older primary pupils recognized that there were 'holes' in their substantive subject knowledge (that is, their knowledge of facts, concepts and the like) in some of the curriculum areas they were required to teach. This, as noted above, did appear to have an impact on mentors' self-esteem and on their job satisfaction.

Even so, mentors claimed that their lack of subject understanding was not of particular importance to their effectiveness as early years teachers. Partly this was because, as I noted earlier, mentors' main concern was not with subject knowledge itself, but with how effectively and appropriately to represent ideas to children: not with *what* they taught but *how* they taught. In addition, mentors believed that even if their own understanding was a little 'shaky' it was still likely to be greater than that of their pupils: in terms of personal subject knowledge, mentors (unlike McDiarmid *et al.*, 1989) claimed that they only needed to be 'one step ahead' of their pupils. As one mentor commented, 'In early years, I don't think that subject knowledge is such an issue. What's difficult is how you get it across ... not "it" itself ...'

But what were mentors' views about the role of subject knowledge in their pupils' learning? Did this appear to be influenced by mentors' difficulties with subject understanding? Mentors' attitudes in this respect were particularly apparent in their comments about the teaching of science. It is to this, therefore, that we briefly turn.

Teaching Science

It should be remembered that one of the basic tenets to which all the mentors subscribed was 'teaching for understanding'. Mentors maintained that, for example, teaching pupils the *names* of the 'materials' they were studying (factual knowledge) was insufficient and inappropriate. Rather, pupils needed first, and above all, to understand something of the *properties* of those materials. But mentors admitted that when dealing with more complex, abstract scientific concepts they did not, in general, aim to provide pupils with a greater conceptual understanding — that is, an understanding of 'why' things happened. Rather, they focused on skills and processes — not on formal scientific investigation, but on developing pupils' common-sense understandings. That is to say, mentors' science teaching appeared to be based not on developing pupils' understanding of 'this is why it happens' but on 'let's find out what happens when ...'.

Mentors maintained that the reason they adopted this approach was that young children were not interested in formal scientific explanations: such explanations were not of any relevance to them. In addition, mentors claimed that many scientific concepts were far too complex for KS1 children to understand. The fact that early years teachers may also have difficulty in understanding these concepts was seen as irrelevant: mentors maintained that even an 'expert' would not be able to make this knowledge accessible or of interest to young children. One mentor explained, 'With science a lot of things you do are abstract . . . you can't see them. We talked about skin on top of the water and OK they can see that to a certain extent . . . but they can't really see . . . If you do dissolving they ask where has it gone? Well where *has* it gone? Scientifically it's gone between the molecules in the water hasn't it. But how do you explain that to a 6-year-old? They can't see it. It's really difficult.' Another added, 'What would be the point of explaining about molecules, it doesn't matter to them about molecules because, frankly, it's snowing outside and they'd rather be thinking about that.'

One point needs emphasis here. Even though these mentors maintained that subject knowledge was largely irrelevant to early years teaching this is not to suggest that they did not think about the subject content of their activities — that would, in any case, be impossible since the implementation of the National Curriculum. But these mentors' primary consideration was not how best to represent accurately the subject content for their pupils. Nor did they, to use McDiarmid *et al.*'s (1989) analogy, engage in a 'bifocal' consideration of subject matter and pupils. Rather mentors, as teachers in a previous project (Furlong and Maynard, 1995), looked at the subject-matter content they were required to teach through the 'lens' of their child-centred understandings about children and how they best learn.

Challenging Attitudes

During the action research team meetings, mentors' attitudes towards subject knowledge were frequently challenged. It was noted that these challenges were seen as of particular importance by the one mentor who, in her training and professional experience, had worked exclusively with early years children. This mentor maintained that the reason she had never considered a 'good' personal subject knowledge as being of any significance to her practice was that in working with very young children she could rely, essentially, on her 'common-sense' understandings. This mentor stated, 'It is only through the project and looking closely at the students who have got holes in their subject knowledge, that I can see it now. At KS1 I didn't come up against the content, so I didn't see teaching as *needing* any knowledge about subjects.'

But being asked to mentor subject knowledge made demands on other aspects of personal subject knowledge which had not been apparent to mentors in their day-to-day teaching. In attempting to develop student teachers' subject understandings, mentors found that they needed to 'bring to their consciousness' and articulate how the activities they devised for their student teachers reflected more principled 'theoretical' subject understandings. These understandings incorporated knowledge of the subject's key ideas and concepts; its underlying processes; beliefs about the nature of the subject area; and also about why the subject area is considered to be important in pupils' development. This was an aspect with which all mentors found they had difficulty. One mentor, who was devising art-based activities for her student commented, '. . . What's struck me the more I've talked to people about this is how hidden inside teachers the reasons why we teach anything are. I wasn't alone in not really being able to say . . . clearly . . . what I did printing for. Is the information there and it's so underneath that we just don't recognize it or don't people know?'

This mentor eventually maintained that when she reviewed the activities she planned for her pupils these understandings were 'all there', they had merely been assimilated as generalized approaches to teaching and were therefore unavailable to conscious thought. Others, however, maintained that they had never held these understandings. One mentor commented, 'I don't know why I do half the things I do. I do them because it seems like a good idea at the time . . . If someone asks me why do you do it, I just wouldn't be able to give them an answer. My answer would be, it says I've got to do it in the National Curriculum or I've done it before and it worked really well and the children got a lot out of it. But I wouldn't know intellectual reasons why I did certain things. And I don't think most teachers do.'

Confronting this difficulty with their subject understanding left all the mentors feeling vulnerable and shaken. One mentor commented, 'As I've been looking at subject knowledge I've realized what huge holes there are in my subject knowledge and whereas before I wouldn't have really thought about it so much and just got on with it, now I think, 'How can I teach this when I don't really know anything about it?' — especially with science and technology. I don't think I have the subject knowledge to teach it properly.' Another stated, 'Student teachers had to think about how children learned. That was the most important thing. Everything had to be planned that way. I never thought any further than that. Well suddenly I realize that there's this other element to it. It's really shaken me. If I had not seen the relevance of subject knowledge, what else don't I know?'

Changing Attitudes

In the action research team meetings mentors not only discussed their difficulties with subject understanding but were encouraged to consider the ways in which greater subject knowledge influenced both their actual practice and how they felt about their teaching. One mentor commented in this respect, 'If I feel secure, I can take a little fact and make a lot of it . . . I can make it last a whole lesson. I feel strongest in the areas I feel most confident in . . . because I know what I am doing.'

Over time mentors appeared, gradually, to change their attitudes towards the importance of subject knowledge for early years teachers. As one mentor explained, 'I think that you have got to know what it is you're teaching. I feel a real conversion in those terms. Unless you know the basis of the subject you are teaching then whatever you are teaching isn't done properly.' Another maintained, 'Originally I can remember saying, "It's not what you say it's the way that you say it", but I don't agree with that view any more. You have got to have good subject knowledge yourself if you're going to teach properly.'

Seeing subject knowledge in more complex ways, mentors were also able to consider the value of different aspects of subject knowledge in effective teaching. Interestingly, given the research cited earlier by Hashweh (1985) and Grossman *et al.* (1989), it was the broader, more 'theoretical' subject principles that they had found so hard to articulate in respect of their own practice that mentors maintained were of most importance for student teachers to understand. One mentor maintained, 'Students need to . . . have a sense of what the subject is and why it is important.' Another commented, 'In early years you may not need to know about, for example, multiplying fractions, but you do need to know as much "about" that subject as you do if you were teaching Y6.'

In addition, mentors began to interpret students' 'difficulties' in new ways. Mentors maintained that previously they had not even considered lack of subject knowledge when students had problems with their practice. For example, the comment was made, 'I don't know what I used to think students were lacking . . . perhaps knowledge about pupil learning. I wasn't in touch with the subject.' Lack of subject knowledge, it was claimed — in particular their lack of understanding of the nature and key ideas of a subject — now 'made sense of a lot things that students do wrong.' One mentor commented, for example, 'I was just staggered by the holes in the students' subject knowledge. Whenever I tried to push J into questions of why she was doing it there was no understanding of the subject at all. There was nothing there. She just had a top up of good ideas for activities. When I was asking, "Why do we teach art?" It was, "Well they like it, they like to express themselves", it was at a basic level. There was nothing else there.'

But it was not only students' difficulties but their *own* understandings that mentors began to interpret differently. In particular, mentors became aware of the subject understandings on which they already drew — if unconsciously — in planning pupil activities. As one mentor explained, 'I had seen it as general knowledge about teaching. Now I see it as knowledge about the subject which enables me to plan effective teaching from it.'

Changes in mentors' attitudes were not only concerned with the role of subject knowledge in their teaching but also with the importance of subject knowledge in their pupils' learning. For example, while initially mentors had maintained the fundamental importance of 'process' rather than 'content', mentors now maintained, 'They need to know some facts, don't they. The only point of investigation is to increase their knowledge . . . you can't *just* have process . . .' In addition, aspects such as enthusiasm, independence and thinking — which had been 'free-floating', now became rooted in subject knowledge. Instead of wanting the children simply to become 'thinkers', mentors now maintained, 'I think you want to train children to think like mathematicians not just do mathematics, and think like scientists and craftsmen, it is those aspects you're trying to develop . . .'

At the end of the project mentors appeared to have found ways in which to integrate their more complex understandings about subject knowledge into their child-centred thinking and practice. As one mentor explained, 'It's got to be a *balance* at primary level, between the content . . . and . . . the values and attitudes and ways of working are equally important.' Another mentor commented, 'If the children came out without knowledge in certain subject areas then, even if they came out keen and enthusiastic, I would still think I hadn't done my job, I had failed somewhere. But equally if they had just been prepared for KS2 with no understanding, with no way of using that information, equally I would feel I'd failed.'

Summary and Conclusion

In the early stages of the project mentors had appeared to view learning as 'natural' — it was seen as a gradual and emergent process of development. Indeed, we have seen that this perspective was also extended to incorporate how mentors viewed teachers and their own teaching. Mentors maintained, for example, that some individuals were 'naturally' good teachers, and that the National Curriculum pushed them to teach beyond the point at which they were 'naturally' enthusiastic. I noted that while the National Curriculum may have required mentors to teach subject content, mentors' *commitment* was to providing their pupils with what they considered to be relevant and meaningful 'experiences'. I noted also that mentors maintained that they valued pupils' emotional and social development and the encouragement of positive attitudes towards learning at least as highly as pupils' intellectual development. Subject knowledge, and the demands of individual subject areas, were therefore seen as of little significance to effective teaching and as unhelpful or even detrimental to their pupils' learning.

Through involvement in this project — through working with students and colleagues and, importantly, through time away from the classroom in which to discuss and reflect on their practice — 'subject knowledge' appeared to become 'visible' to the mentors. For example, mentors became aware of their own difficulties with subject knowledge — both with substantive knowledge and with the principles and processes underlying the activities they taught; they became aware of the positive influence of a more thorough subject knowledge on their practice; and they became aware of the subject knowledge on which they already drew when devising pupil activities. Indeed, towards the end of the project, mentors generally agreed that subject knowledge had been 'the missing element' in their thinking and practice.

Ultimately, mentors appeared to accept not only the importance of subject knowledge for themselves as teachers, but also the importance of subject knowledge for their pupils. But this is not to say that they completely relinquished their child-centred beliefs. Mentors found that seeing early years education as a process of inducting children into the 'discourse and disciplines of subjects' did not negate their beliefs about children's learning or their commitment to promoting children's social and emotional development. Similarly, acknowledging the integrity and demands of individual subject areas did not mean that they could no longer provide their pupils with worthwhile and meaningful experiences. The mentors had thus, for themselves, found a way in which to resolve the apparent tension between the subject-centred and child-centred approaches to teaching.

At the beginning of this chapter it was noted that the government appears to be trying to improve teachers' subject knowledge and bring about a more subject-centred approach to primary school teaching through initiatives such as the implementation of a national curriculum and assessment system and reforms of ITT. But if early years teachers are not aware of their difficulties with subject understanding, if they do not see subject knowledge as of any relevance to effective practice or of particular importance in their pupils' learning then these initiatives are likely to count for nothing. If there is to be any possibility of change, it is teachers' *attitudes* towards subject knowledge that need to be addressed first and foremost.

I conclude, however, with a cautionary note. It will be remembered that the teachers in this study ultimately maintained that if students were to be effective primary practitioners then an understanding of the nature and key ideas of the subjects they were required to teach was of fundamental importance. It may be of significance, therefore, that this was not what they chose to mentor to their students — rather, teachers continued to induct their students into child-centred ways of thinking and teaching. At the beginning of this chapter I commented that although attitudes may predispose us to behave in certain ways, our behaviour in real life situations will be subject to other influences. Even changing teachers' attitudes towards subject knowledge, therefore, will not *guarantee* any change in their classroom practice!

Note

1 It is important to note that this research was undertaken before the government reforms of the National Curriculum following the Dearing review.

References

ALEXANDER, R. (1984) *Primary Teaching*, Eastbourne, Holt, Rinehart and Winston.
ALEXANDER, R., ROSE, J. and WOODHEAD, C. (1992) *Curriculum Organisation and Classroom Practice in Primary Schools*, London, HMSO.
ANNING, A. (Ed) (1995) *A National Curriculum for the Early Years*, Buckingham, OUP.
BENNETT, S.N. and CARRE, C.G. (Eds) (1993) *Learning to Teach*, London, Routledge.
BLENKIN, G. and KELLY, A. (Eds) (1994) *The National Curriculum and Early Learning*, London, Paul Chapman Publishing.
COX, T. and SANDERS, S. (1994) *The Impact of the National Curriculum on the Teaching of Five Year Olds*, London, Falmer Press.
DEPARTMENT FOR EDUCATION (DFE) (1993) WO (1993) *The Initial Training of Primary School Teachers: New Criteria for Course Approval* (Circular 14/93) London, DFE; *Circular 62/93*, Cardiff, The Welsh Office.

FURLONG, J. and MAYNARD, T. (1995) *Mentoring Student Teachers: The Growth of Professional Knowledge*, London, Routledge.

GROSSMAN, P.L., WILSON, S.M. and SHULMAN, L. (1989) 'Teachers of substance: Subject matter knowledge for teaching', in REYNOLDS, M.C. (Ed) *Knowledge Base for the Beginning Teacher*, New York, Pergamon.

HASHWEH, M.Z. (1985) 'An exploratory study of teacher knowledge and teaching: The effects of science teachers' knowledge of subject matter and their conceptions of learning on their teaching', Unpublished doctoral dissertation, Stanford University, Stanford, CA.

LAWLOR, S. (1990) *Teachers Mistaught*, London, Centre for Policy Studies.

MAYNARD, T. (1996) 'Mentoring subject knowledge in the primary school', in MCINTYRE, D. and HAGGER, H. (Eds) *Mentors in Schools: Developing the Profession of Teaching*, London, David Fulton Publishers.

MCDIARMID, G.W., BALL, D. and ANDERSON, C. (1989) 'Why staying one chapter ahead doesn't really work: Subject specific pedagogy', in REYNOLDS, M.C. (Ed) *Knowledge Base for the Beginning Teacher*, New York, Pergamon.

MCNAMARA, D. (1994) *Classroom Pedagogy and Primary Practice*, London, Routledge.

OFFICE FOR STANDARDS IN EDUCATION (OFSTED) (1994) *Primary Matters: A Discussion on Teaching and Learning in Primary Schools*, London, Ofsted Publications Centre.

OFFICE FOR STANDARDS IN EDUCATION (OFSTED) (1995) *The Annual Report of Her Majesty's Chief Inspector of Schools, Part 1: Standards and Quality in Education*, London, HMSO.

O'HEAR, A. (1988) 'Who teaches the teachers?', London, Social Affairs Unit.

SANDERS, S. (1994) 'Mathematics and mentoring', in JAWORSKI, B. and WATSON, A. (Eds) *Mentoring in Mathematics Teaching*, London, Falmer Press for the Mathematics Association.

SCHWAB, J. (1978) 'Education and the structure of the disciplines', in WESTBURY, I. and WILKOF, N.J. (Eds) *Science, Curriculum and Liberal Education*, Chicago, University of Chicago Press.

SHULMAN, L. (1986) 'Those who understand: Knowledge growth in teaching', *Educational Researcher*, **15**, 2, pp. 4–14.

WILSON, S., SHULMAN, L. and RICHERT, A. (1987) '150 Different Ways of Knowing: Representations of Knowledge in Teaching', in CALDERHEAD, J. (Ed) *Exploring Teachers' Thinking*, London, Cassell.

WRAGG, E.C., BENNETT, S.N. and CARRE, C.G. (1989) 'Primary teachers and the National Curriculum', *Research Papers in Education*, **4**, pp. 17–37.

4   Parents and the National Curriculum

Felicity Wikeley

This chapter addresses the issues raised by parents in response to the introduction of the National Curriculum and its accompanying standardized assessment. The research described interviewed a sample of parents of the first cohort of 7-year-olds to be assessed using Standard Assessment Tasks. Their attitudes and opinions were recorded over a period of three years throughout their children's experience of Key Stage One

The parents' desire for a fair system that not only worked to the benefit of their own children but for all children regardless of prior skills and ability was clearly apparent. A view of assessment as a useful diagnostic tool rather than performance indicator indicated their wish to be involved in their children's education, discussing strengths and weaknesses with teachers which would enable them to offer real help and support at home.

Introduction

The rhetoric surrounding the 1988 Education Reform Act (1988a) which introduced a national curriculum and its accompanying assessment was very much about parents and their supposed concerns about declining standards in the education of their children. Language such as 'parent power' and 'parentocracy' was often associated with its perceived aims and objectives. Until that time much of the previous research involving parents evolved from the findings of the Plowden report in which parental interest had been shown to be influential in their children's educational attainment (Douglas, 1964) and focused on how this interest could be enhanced and encouraged for the benefit of their children. Over the years this has resulted in numerous parental involvement programmes of varying types with accompanying research into the effects of such initiatives on children's learning (Topping, 1986; Griffiths and Hamilton, 1984; Hannon and Jackson, 1987). The 1988 Education Act which introduced the National Curriculum inspired a different type of research about parent and education. This was mainly concerned with the relationship between parents and education policy (Gewirtz *et al.*, 1995; Woods, 1993; Edwards and Whitty, 1992) particularly in terms of school choice and the consumer role for parents within the education system. There were few studies, of which the work described here was one, about parents' expectations of their children's schools and their actual opinions and attitudes towards the changes in the education their children were receiving. The reaction of the parents in this study reflected this lack of consultation.

I was glad to do it. It gives credence to the fact that everyone is not happy with the National Curriculum and what's going on. It's given me the confidence to say I don't like the National Curriculum. Because the National Curriculum was imposed and I was really glad there was the opportunity to find out what opinion parents really had — no political body has ever asked us if we wanted what they have done. (Mother on being asked if being part of the project had had any effect on her interaction with the school)

However as early as 1987 the politicians were using parents' concerns as the *raison d'être* for the new legislation. In proposing the Act to the House of Commons, Kenneth Baker, the then Secretary of State for Education claimed it would '... free schools and colleges to deliver the standards which parents and employers want' and in 1992 another Secretary of State for Education, John Patten, said 'our proposals are radical, sensible and in tune with what parents want.' (*Times Educational Supplement*, 7 August 1992.) This chapter explores how true these statements were.

It draws on research carried out at the time of the introduction of the National Curriculum which collected the views of a group of parents who were to be particularly affected by the new legislation in that their children would be amongst the first cohort to go through their whole school lives with a national curriculum and its accompanying standardized assessment. It identifies two underlying themes to the parents' responses. These are a desire for a fair system of education for all children that acknowledges their differences, and secondly a desire to be actively involved in their own child's education at an individual level.

The National Curriculum and Assessment

Much of the information directed at parents from the Department of Education and Science prior to the introduction of the National Curriculum took the line that it could only be to their benefit and their children's. In a pamphlet entitled *Our Changing Schools: A Handbook for Parents* distributed in 1988 they were told:

The National Curriculum is designed to help raise standards for all pupils. It will be brought in over the next few years. It means that your child will receive a broad, balanced education throughout primary school, but one which is based on his or her needs. (DES, 1988b, p. 11)

Again, in 1991 the new Secretary of State for Education, Kenneth Clarke wrote:

Your child has the right to a good education, and you have the right to know both what is being taught in your child's school and how your child is progressing. That is why we now have a National Curriculum which sets out for the first time what children should know, understand and be able to do at each stage of their education from 5 to 16. (DES, 1991: inside front cover)

and later in the same document the advantages for parents were further elaborated:

The National Curriculum guarantees that all children will be taught what they really need to know, with checks on their progress at every stage. This means that you as a parent can find out what your child is doing at school and why . . . This combination of clear targets and national tests will help ensure that:

- teachers have the highest possible expectation of their pupils;
- standards are raised in schools right across the country;
- pupils can move from one school to another without disrupting their education; and
- you, as a parent, can hold your chid's school to account for the progress your child is making and for the standards of the school generally. (DES, 1991)

From such documents it would not have been an unfair conclusion to assume that the new legislation had been a response to an outcry from parents about falling standards, lack of information from schools and incompetent teachers making wrong judgments about children's potential. However in reality, prior to its introduction there appears to have been very little research into what parents did or did not have concerns about and secondly, even less research into whether the proposed reforms were 'in line with what they wanted'.

At the same time another debate was being conducted in the media as to the efficacy of 'traditional' or 'progressive' methods of teaching. There was concern about the 'real books' methods of teaching and the use, or not, of phonics in the teaching of reading. This often spilled over into a general dismissal of 'trendy' teachers who used topic work to the exclusion of traditional teaching of the basics. 'Back to basics' was a phrase adopted by the political right and used with relish by the media. Because it was part of the Education *Reform* Act the implication was that education had got into such a bad state that it needed a major reform such as the introduction of the National Curriculum to restore these traditional methods. Even today, nearly seven years later, there are those who believe that the National Curriculum was introduced to make 'trendy teachers' return to 'traditional' methods of teaching

The national curriculum was never meant to increase the time spent on the three Rs, but to improve the way they are taught. (*Daily Telegraph*, 21 February 1996)

In reality methods of teaching were not mentioned in the DES literature or in the ministerial statements. The National Curriculum was about curriculum content not the methods by which it was taught. Similarly the media's portrayal of parents' concerns about education was not based on reliable evidence. Did parents really have concerns about falling standards? Did they want to know more about what their children were doing at school? Were they feeling uninformed about their children's progress? Did they relate any concerns about their children's progress to the inefficient teaching methods being used in schools?

To try and answer some of the questions posed above 138 parents, whose children started school during the 1988–9 school year, were interviewed in some depth over the first three years of its implementation. Their children entered Year 1 in September 1989, as the National Curriculum was introduced and were not only part of the first cohort to be taught the National Curriculum throughout their school lives but also were the first to participate in the Standard Assessment Tasks (SATs) for 7-year-olds in 1991. The aim of the project was to find out these parents' opinions and attitudes to the changes that had been introduced in their name and would affect the whole of their children's school lives. They attended eleven primary schools in the South West of England, selected to ensure the sample included parents from a wide range of socio-economic background and experience of differing school organization and setting.

Although the study covered a wide range of issues connected with the 1988 Act (Hughes *et al.*, 1994) this chapter concentrates on the parents' opinions and attitudes towards the National Curriculum and assessment itself. They were asked about whether or not they approved of the National Curriculum or even the concept of a national curriculum. They were asked what they knew about what their children were taught in various subject areas and whether they felt this was what they should be taught. They were also asked about their views on the assessment of their children against national norms. Because of the public interest in methods they were asked about the methods being used to teach their children and whether they had concerns about falling standards. The interviews were carried out over a period of three years, whilst their children completed Key Stage 1 and entered Key Stage 2 and the parents' changing views, as they and their children's teachers became more familiar with the new curriculum, noted. This chapter discusses those views and the challenges and opportunities they offer schools in the creation of a true partnership with parents.

Fairness

Whatever the rhetoric implied as to the reasons for reform there was some evidence that parents took on board the arguments they were being exposed to and believed that the new policy would improve their relationship with their children's schools.

The first interviews took place in the Autumn of 1989. The National Curriculum had only been introduced in the September and even then only partially.

All children entering Year 1 had to follow the National Curriculum in English, maths and science (the core subjects) although the 'foundation subjects' (history, geography, technology, music, art and PE) would be brought on line in subsequent years. Although the parents had been the recipients of national advertising with regard to its introduction it would have been understandable if they did not feel fully informed at this stage. However all the parents said that they had heard of the National Curriculum and even though 30 per cent felt that they did not know enough about it to either approve or disapprove, the rest were prepared to form some sort of judgment. The majority approved of its introduction even if they felt it had disadvantages as well as advantages. By the third year of the study only about 10 per cent were openly ambivalent because of a perceived lack of knowledge. Children were often parents' main source of information; they learned about the National Curriculum as their children experienced it.

One main advantage cited by parents of the introduction of a national curriculum was that it would prevent their children being subject to the vagaries of individual teachers and schools. Some parents saw this in terms of teachers with particular interests or even political viewpoints and others in terms of progress through school being less likely to involve the repetition of the same topics year after year due to the lack of whole school curriculum planning. Moving schools was also regarded as being something that would benefit from the existence of a national curriculum, in that children would be able to slot into the same teaching programmes in their new school without any disruption to their progress. In broad terms parents saw some of the inequalities of experience being ironed out in that all children would be receiving the same experience of education regardless of where they went to school or by whom they were taught.

It will give everyone a fair chance

It's a good idea, getting children to compete on equal terms

It will prevent waste of pupil time on irrelevant issues such as political sympathies of staff. It allows debate nationally.

The emphasis on English and maths was also approved of by over two-thirds of the parents. This was because they saw them as the basis for all learning, giving all children a fair chance

You can get on if you can read and write and do maths

Science was more problematic. At the beginning of the study it was a new subject area for this age group or at least in an explicit form and many were unsure of what it would look like in practice. For many this was the most innovatory introduction at Key State 1 and was the subject that a large number of parents had some ambivalence about. It was the one they found most surprising but often this related to what the children were doing — topics parents associated with their own secondary education now being covered by their 5-year-olds.

As will be discussed later, as the study progressed they became more enthusiastic, mainly taking their lead from their children.

> She wants to be involved — I didn't think she would be — the questions she asks are surprising — if I'm measuring etc.

> She amazed me. Her eating changed. We had discussions at every meal. What was danger food? Anything with sugar is danger. Her attitude to sweets changed. I was surprised at how much she had taken in. She is very keen.

It was accepted as one of the core subjects but less readily than English and maths.

An integral part of the National Curriculum was the accompanying standardized assessment. At the start of the study although most of the parents appeared to know that their children would be assessed at the end of their infant stage — Key Stage 1 was not a term with which they were familiar in 1989 — they were unsure of what would be involved. In common with many professionals, they were unsure how much was to be based on teacher assessment, how much on standardized tests and what form these tests would take. However the majority of parents felt that assessment would be a good thing. This was a view that changed over the period of the study.

Originally their concerns were expressed as reservations about pressure being put on children. Memories of their own experiences of the 11+ examinations still loomed large for several parents and they were concerned about children being labelled failures at the age of 7. There was also some concern as to what the outcomes of assessment would be. Would children be expected to repeat years? Would they be held back if they did not achieve the required standard? There was some confusion as to whether the results would be made public. Just over 50 per cent of the sample were aware that their children would be assessed during 1991 although half of these did not know if they would be told their child's results. The majority thought this should be available to them but the publication of results — still a possibility at that stage — created even more confusion and concern. Within the sample there were two very small schools and within the primary sector as a whole there are many. Parents in these schools were concerned that public results would lead to the identification of individual children within those schools. Children would then stand in danger of being 'blamed' for a school's low performance. This they saw as exerting unnecessary pressure on young children.

The second concern relating to the equity issue was the age range of the children involved. Children who were only just 7 would be assessed at the same time as those who were nearly 8. Some parents expressed concern that the use of such tests as performance indicators rather than as purely diagnostic tools would disadvantage those children whose birthdays fell later in the school year. There was some discussion during the life of the project that the government would introduce paper and pencil tests because of the difficulties of administering the SATs and for similar reasons many parents expressed their concern that this could disadvantage

Table 4.1: Children's 'Actual' and 'Expected' Results (Year 3)

	English (n = 97)	Maths (n = 96)	Science (n = 92)
Did better than expected	22%	9%	24%
Did same as expected	65%	75%	68%
Did worse than expected	13%	16%	8%

some children. Parents were not just concerned with benefits for their own children but also expected a system that was fair for all children.

> My own child could cope quite well, but others who are not so good at reading and writing would be put under pressure. It's not fair. There's enough pressure at the 11+.

This reaction was at odds with the response of the teachers interviewed in the study who felt that parents were only interested in the success of their own children. Teachers quoted examples of parents who frisked children invited home for tea to find out if the reading book they were taking home was of a higher level than that of their own child and cited examples of 'pushy' parents who had unreasonably inflated views of their children's abilities. This view could imply that the parents' belief in their own children's success allowed them to be magnanimous towards those they regarded as being less able. However this view was not borne out by evidence from another source.

During the Summer term of 1992, immediately after their children had completed the SATs, the parents had been interviewed by telephone and asked what level (i.e., 1, 2 or 3) they expected their child to achieve in English, maths and science. These expectations were compared with the child's actual results as reported to them at the end of the Summer term. Table 4.1 shows the high percentage of parents who were right in their expectations of their children's results and where they were wrong. In English and science they were more likely to underestimate their child's performance than overestimate it.

This would make their desire for a fair system genuine and was illustrated by the parent who complained to the teacher that her son was not being heard to read often enough. The response she received was that to hear all the children every day would take four hours. A few days later the teacher reassured her that she had managed to hear her son more often now. The parent was unsure whether she should be pleased for her own son or concerned that the other children in the class were losing out. A dilemma she acknowledged and did not feel comfortable with.

Involvement

The other advantage that most parents saw in the National Curriculum centred on a feature that had been prominent in the DES literature. It would enable them to know more about what their children were doing and consequently they would be able to help their children when they needed it. Since the Plowden Report (Central Advisory Council for Education (England), 1967) in the 1960s it has been generally accepted that parents *should* be involved in their children's education and many studies show how influential they can be on their children's progress (Tizard *et al.*, 1982; Widlake and Macleod, 1985). However most of these have been directed at teachers and schools and parents' understanding of, and the part they can play in, the school's aims and objectives. Very little has been addressed at harnessing parents knowledge of their own children and their natural desire to help. Parents are rarely, if ever asked what they know about their own children's abilities or ways of learning. Being able to help their children in a more productive, focused way was the main perceived advantage of assessment as well as the National Curriculum. They expected the National Curriculum to give them more information about what their children were doing. They expected assessment to give them and teachers more detail about their children's progress within that curriculum so that support could be focused. Neither the National Curriculum nor assessment fully lived up to this expectation.

Although the majority of parents were happy that English, maths and science were the core subjects they were less sure about the foundation subjects at this early stage. In the first year these had not been introduced in any formal sense so the parents were asked about each foundation subject separately; was it and should it be part of the curriculum for this age group. In subsequent years they were asked if they had noticed any changes in the amount of each subject being experienced by their children. Art, PE and music appeared to be regarded as an accepted part of the early years curriculum. History, geography and technology caused more of a problem. Their understanding of a particular subject area often related to their own school experience which many thought was not appropriate for this age group. As with science some parents had problems in identifying what history, geography or technology looked like at this age.

Well they are always cutting things out — making boxes. Is that technology?

From the things he says they must do geography. All this business with the ozone thing. They talk about different countries.

[Design and Technology] Computing — I suppose that comes into it.

Those who could conceive of them as cross-curricular themes were more approving of their inclusion than those who saw them as discrete subjects as in the secondary curriculum.

They did a whole thing on water — water treatment works, reservoir — they combine it all and then go back and write about it.

Do all those — do it as part of a project — I agree with that — they also do country dancing.

For the core subjects the parents were asked about the content of the curriculum and teaching methods being used in their children's schools. They were asked if they thought there was anything surprising about either the curriculum or methods. There was a close relationship between what they felt was being taught and what they felt should be taught. It was a difficult question in that the parents did not seem to be able to easily separate the two concepts and would answer the 'should be' question with descriptions of what happened in the classroom. The National Curriculum did not appear to make them feel more informed about what their children were doing than before its implementation.

spelling — but they are very good at that here . . .

the basics — they spend a lot of time on that.

Although parents continued to ask until the end of the project for more information about what their children were doing they probably knew more than they thought. In the second year the parents were asked to complete a daily diary for two weeks of the contact they had with the school including information that came home. The research team's intentions had been to look at how schools and parents interacted and how parents learned about school matters. What was really learned was how much information comes home with the children about what they are learning at school. Diaries gave us vast amounts of information about curriculum areas covered at school and often continued at home. It is therefore not surprising that the parents' expectations as to what should be taught is based on their knowledge of what is taught as conveyed by their children.

The final interviews with the parents took place in the Autumn of 1992, when the children were in the first term of Key Stage 2. A real advantage of assessment would have been to give them, and the teachers, useful information to be used to help the child's future progression. With hindsight they felt that the Key Stage 1 assessment and the reports they had received from the schools on their children's progress did not do this. When interviewed after receiving the report, one parent counted the number of times 'satisfactory' appeared and asked the interviewer what that told him about his son.

Another disappointment for some parents had been the lack of opportunity to talk directly to their children's teachers about their child's progress. Some of the schools, owing to the increased workload presented by the SATs and written reporting procedures had either cancelled parents evenings or discouraged parents from attending unless they had a problem they wished to discuss. Although appreciating the extra workload that SATs had caused the teachers the parents regarded meeting the teacher face to face as an important aspect of sharing information about the child's progress and learning about how they could help their child at home. Written reports on their own did not give the same feeling of sharing in that they were more one way. One mother commented that she wanted to talk to the teacher but had been told that she was only available if there was a problem or something the parent was worried about. If she saw the teacher the implication was that she was a 'worrying mother' as her child was reported to be at Level 2 in all subjects. Although she wanted to discuss her child's progress in more detail with the teacher she was concerned about giving the impression that she was a 'pushy' parent with inflated expectations of his attainment. The face to face contact with the teachers appeared to mean more to the parents than just the receiving of information. It was part of their involvement with their child's education.

Another aspect of this desire to share information about the child was explored in questions at beginning of the project when the parents were asked about being involved in the assessment of their children. Several had thought that they should be involved — they know their children and could offer a complementary insight into their learning. The fact that they know their children was borne out by the evidence in Table 4.1 but how this knowledge can be tapped by the teachers has yet to be shown.

Unlike their desire for a fair system which is based on a concern for all children, the parents' desire for involvement in their children's education was very much directed towards their own children. They wanted to know about their children's progress so that they could help them with their weaknesses. They wanted to speak to teachers so that they know the help they were offering was in line with what they were doing at school but several parents commented that they were not interested in being involved in all children's education. Although helping in school is common at this age, several parents reflected that they did not want to go into school to hear other children read, help with cooking or supervise swimming but to work with their own child either in school or at home. The teachers in the study had a tendency to describe parental involvement as parents in school and in some schools parents were specifically not allowed to help in their own children's classes for fear of favouritism.

Conclusion

The parents' concern for a fair system that works to the advantage of ALL children could be seen to be at odds with the government perception of the sole concern of parents being the desire to gain the best for their own child. The push for more selective schools as being attractive to parents ignores the fact that for every grammar school created four secondary modern schools would also have to exist. 'Opting-out' ballots have been lost because of parental awareness that financial advantage for their children's schools could mean disadvantage for others around them. However, it would be wrong to imply that all parents saw the legislation as bad. The majority of the parents were in favour of the National Curriculum and the changes it had brought about to their children's education even if they were more ambivalent about assessment.

It would also be wrong to assume from these findings that parents are at odds with the teachers of their children's' schools. It must not be forgotten that by asking the questions minor irritations or small reservations can, purely by the fact of being articulated, appear to be major concerns. However it would also be wrong for schools to believe that there was no way parents' interest and understanding of their own children could be used to the benefit of the child more effectively.

Parents' relatively modest expectations of the National Curriculum gleaned from the publicity that surrounded it were not met. They wanted it to provide really useful information, more than had been available before, about their children's strengths and weaknesses that they could use to give their children real support. Ultimately they felt they were more likely to get this from personal detailed discussions with teachers about their children's progress than from standardized tests which they could see would not necessarily be fair to all children.

It has to acknowledged that these interviews were carried out during the first years of the National Curriculum and it would be interesting to see how similar parents feel now that the Dearing review has been implemented.

Although the review does not address reporting procedures as such it does encourage more qualitative reporting of art, PE and music which will facilitate discussions between parents and teachers. Absolute measures of progress were less important than detailed formative discussions with teachers which were seen as beneficial to the children. The parents did not appear to have a problem with teacher assessment but wanted the opportunity to use it as the basis of a genuine two way dialogue. In line with other studies (MacBeath and Weir, 1991) the children were shown as the major source of information and knowledge and this was extended further in that parents were shown to be taking their lead from their children in terms of their learning. Children share things at home and there were instances of discussions between parents about what constituted learning, how important written work was etc. being conducted in front of the researchers.

Another positive outcome of the review from the parents' point of view might be the changes in assessment procedures, particularly the simplification of SATs. As was shown in their reaction to the assessment procedure and concern for the pressure it was putting on teachers, they were not keen on the concept of assessment being used as a performance indicator rather than a diagnostic tool. Another concern was the loss of teaching time during that period. They felt their children had lost time with their teachers during the assessment period. Interestingly, although it was intended differently, these children were also amongst the first cohort to undergo Key Stage 2 assessment in 1995. Although this particular project was unable to interview their parents at that stage in one of the schools involved they did organize a protest and try and withdraw their children from the SATs claiming that valuable teaching time would be lost without any substantial gain in useful diagnostic information. They were almost unanimous in their belief that their children had not experienced any real stress or been put under any pressure by the assessment procedures but they talked of their children 'missing' their teachers'. Teachers are very important to the children in Year 1 and the constant time out of the classrooms doing one to one assessments of reading or supervising science SATs in small groups meant that they were not available to the children. Children were reporting to their parents that they had been told not to bother Mrs . . . and if they wanted any help to go to the classroom assistant or, in some cases, supply teachers were bought in for what seemed to the children considerable periods of time. The fact that the teacher's workload has also been reduced by the review, in that the number of SATs has been reduced by science only being assessed through teacher assessment, will also help in this.

These are the sorts of opportunities schools and teachers could be picking up on. Parents' understanding of how their children learn is an issue rarely discussed with teachers. Tasks may be shared as in Impact maths or paired reading schemes but there is little opportunity for parents to share with teachers their own learning theories or strategies. Parents liked the idea of building relationships with the teachers of their children. In fact it was one of their most favoured characteristic of a 'good' school but they appreciated that time was needed to do that. Teachers who were grappling with innovations did not have time to talk to parents at length or to build relationships. The parents would be pleased that their children's' schools were to have some stability to help them in this task.

Finally, although their opinions about providing a level educational playing field for all and a desire to be directly involved with their own child's education predominated, the parents also wanted the first few years of schooling to contain an element of fun and spontaneity. Some schools had cancelled the Christmas concert because of the introduction of the National Curriculum and, whilst being sympathetic to the teachers' workload, it was seen as a loss. Things were returning to normal as the study finished but it is to be hoped that the push to raise national standards does not supersede parents' wishes to instil in their children a love of learning.

References

CENTRAL ADVISORY COUNCIL FOR EDUCATION (ENGLAND) (1967) *Children and Their Primary Schools: A Report of the (England) (Plowden Report)* London, HMSO.

CLARE, J. (1996) 'Teach us what we don't know', *The Daily Telegraph*, 21 February.

DEPARTMENT OF EDUCATION AND SCIENCE (DES) (1988a) *Education Reform Act*, London, HMSO.

DEPARTMENT OF EDUCATION AND SCIENCE (DES) (1988b) *Our Changing Schools: A Handbook for Parents*, London, HMSO.

DEPARTMENT OF EDUCATION AND SCIENCE (1991) *Your Child and the National Curriculum*, London, HMSO.

DEARING, R. (1994) *The National Curriculum and its Assessment: Final Report*, London, School Curriculum and Assessment Authority.

DOUGLAS, J.W.B. (1964) *The Home and the School: A Study of Ability and Attainment in the Primary School*, London, MacGibbon and Kee.

EDWARDS, A. and WHITTY, G. (1992) 'Parental choice and educational reform in Britain and the United States', *British Journal of Educational Studies*, **30**, pp. 101–17.

GEWIRTZ, S., BALL, S. and BOWE, R. (1995) *Markets, Choice and Equity in Education*, Buckingham, Open University Press.

GRIFFITHS, A. and HAMILTON, D. (1984) *Parent, Teacher, Child: Working Together in Children's Learning*, London, Methuen.

HANNON, P. and JACKSON, A. (1987) *The Belfield Reading Project*, London, National Children's Bureau.

HUGHES, M., WIKELEY, F. and NASH, T. (1994) *Parents and Their Children's Schools*, Oxford, Blackwell.

MACBEATH, J. and WEIR, D. (1991) *Attitudes to School*, Glasgow, Jordanhill College.

PATTEN, J. (1992) *Times Educational Supplement*, 7 August.

TIZARD, J., SCHOFIELD, W.N. and HEWISON, J. (1982) 'Collaboration between teachers and parents in assisting children's reading', *British Journal of Educational Psychology*, **52**, pp. 1–15.

TOPPING, K. (1986) *Parents As Educators: Training Parents to Teach Their Children*, London, Croom Helm.

WIDLAKE, P. and MACLEOD, F. (1985) *Raising Standards*, Coventry, CEDC.

WOODS, P. (1993) 'Parents as consumer-citizens', in MERTTENS, R., MAYERS, D., BROWN, A. and VASS, J. (Eds) *Ruling the Margins: Problematising Parental Involvement*, London, University of North London Press.

Part 2

*Pedagogical, Curricular and
Assessment Issues*

5   Teaching Subjects, Teaching Children: Topic-based Teaching within a Subject-based National Curriculum

Susan E. Sanders

One interpretation of a national curriculum organized into discrete subjects is that lessons should focus on individual subjects. The aim of this chapter is to explore the extent to which the teaching of early years pupils has moved and should move from the traditional rhetoric of the thematic, cross-curricular approach of the post-Plowden pedagogues towards subject focused teaching.

The chapter begins by outlining the origins of the current debate about thematic approaches and discrete subject teaching. It attempts to give a picture of the reality compared with the rhetoric of the organization of the early years curriculum prior to the National Curriculum and follows teachers' perceptions and attitudes towards it through its implementation and up to the Dearing reforms. This is followed by a discussion of two current challenges to, and realities of, early years teaching: teachers' subject knowledge and their ideological approaches to the curriculum. The chapter concludes with an examination of the implications of these current tensions for early years education and this author's position with regard to possible new approaches which offer solutions.

Introduction

Soon after the advent of the National Curriculum an article entitled 'Will there still be time for Rainbows?' was published. This title crystallized the concerns of many teachers of early years pupils; that the National Curriculum would dictate so much about what should be taught, how and when, that there would be no possibility for them to adhere to one of the tenets of child-centredness to respond to a stimulus when it presents itself. In this chapter I examine the extent to which the National Curriculum has challenged another tenet of primary pedagogy; that the curriculum should not be taught in discrete subject packets but in an integrated way through a thematic approach or topic work.[1]

From the Plowden Report (Central Advisory Council for Education (England, 1967) and the Gittins Report (Central Advisory Council for Education (Wales), 1967) onwards the thematic approach was as central to the early years curriculum as it was to primary education. Advisors, primary educationalists and teachers all publicly endorsed its virtues. During the late 1980s however, as I detail in Cox and

Sanders (1994) teachers perceived this approach to be under attack not only from the structure of the National Curriculum but from government through sponsored discussion such as that by Alexander, Rose and Woodhead (1992) in a document known as 'The Three Wise Men Report'. As Anning (1995) highlights

> ... for Early Years teachers with a deep-rooted belief in a curriculum based on children's developmental needs and interests, the dominance of subject knowledge in the professional discourse about the reforms left them feeling alienated and undervalued. (Anning, 1995, p. 6)

What has interested me since I first worked in a famously 'progressive' school in the early 1970s is the extent to which primary school teachers (and in particular teachers of early years pupils) really do teach in 'Plowdenist' ways. This was critically refocused for me when I joined a Higher Education Institution (HEI) situated in an area where the local advisors wholeheartedly espoused thematic approaches but my informal observation revealed a range of teaching approaches employed in many schools. In the next section I revisit some of the arguments in Cox and Sanders (1994, Chapter 9) and discuss them in light of our (and others') more recent research in an attempt to clarify the reality of early years classrooms.

The Thematic Approach: Rhetoric or Reality?

In Cox and Sanders (1994) we gave an account of the ways in which teachers expected the National Curriculum to lead to a change from the thematic, cross-curricular approach which they equated with child-centredness, to one of discrete subject teaching. We also detailed how support for the cross-curricular approach changed over the early years of the implementation of the National Curriculum and the possible driving forces for this sea change. Prior to the National Curriculum the topic web was a central focus of primary teachers' curriculum planning. Initial Teacher Education (ITE) students would be initiated into the mysteries of the topic web as a rite of passage into the profession. Teachers would send students back to their HEI with a copy as fundamental documentation prior to their teaching practice. In 1989 40 per cent of the schools in our survey of a random sample of primary and infant schools in a South Wales Local Education Authority stressed that they were using a cross-curricular approach (Cox and Sanders, 1994). Given the commitment of the local advisors and others (Curriculum Council for Wales, 1992) to such approaches I considered this surprisingly low. However both Simon (1981) and Delamont (1987) had already exposed the 'myth of the primary revolution'. Rather than a single-minded approach, observational research in the 1980s revealed a great deal of variety in teaching approaches employed in English primary schools.

Teachers and educationalists had expected the National Curriculum to affect thematic, cross-curricular and topic-based approaches to the curriculum as they perceived such an outcome as part of the government's agenda. Coulby (1990) warned that

A further major difficulty for the National Curriculum in primary schools is that it is perceived and described in terms of subjects. (Coulby, 1990, p. 14)

From Cox and Boyson (1977) to the Hillgate Group (1986, 1987) a derisory and ill-informed attack on many aspects of education including 'progressiveness' paved the way for the reforms which included the National Curriculum.

. . . in many places there is a serious risk of disciplined study being entirely swamped by an amorphous tide of easy-going discussion and idle play. (Hillgate Group, 1986, p. 2)

At its weakest there is a lot of sticking together of eggboxes and playing in the sand. (Kenneth Clarke, sometime Minister/Secretary of State for Education, reported in Anning, 1995, p. 3)

Indeed just prior to the introduction of the National Curriculum, Michael Fallon, a junior minister of Education in the Thatcher Government, warned that

The days of group project work were numbered, [that] teachers should forget the 'fiction of child centred learning' and 'the pursuit of happiness' and concentrate instead on individual subject learning and whole class teaching. (Quoted in Simon, 1993, p. 13)

And Galton (1995) asserts that:

One of the aims of those who conceived the idea of a National Curriculum was to raise standards by ending the influence on primary practice of what was referred to as 'Plowdenism'. (Galton, 1995, p. 73)

These attacks are often dismissed as being 'politically motivated'. More difficult for teachers to dismiss are the concerns of professional educators. Often the educators who expressed concerns were respected and I believe their concerns were certainly worthy of consideration by the teaching profession but somehow they too came to be seen as playing into the hands of the politicians and the once darlings of the profession became the focus of mistrust. Perhaps the most distressing example of these was that of Robin Alexander who first highlighted many of the flaws in what 'Plowdenism' had become in practice in many primary schools (Alexander, 1991). In fact his criticisms were foreshadowed some sixteen years earlier by Bruner.

A generation ago the progressive movement urged that knowledge be related to the child's own experience and brought out of the realm of empty abstractions. A good idea was translated into banalities about the home, the friendly postman and dustman, then the community, and so on.

It is a poor way to compete with the child's own dramas and mysteries. (Bruner, 1974, pp. 79–80)

In the early stages of the implementation of the National Curriculum teachers modified their interpretation of the thematic approach, often in line with the vilified 'Three Wise Men's' recommendations (Alexander, Rose and Woodhead, 1992). In Cox and Sanders (1994) we speculated as to the future of the thematic approach suggesting that perhaps it would lie with teachers of early years pupils. Since then a follow up to our research in 1994 (see Chapter 2) has shown that at Key Stage 1 the balance between thematic and subject specific teaching had, in the majority of classes, not shifted.

There has not been so much of a shift, we are still topic based. Possibly mathematics might be the most difficult subject to integrate into a theme. (Headteacher).

No, we still do the topic as much as before, except for mathematics. (Headteacher)

No major change. The cross-curricular approach was well in hand prior to the National Curriculum, we wish to continue to deliver in this way. Planning of work is informed by attainment targets but the approach is much as before. However there was always some subject specific teaching in mathematics, science and English. (Headteacher)

However at Key Stage 2 this situation was reversed, affirming our earlier speculation.

Not so much (change) at Key Stage 1, it's still topic based . . . (Headteacher)

Yes. Subjects are far more specific and difficult to bring into a theme. More and more teachers are specifying history or geography for that term. (Same Headteacher about Key Stage 2)

Another headteacher reported that at Key Stage 2

Teaching approach was cross-curricular until this year but it is no longer feasible and will now change. For example history, geography and science are to be taught specifically but there will be some ongoing thematic work.

Classteachers also indicated a difference between Key Stage 1 and Key Stage 2.

We still teach thematically. The infant curriculum adapts itself better to this than the junior. At Level 1 all aspects can be filled in (except for some areas of maths (sic) and science). (Classteacher)

OFSTED (1996) reporting on findings from school inspections for 1994–5 also distinguish between Key Stages 1 and 2 with regard to curriculum planning.

> Most primary schools plan the curriculum to meet National Curriculum requirements through a blend of separate subject teaching and topic work. Thematic and broad-based topic work is often prevalent in KS1. In KS2, work is increasingly focused on subjects either through subject-specific topics, particularly for history and geography, or separate subject lessons. (OFSTED, 1996, p. 39)

Interestingly our teachers were still emphasizing their unsolicited commitment to a cross-curricular approach in responses to questions when interviewed about the future of subject specific teaching after the Dearing Review (Dearing, 1994).

> There are pressures towards subject specific teaching but I'm a firm be-liever in the thematic approach. (Key Stage 1 Class teacher)

Unlike our earlier research, these findings, from our study of teachers in one LEA in Wales were not congruent with the findings of the larger scale PACE project (Pollard *et al.*, 1994). They found that

> In 1991 the curriculum experienced by (these) 6- and 7-year-old children was taught *far more* as single subjects than it had been in 1990. (Pollard *et al.*, 1994, p. 20)

One difference between our research and that of PACE is that their evidence is partly based on classroom observation whereas ours was gathered by question-naire. The differences could be explained by teachers' reticence to admit to 'giving up on thematic work'. However OFSTED base their findings on classroom obser-vations but their findings are three years later than those of PACE.

Stannard (1995) reported that most primary schools had a commitment to topic work, partly because the teachers saw topic planning as an economical way to manage the curriculum. He does not distinguish between usage at Key Stages 1 and 2 but suggests that at Key Stage 1 the topics are more general and at Key Stage 2 more subject focused.

However our teachers did not always see the shift in balance between thematic and subject specific teaching as beneficial or the only solution to the National Curriculum.

> Yes there has been a shift in balance. We've become more subject specific in teaching some National Curriculum subjects in both Key Stages but the way forward is by increasing the thematic coverage — we've lost more than we have gained. (Teaching Head)

Anning (1995) also reports other significant changes in the practice of primary school teachers in that

The choice of a topic is no longer the 'property' of individual class teachers. They have lost the freedom and spontaneity of curriculum planning they had previously enjoyed. Broad themes, usually to last a half-term in rolling two-year cycles, are determined at whole-school planning meetings. (Anning, 1995, p. 7)

Pedagogical Challenges for Early Years Teaching

Many teachers contend that the only way to approach coverage of a national curriculum as broad as that in England and Wales is by adopting a thematic, cross-curricular approach.

Yes there has been a shift in balance, we've become more subject specific in teaching some of the National Curriculum in both Key Stages but the way forward is by increasing the thematic coverage . . . (Headteacher)

Palmer and Pettit (1993) were committed to the retention of topic work in the early years despite the acknowledgment that:

The introduction of a subject-based curriculum in England and Wales has led to intense questioning of that assured position. Teachers and others are wondering whether in any case it is necessarily the best way of teaching young children. (Palmer and Pettit, 1993, Frontispiece)

Arnold (1991) articulated the same sentiment;

Topic work has been strongly criticised as being ineffective in promoting effective learning . . . from our own professional experience and our work with whole schools and groups of teachers we strongly disagree! (Arnold, 1991, p. 1)

However I contend that there still exist two major challenges to teachers which affect their desire to maintain a thematic approach to the early years curriculum. These are criticisms of their subject knowledge and the previously outlined politically motivated attack on post-Plowden primary practice.

Recently the New Right have taken a deficiency in teachers' knowledge of subject content as a focus for criticism of the profession. Galton (1995) convincingly asserts that this is based on a perspective from HMI:

That the weaknesses in primary practice that were observed and reported on by Her Majesty's Inspectorate stemmed largely from teacher's ignorance of the subject matter. As teachers improved their knowledge base, their confidence would increase and they would be prepared to be more flexible in their use of teaching strategies. (Galton, 1995, p. 94)

Research evidence exists to support the view that primary teachers have deficiencies in their knowledge as well as misconceptions (e.g., Bennett and Carré, 1993; Summers, 1994) (see also Chapter 3). However this is not unique to England and Wales (Borko and Livingston, 1989) neither is it surprising given the breadth of the current curriculum (eleven subjects in England, twelve in Wales including Religious Education).

The government has once again sought to tackle this deficit through regulations for ITE. Although, as we reported in Cox and Sanders (1994) the 1993 regulations (Welsh Office, 1993) suggested that Newly Qualified Teachers (NQTs) might have a limit to the National Curriculum subjects they would have studied, the Welsh Office indicated that they expected that *for the time being* most courses would continue to prepare students to teach the whole curriculum. Consider then the implications of the recently developed entry profile for NQTs currently being piloted in England (and under consideration in Wales) which require a subject knowledge equivalent to that of Level 7 in all National Curriculum subjects. No doubt this is a strategy for overcoming the problem highlighted by the influential Alexander, Rose and Woodhead's (1992) statement:

> The subject knowledge required by the National Curriculum makes it unlikely that the generalist primary teacher will be able to teach all subjects in the depth required. This is particularly the case in Key Stage 2, but is true also in Key Stage 1. (Alexander, Rose and Woodhead, 1992, p. 35)

But does this not also have implications for the approach to the early years curriculum? If an NQT has to achieve Level 7 in a subject to be considered 'competent' then this might well lead to a limit to the number of subjects an NQT could be deemed 'competent to teach'. If a teacher is not 'licensed to teach' all subjects in the National Curriculum then how can he or she adopt a truly thematic approach? Or does this extend the conspiracy too far? Woodhead in his role as Chief Inspector of Schools for England laments that in 1993/94

> Too few primary schools made the most of teachers who had particular subject expertise ... (OFSTED, 1995, p. 27)

If the conspiracy theory holds (and I believe there is a subject agenda) then the lack of subject knowledge must be addressed.

The political attack on post-Plowden primary practice as a contributory factor to low standards has been long and the media has been instrumental in reaffirming the myth. In the previous section I outlined this attack in the run up to the 1988 ERA. The attack continues:

> For too long our children have been at the mercy of trendy 'experts' ... (*The Sun* 29 July 1992 reported in Anning, 1995)

Unfortunately many of the defences offered to these attacks have not been based on rigorous research but on 'a gut feeling' such as that expressed by Gammage (1994) when he exhorted a meeting of a local branch of National Association for Primary Education 'We know its right don't we!.' There also exists a series of statements from the Plowden Report for which it is difficult to track the research base for example:

Children's learning does not fit into subject categories. (Curriculum Advisory Council for Education (England) 1967, para 555)

However this idea has been internalized by the profession and is now taken as a self-evident truth.

This is illustrated by comments such as this from a classteacher during our follow up research

Children do not see knowledge as compartmentalized.

and this from The Early Years Curriculum Group (EYCG) (1989)

Learning is holistic and for the young child is not compartmentalised under subject headings. (EYCG, 1989, p. 3)

If teachers of early years pupils are to maintain their allegiance to a child-centred ideology they must take one of two courses of action. They must either dispel criticisms of their approaches to learning e.g., regarding the use of a thematic approach *or* they must resolve their personal conflict about subject specific teaching. In either case they must address the issue of their lack of subject matter knowledge, although there are inferences that I draw above that the breadth of subjects they might be expected to have deep knowledge about could be less and thus more realistic.

Supporters of the thematic approach produced works to assist the improvement of topic work under the National Curriculum (Arnold, 1991; Palmer and Pettit, 1993) and these have no doubt been instrumental, along with a great deal of localized INSET for the advances made in the planning of topic work since Alexander, Rose and Woodhead (1992).

Many primary schools were continuing to review the relative contributions of topic work and separate subject teaching in meeting NC requirements. . . . Improvements found now in most schools included agreed long-term topic frameworks for each Key Stage and a move from broad-based topics in KS1 to a sharper subject focus in KS2. (OFSTED, 1995, p. 26)

However such improvements have not necessarily resulted in the advances in attainment in all subjects that might have been expected. The dissatisfaction with Welsh and English pupils' performance in reading and mathematics is well documented.

Many pupils need continuing support to master early reading skills. (OFSTED, 1996, p. 19)

There are, for example, too many pupils who remain unnecessarily reliant on their fingers for counting, are unable to use a ruler correctly and are wild in making estimations. (OFSTED, 1996, p. 20)

In the next section I present my belief that the second of the solutions offered above, i.e., confronting the heresy of subject specific teaching, is the one that should be given serious consideration for the sake of children we are seeking to teach.

Coming Out of the Closet: This Author's Position

It is often difficult for someone involved in ITE to speak publicly about their views when these conflict with the accepted stance within the profession. So much of work in ITE relies on the goodwill of local schools and teachers. To publicly challenge beliefs can lead to a loss of that goodwill. However in the rest of this chapter I intend to argue that subject specific teaching can be child centredness at its best.

The ideology of the complete curriculum being delivered in a cross-curricular or thematic way was never a reality even with very young children. Mathematics, for example, has typically been introduced as a discrete subject. It has of course been applied in the service of other subjects; measuring the height of a seedling in science, drawing a graph of how pupils travel to school for a project on transport, calculating the age of a monarch when they died but seldom were such 'problems' used as a way of introducing the knowledge, skills and concepts associated with measurement, data-handling or subtraction. However for the large majority of early years pupils mathematics has been the focus of the activity; counting with unifix cubes, sorting geometric shapes, 'doing sums in workbooks'. There have been subjects in the curriculum that have been taught in an integrated way for example; history and geography through a study of 'Our Town', illustrated by stories, poems and pictures or science and technology through building a model lighthouse in a project on the sea. But the main teaching of subjects like mathematics, physical education or religious education (and to a large extent English) has always been discrete. The reality of early years teaching is a combination of subject specific teaching, topic focused studies and the application of knowledge and skills learnt through subject specific teaching to other subjects.

(Nevertheless) we suggest that it is neither possible nor desirable to attempt to deal with the whole of the curriculum in topics. In practice this has very rarely been done, for very good reasons. (Palmer and Pettit, 1993, p. 16)

Susan E. Sanders

Yes there has been a shift. We don't have the same flexibility as five years ago. In the past if something didn't fit you would defer it. Now we use a mixture of thematic and discrete teaching. (Headteacher in our 1994 study)

The image used by the New Right; children tripping through the damp grass like Isadora Duncan, picking up disassociated crumbs of knowledge when the whim took them or the teacher, who did not actively teach but 'facilitated learning' in what ever area the child showed an interest, was always a myth.

Tensions for Teachers in Subject Specific Teaching

Of course many teachers, particularly those of young children, will find the subject specific solution difficult. Maynard, in Chapter 3 of this book and elsewhere (1996) articulates the tension as teachers of early years pupils struggle to address their deep-rooted belief that they are child-centred pedagogues who teach children and not subjects and that even to discuss subject knowledge is to sell their souls to the devil, in this instance the government agencies that support subject teaching and criticize teachers for their lack of knowledge. When Maynard, Furlong and I obtained Welsh Office funding to research and develop the mentoring of subject knowledge to primary ITE students we experienced criticism and distrust from teacher colleagues who accused us of selling out to those agencies. Teachers who worked on the project however, like Maynard's teachers in an earlier project (Maynard, 1996), found it possible to resolve the dilemma by seeing the connections between the construction of the individual child's knowledge, however this is achieved, with a child centred pedagogy. The tensions appear when a certain view of 'child-centredness' is taken. As Maynard (1995) argues child-centredness has been taken to have several definitions and to encompass a variety of teaching approaches. The criticisms of Alexander, Rose and Woodhead (1992) are not aimed at child-centredness *per se* but at poor planning, teaching and management that militate against children's learning. Surely weaknesses that militate against children's learning cannot be adhered to as part of a child-centred pedagogy. Pollard *et al.* (1994) suggest that some teachers of early years pupils may no longer feel that subject-based teaching undermines essential characteristics of childhood and children's learning.

I have argued extensively elsewhere (Sanders, 1994, 1995; Maynard, Sanders and Furlong, 1996) that a key element in successful teaching is the teacher's conceptions of the nature of the subject. The extent and style of study required to ensure that teachers have this central pillar in their subject knowledge should not be underestimated. Extend this over the eleven or twelve subjects taught in the primary school and consider whether or not this is a realistic task in any style of teacher preparation programme currently accredited in Wales or England.

If we acknowledge the limitations of the preparation of our NQTs then this begins to have implications for the type of teacher that will be available for employment. I suggest that we can realistically produce 'generalist teachers' for Key

Stage 1 only if we limit the number of subjects in the curriculum or lower the level required of entrants to the profession. The former may be achieved anyway by the current status of the non-core subjects which seem to have been weakened by the revisions to the National Curriculum, both in the reduction of the content and in the fact that at least for the time being there is no statutory assessment of them. The latter may well be an illogical suggestion for only recently the profession rebelled against proposals for a less well qualified 'Mum's Army' of teachers of young children (see *Times Educational Supplement*, 5 March 1993, Junior Education, August 1993). If the full spread of the current curriculum is to be maintained then more than one teacher must share responsibility for its delivery. The way in which the curriculum is taught is open to debate. There is too little hard research data comparing the outcomes of well structured and planned thematic approaches with the outcomes of 'expert' subject teaching at Key Stage 1 (or Key Stage 2) for this author to exclusively embrace one approach. Extensive funding would be required, there would have to be a longitudinal element to the research: neither of these are likely while much research funding available is policy driven and the current style of research auditing exists in our HEIs. However we must continue to emphasize that the evidence presented by both sides has in the main been subjective and anecdotal.

> A tide of romantic traditionalism, a gut response to ministers' own school-days, and an over reaction to anecdotal evidence of the perceived dangers of extreme teaching methods. (Graham, 1993, p. 119)

The supporters of 'progressive' education have more recently replied to criticisms with well argued, theoretical and research based discussions (Gammage and Meighan, 1993; Galton, 1995).

However, as Alexander (1994) pleads

> We will need to remove the ideological baggage from the debate about the place of subjects in the primary curriculum and ask questions about the relationship between children's ways of thinking and the culturally-evolved forms of understanding which acknowledge the reality of both, and exploit and reconcile them to the advantage of both children and society, rather than pursue one at the expense of the other. (Alexander, 1994, p. 30)

Conclusion

This author believes that the time has come for teachers of early years pupils to refocus on the child whom they claim to be at the centre of their ideology. Every child has the right to the best techniques to enable them to learn. Why must the same technique be optimum for every subject? Subjects have unique elements in their nature, some subjects have congruent elements. Investigation is part of the nature of both mathematics and science. However mathematical proof and scientific proof have different elements. Dogmatic and close-minded adherence to an approach to teaching that may only be of benefit in certain areas of learning cannot be 'child-centred'. In fact it could be construed as 'teacher-centred'. The teacher feels comfortable with the approach and stays committed to it even when evidence from research, assessment and their own observations demonstrate that many children are not learning. This is of course not only true of a teacher's commitment to a thematic approach, the teaching of arithmetic for example suffers from a similar lack of reflection on the part of some teachers (OFSTED, 1993).

The National Curriculum itself is not responsible for the decline in the pretence of a completely thematic approach. It has perhaps allowed teachers to attribute their subject teaching, not to their own lack of commitment to an ideology but to a government directive. It has perhaps allowed them to salve their conscience that they cannot teach children all knowledge, skills and concepts in the way that their training courses espoused.

I suggest that the moment is right for teachers of young children to consider how best their pupils learn the concepts, skills and knowledge in each subject as well as the ways in which they could best develop the broader objectives of early education. The opportunity of the five-year moratorium on changes to the National Curriculum will allow them to develop the most appropriate approaches to the teaching of young children from an informed viewpoint rather than from dogma. The beneficiaries of this will be the children. It will be a truly 'child-centred approach'.

Note

1 Primary teachers will use interchangeably words and phrases such as thematic approach, topic or project work, cross-curricular approach. In this chapter they are taken to cover an approach to teaching which does not present subjects as discrete packets of knowledge. Where it is necessary to distinguish between such approaches it is done so in the text.

References

ALEXANDER, R. (1991) *Primary Education in Leeds*, Leeds, University of Leeds.
ALEXANDER, R. (1994) 'What primary curriculum?: Dearing and beyond', *Education 3–13*, **22**, 1, pp. 24–35.
ALEXANDER, R., ROSE, J. and WOODHEAD, C. (1992) *Curriculum Organisation and Practice in Primary Schools: A Discussion Paper*, London, HMSO.
ANNING, A. (1995) *A National Curriculum for the Early Years*, Buckingham, Open University Press.
ARNOLD, R. (Ed) (1991) *Topic Planning and the National Curriculum*, Harlow, Longman.
BENNETT, N. and CARRÉ, C. (Eds) (1993) *Learning to Teach*, London, Routledge.
BORKO, H. and LIVINGSTON, N.C. (1989) 'Cognition and improvisation: Difference in mathematics instruction by expert and novice teachers', *American Educational Research Journal*, **5**, 1, pp. 473–98.
BRUNER, J. (1974) *The Relevance of Education*, Harmondsworth, Penguin.

CENTRAL ADVISORY COUNCIL FOR EDUCATION (ENGLAND) (1967) *Children and Their Primary Schools: Volume 1 Report* (The Plowden Report) London, HMSO.

CENTRAL ADVISORY COUNCIL FOR EDUCATION (WALES) (1967) *Primary Education in Wales (The Gittins Report)*, London, HMSO.

COULBY, D. (1990) 'The construction and implementation of the primary core curriculum', in COULBY, D. and WARD, S. (Eds) *The Primary Core National Curriculum: Policy into Practice*, London, Cassell.

COX, C.B. and BOYSON, R. (Eds) (1977) *Black Paper 1977*, London, Temple Smith.

COX, T. and SANDERS, S.E. (1994) *The Impact of the National Curriculum on the Teaching of Five Year Olds*, London, Falmer.

CURRICULUM COUNCIL FOR WALES (1992) 'A report on the primary education review in Wales 1992', Unpublished [but copies were available from] Cardiff, CCW.

DEARING, R. (1994) *The National Curriculum and Its Assessment: A Final Report*, London, SCAA.

DELAMONT, S. (1987) 'The primary teacher 1945–90: Myths and realities,' in DELAMONT, S. (Ed), *The Primary School Teacher*, Lewis, Falmer Press.

EARLY YEARS CURRICULUM GROUP (1989) *The Early Years and The National Curriculum*, Stoke-on-Trent, Trentham Books.

GAMMAGE, P. (1994) *Meeting of the Swansea Branch of the National Association for Primary Education (NAPE)*.

GAMMAGE, P. and MEIGHAN, J. (Eds) (1993) *Early Childhood Education: Taking Stock*, Ticknall, Education Now Books.

GALTON, M. (1995) *Crisis in the Primary Classroom*, London, Fulton.

GRAHAM, D. (1993) *A Lesson for Us All: The Making of the National Curriculum*, London, Routledge.

HILLGATE GROUP (1986) *Whose Schools?: A Radical Manifesto*, London, Claridge Press.

HILLGATE GROUP (1987) *Reform of British Education*, London, Claridge Press.

JUNIOR EDUCATION (1993) 'News round-up', *Junior Education*, **17**, p. 7.

MAYNARD, T. (1995) 'Child-centred or subject centred: A resolution?', Paper presented to *The Annual Conference of The Australian Association for Research in Education*, Hobart, Tasmania.

MAYNARD, T. (1996) 'Mentoring subject knowledge in the primary school', in MCINTYRE, D. and HAGGER, H. (Eds) *Mentors in Schools: Developing the Profession of Teaching*, London, David Fulton Publishers.

MAYNARD, T., SANDERS, S.E. and FURLONG, J. (1996) *Subject Mentoring in the Primary School: The Core Curriculum*, Swansea, University of Wales, Swansea. (Currently not available outside Wales)

OFFICE FOR STANDARDS IN EDUCATION (OFSTED) (1993) *The Teaching and Learning of Number in Primary Schools*, London, HMSO.

OFFICE FOR STANDARDS IN EDUCATION (OFSTED) (1995) *The Annual Report of Her Majesty's Chief Inspector of Schools 1993/4*, London, HMSO.

OFFICE FOR STANDARDS IN EDUCATION (OFSTED) (1996) *The Annual Report of Her Majesty's Chief Inspector of Schools 1994/95*, London, HMSO.

PALMER, J. and PETTIT, D. (1993) *Topic Work in the Early Years*, London, Routledge.

POLLARD, A., BROADFOOT, P., CROLL, P., OSBORN, M. and ABBOT, D. (1994) *Changing English Primary Schools?: The Impact of the Education Reform Act at Key Stage One*, London, Cassell.

SANDERS, S.E. (1994) 'Mathematics and mentoring', in JAWORKI, B. and WATSON, A. (Eds) *Mentoring in Mathematics*, London, Falmer Press.

SANDERS, S.E. (1995) 'Knowledge and nature of subject', Paper presented to *The Annual Conference of The Australian Association for Research in Education*, Hobart, Tasmania.

SIMON, B. (1981) 'The primary school revolution: Myth or reality?', in SIMON, B. and WILCOCKS, J. (Eds) *Research and Practice in Primary Classrooms*, London, Routledge and Kegan Paul.

SIMON, B. (1993) 'Primary education', *Education Today and Tomorrow*, **44**, pp. 13–14.

STANNARD, J. (1995) 'Managing the primary curriculum after Dearing: A rationale', *Education 3–13*, **23**, pp. 3–6.

SUMMERS, M. (1994) 'Science in the primary school: The problem of teachers' curricular expertise', *The Curriculum Journal*, **5**, pp. 179–94.

TIMES EDUCATIONAL SUPPLEMENT (1993) 'Ministers seek non-graduate staff', *Times Educational Supplement*, 5 March, p. 11.

WELSH OFFICE (1993) *The Initial Training of Primary Schools Teachers: New Criteria for Course Approval*, Cardiff, Welsh Office.

6 Assessment Issues and the National Curriculum I: National Curriculum Assessment at Key Stage 1

Theo Cox

This chapter outlines the main developments in National Curriculum assessment and record keeping and the impact that these have had upon teachers and their existing professional practices and their attitudes to assessment. Through a combination of statutory orders, advice and guidance the government has put in place a programme of summative end of key stage assessment of attainments in the core subjects based upon both standardized tests/tasks and teacher assessment. In addition teachers are being encouraged to carry out formative, ongoing assessment of children's progress through the various programmes of study during each key stage. The summative, 'snapshot' assessments at the end of each key stage are designed to provide objective evidence of the national standards of achievement in the core subjects. A number of key questions about the future form of both teacher assessment and standardized assessment are discussed in the light of the recent major revision of the National Curriculum.

Introduction

One major consequence, among several, of the introduction of the National Curriculum at Key Stage 1 was to confront early years teachers with the requirement to carry out assessments of their pupils' academic progress and attainments in a far more systematic and explicit way than most of them had done before. This was a major challenge to the profession for, as Gipps *et al.*, 1995 described, British primary teachers, traditionally, were relatively unsophisticated in their approach to assessment. The evidence from studies of assessment practice prior to the National Curriculum showed that the ongoing, day to day classroom assessment carried out by the majority of primary teachers was of a highly intuitive 'in the head' kind. This was not surprising, as Gipps *et al.* point out since there was an absence of a syllabus, bench marks or criteria for teachers to focus on when evaluating their children's classroom performance. Schools sometimes apply standardized tests, usually in reading and mathematics, but the information they yielded rarely influenced teaching decisions (Gipps *et al.*, 1983). In addition, of course, teachers used their own informal classroom tests, marked children's work and kept some form of progress record. On the whole though early years teachers adopted an essentially informal holistic approach to their assessment with the aim of finding out 'where to go next' in their teaching (Pollard *et al.*, 1994).

Given this low key, predominantly subjective and intuitive approach to assessment among primary and early years teachers it is hardly surprising that many of them felt bewildered and threatened by the demands of the new National Curriculum for a much more hard headed explicit and systematized form of assessment of children's progress and attainments which were to be judged against national performance criteria.

Assessment under the National Curriculum

With the clear aims of raising standards in education, particularly in the '3Rs' and of making schools more accountable to the public for their effectiveness, the government of the day introduced the National Curriculum and its associated assessment requirements in 1989 for Key Stage 1. The key features of the assessment programme and the thinking underlying it are well described by Gipps *et al.*, 1995. The programme, as originally put forward in the Task Group on Assessment and Testing (TGAT) Report (DES, 1988), required that pupils should be assessed against National Curriculum attainment targets, both through external tests, called Standard Assessment Tasks (SATs), and by their teachers through teacher assessment, with the results to be published at the ages of 7 (Key Stage 1) 11 (Key Stage 2), and 14 (Key Stage 3). The results from the two aspects of the assessment programme were to be combined using a system of moderation aimed at bringing the teachers' assessments into line with the test results where the two did not match.

As Gipps *et al.* (1995) point out an important aspect of the TGAT framework was that teachers' assessments would be central to the system; teachers were to assess pupils' performance continuously using their own informal methods which would provide both formative and diagnostic information to support ongoing teaching. These teacher assessments would be summed up at the end of each key stage and used as part of the public reporting programme.

In order to distinguish between the informal ongoing kind of formative assessment that was now to be expected and the higher profile, end of key stage 'snapshot' summative assessment Gipps *et al.* called the former kind teacher assessment (ta) and the latter Teacher Assessment (TA) and this seems a useful distinction, albeit a relative one since the two forms of assessment were closely linked in the TGAT model.

The end of key stage arrangements for testing through SATs and Teacher Assessment were regulated in detail through government orders which included the arrangements for external 'audit moderation' of these assessments. In addition funding was provided to support LEA in-service training in how to carry out the summative judgments required, usually for Year 2 teachers. This was backed by the publication of such guidance documents as the 'School Assessment Folder Key Stage 1' (School Examination and Assessment Council (SEAC, 1993) which included exemplars and advice on judging attainment levels in the various core subject attainment targets using the new ten-level scale. In contrast the government provided relatively little guidance for teachers on how they could carry out the ongoing assessment and record keeping *during* Key Stage 1, with the result that there was a very wide range of assessment practice throughout England and Wales and a lack of confidence amongst teachers regarding its adequacy and relevance. This confused situation was well described by Pollard *et al.* (1994) in their report on the PACE Project at Key Stage 1 (see Chapter 2):

> In 1990 the picture that emerged was of teachers spending a considerable amount of time devising and completing their own records or completing records imposed on them from outside, such as from their LEA. Much of this work was carried out in the teacher's own time and against a background of anxiety or even panic about how to do it, guilt about not doing it well enough, cynicism about its potential value for pupils' learning and resentment about being made to feel inadequate. (Pollard *et al.*, 1994, p. 196)

Nevertheless some common components of primary schools' ongoing assessment programmes gradually emerged, such as the use of 'tick lists', where teachers recorded pupils' attainments in the various core subject attainment targets using ticks, symbols or comments, the keeping of 'evidence' to support teachers' judgments, often in pupils' 'portfolios', and the compilation of 'school portfolios' consisting of selected samples of children's work as agreed exemplars of performance levels. In addition many schools developed their own assessment policies with the aim of coordinating and standardizing the National Curriculum assessment programmes of the teachers.

Studies of National Curriculum Assessment up to the Dearing Review and the Revised National Curriculum

During the period between the introduction of the National Curriculum in 1989 and the government commissioned review of it by Sir Ron Dearing in 1993, major studies of Key Stage 1 teachers' assessment practice in England were set in place by Caroline Gipps at London University, entitled 'National Assessment in Primary Schools: an Evaluation' (NAPS), and by the PACE team at the Universities of Bristol and South West England. The NAPS study focused upon Year 2 teachers since they were responsible for the end of Key Stage 1 assessments, while the Bristol study included both Year 1 and Year 2 teachers. In Wales the Swansea University Impact Study (see Chapter 2) included an investigation of National Curriculum assessment practice in the sample of primary and infant schools in the participating LEA with a focus upon Year 1 teachers.

In addition to these university studies both of the curriculum and assessment bodies, SCAA in England and ACAC in Wales, carried out consultations with teachers and LEAs on the government's proposals for the streamlining and revision of the National Curriculum and its assessment following its acceptance of Dearing's recommendations (Dearing, 1994). SCAA also commissioned the National Foundation for Educational Research (NFER) to carry out an evaluation of National Curriculum teacher assessment in maths and science.

The main findings of the Swansea University Impact Study will be presented first and these will be related to those of the other studies and reports. (See Chapter 2 for details of the aims and conduct of this study.)

The Swansea University Impact Study

Introduction

In the course of interviewing the Year 1 class teachers and the head teachers a brief enquiry was made about the nature and scope of the schools' National Curriculum assessment and recording systems. It was clear that there was a considerable variety amongst them, although there were some common elements. One of these was a National Curriculum record which the LEA had produced as a model and which listed all of the statements of attainments under each attainment target in the National Curriculum subjects. For each statements of attainment a box was provided for comments. Some of the schools adopted this record as it stood while others made their own versions of it. There was variation between schools as to whether ticks, comments or symbols were used in the boxes, e.g., for 'introduced', 'practised' or 'achieved'.

In addition since the National Curriculum records were normally entered only at termly or yearly intervals the schools also developed informal systems for recording the teachers' observations of their children's progress, e.g., through individual or class diaries or record sheets. Some schools also devised assessment tasks for the purpose of supporting teachers' judgments of children's attainment levels in the various attainment targets. Schools were also advised to keep selected samples of each child's written or other work in the core subjects as 'evidence' to support their later level judgments. Ideally these samples should be annotated by the teacher to indicate why they were selected, their context, and what level of performance they represented. Some schools also compiled school portfolios of samples of children's work assessed through 'agreement trialling' in order to help teachers in the particular school to achieve some consistency in their judgments.

In addition to the above National Curriculum records and evidence teachers continued to keep their own traditional personal records of children's attainments and progress, particularly in the 3Rs, e.g., pages or books read, sight vocabulary and sounds mastered, sometimes in diary form.

Findings Regarding Assessment and Record Keeping

The Head Teachers' Views

Only a minority of head teachers felt happy or reasonably happy with their current assessment and record keeping systems and even they showed awareness of the need to review and improve them, for example by gathering objective evidence to support teachers' assessments in order to make them more 'accountable'. The remaining head teachers declared themselves unhappy with their current systems even though they felt obliged to maintain them as part of the perceived National Curriculum requirements. Particular criticism was focused on 'tick boxes' which were judged by some to be meaningless unless accompanied by teachers' comments. There was a clear preference among some head teachers for teachers to make qualitative comments on children's learning, whether written in diary form or in the National Curriculum record booklets made available by the LEA, and also for the keeping of evidence in the form of samples of children's written or other work.

Another major concern was over the administrative burden of applying the assessment and recording systems across the whole National Curriculum which fell upon the class teachers. Several head teachers expressed the view that these systems were taking up far too much of the teachers' time without producing practically useful data. Even those head teachers expressing relative satisfaction with their present systems were aware of the need to develop and refine them so as to improve their quality as the following quotations illustrate:

> I am relatively happy in that we have a system in place but it needs further development if teacher assessment is going to be of high quality, e.g., annotated samples of children's work need to be developed and we need more staff discussion of developments.

> Only this term we have started building assessment into actual planning. Teachers found this most difficult, Previously they did it retrospectively.

> County records are fine for recording assessments but we still have to look at how we get the assessment, i.e., getting the evidence. In foundation areas such as physical education and music we are not happy with assessment yet — we are getting to grips with the new content. In project work we are developing a method of assessing different subject areas in the same project. We have not got it thoroughly enough as a school. It is mostly OK but is still under development.

The challenging nature of National Curriculum assessment was expressed by one head teacher as follows:

> Assessment is very difficult — the most difficult part of the National Curriculum. There are very prescriptive requirements for information without enough time and training available to equip teachers to undertake it.

The majority of head teachers predicted or at least expressed the hope that the burden of assessment and record keeping would be reduced following the revision of the National Curriculum and the reduction in the numbers of attainment targets, even if existing forms of assessment were retained. A small minority of them were not expecting any major change and expressed satisfaction with their present systems.

One head teacher showed concern about the proposed shift of emphasis in National Curriculum assessment towards end of key stage judgments through level descriptions.

> It's going to be felt that making general comments at the end of the key stage is the way forward in easing the pressure on teachers through having to assess statements of attainment but it puts an emphasis on the end of the key stage with teachers then having to make the final decision. Other teachers may feel that they have less responsibility but we have to take into account that it puts too much of a burden upon end of key stage teachers.

The Class Teachers' Views

The majority of Year 1 class teachers judged that their assessment and record keeping systems were manageable or fairly manageable although time consuming. It appeared from their comments that much of the recording of children's assessments was done in their own time, either at the end of the school day or at home. Some dissatisfaction was expressed concerning 'tick boxes' unless ticks were accompanied by comments. Many if not all of them kept portfolios of samples of their pupils' work, Ideally these would be annotated by the teacher but time sometimes precluded this.

A minority of class teachers felt that their current systems were unmanageable or extremely time consuming, particularly in large classes with a wide spread of children's abilities. Despite this they were trying to make the system work. The practice of just ticking the boxes in the National Curriculum records was justified by some of these teachers as being a way of coping with the heavy demands on their time.

A few teachers expressed the need for a standardized model form of assessment and record keeping to be provided either locally or nationally.

> There should be a national system of assessment and record keeping, e.g., for children moving from school to school. Similarly there is a case for an LEA policy.

> It's all in a state of flux. I don't think we're sure what people want — what is required. Why haven't they produced some form of model record?

The importance of building assessment into the planning of teaching was expressed by one teacher as follows:

> The whole idea of giving assessment is to make diagnosis regarding the next stage through observation and intuiting. This uses assessment in a planning way. Much assessment is not planned — it just happens.

Despite their burdensome nature the great majority of teachers thought that their assessment records were useful, at least in some respects, for example, as a summary record of what children had completed and what needed to be reinforced. National Curriculum records were particularly useful at the start of a new year or in respect of children transferring from other schools and they were also helpful to teachers when reporting to parents at the end of the school year. A number of teachers felt that, when it came to planning programmes of work for individual children, their own personal records of their children's progress, together with National Curriculum diaries or comments and selected samples of children's work, were more practically useful than the formal National Curriculum records adopted by their schools, as the following quotations illustrate:

> LEA records are not that useful. Our own records on basic skills and pieces of work handed on at transfer are more useful especially for slower children where more detailed records are useful.

> My own records are invaluable. In core subjects when planning work I can consult them to find out what a particular child needs. LEA National Curriculum records have some use, e.g., what they have covered in reception, especially at transfer.

Compared with the head teachers the class teachers were less confident as a group that their assessment and record keeping systems would change under the revised National Curriculum. The main change expected was a reduction in the administrative workload, reflecting the reduced number of attainment targets. Only a few teachers predicted a change in the format or scope of their systems, for example, through building assessment into schemes of work and a greater emphasis upon teachers' judgments in place of statements of attainments.

> Assessment possibly built into schemes of work in a way not done so far. We have a framework to work from and relate to the content of the new slimmed National Curriculum. We need INSET looking at children's work, assessing levels and moderation. Some Year 1 teachers are using intuitive judgments but Year 2 teachers have assessed using SATs as a framework. Year 2 teachers are skilled at making judgments using appropriate criteria.

Other Studies of Teacher Assessment

The PACE Study

As described in Chapter 2 the PACE study is a comprehensive longitudinal study of the impact of the National Curriculum upon primary education at Key Stages 1 and 2. Its findings with regard to the impact of the National Curriculum assessment and record keeping requirements are reported in Pollard *et al.*, 1994 which covers the period from 1990 to 1992. They were based upon interviews with Year 1 and Year 2 class teachers and head teachers plus written questionnaires.

The authors comment that at the outset of the study teachers' views of assessment reflected their existing professional ideologies. They tended to favour formative, provisional and implicit assessment rather than summative forms of explicit and categorical assessment. This meant that the assessment requirements of the National Curriculum posed a severe challenge to their existing beliefs and practices. The study found that the National Curriculum requirements led to large changes in classroom practice, particularly with regard to record keeping. The picture that emerged was of teachers spending a considerable amount of time devising and completing their own records or completing records imposed on them from outside, e.g., from the LEA. An enormous variety of records were being used. As in the Swansea University study teachers showed much concern about the amount of time required by the new assessment and record keeping arrangements and this concern was exacerbated by their general lack of confidence in the appropriateness and value of the systems they were applying. The teachers' resentment and frustration at the amount of time they were having to spend on procedures which they did not value did not diminish during the period of the study despite their increased familiarity with them.

Despite this somewhat negative reaction the study found some evidence for the emergence of improvements in teachers' assessment knowledge and practice as they gained in confidence and knowledge and learned to mediate the external requirements towards their own professional ends. These included becoming clearer about teaching objectives and beginning to use assessment creatively in a diagnostic, formative way to support learning, collaborative approaches to assessment and the use of a wide range of techniques for gathering and storing evidence of attainment.

The National Assessment in Primary Schools (NAPS) Study

This major evaluative study of national assessment in primary schools at the end of Key Stage 1 was carried out by Gipps *et al.*, 1995. Its aim was not simply to study the impact of the national assessment programme on the schools in the research sample but also to find out whether the Year 2 teachers became more sophisticated and knowledgeable in assessment or simply learned to apply an imposed system. A national sample of thirty-two schools from eight LEAs in England was drawn up and the research programme used interviews with head teachers and Year 2 teachers, postal questionnaires and detailed classroom observations of assessment in action.

Like the PACE and Swansea University studies the NAPS study found some evidence for negative feelings among the sample teachers towards aspects of the National Curriculum assessment programme. More specifically there was anger and guilt about the publication of test results, feelings of dissonance and alienation because of the perceived invalidity of the testing programme and feelings of concern about the impact of testing on young children. However this negative finding was strongly offset by the encouraging evidence for a steady improvement in the quality and rigour of the Year 2 teachers' practice and understanding of assessment. These gains are summed up as follows:

> To conclude we believe we have offered evidence that, as a result of the National Curriculum and assessment programme, teachers have redirected the focus of their teaching and this has been reflected in improved national assessment results in the 'basic skills'. Greater care in planning, close observation of children and a more detailed understanding of individual progress impacting on teaching were reported by over half our headteachers, as well as a lasting effect on collaboration and discussion by a smaller number. Many of our Key Stage 1 teachers have moved away from intuitive approaches to assessment towards more systematic, evidence based techniques. The SATs have acted as a training device, and group moderation has broken down barriers. There is a clear picture of enhanced understanding and practice in assessment for the Y2 teachers, and the heads and LEAs are putting these skills to good use further up the system. All this has been achieved, however, at a cost to teachers' lives and ways of working. Finally, we believe our evidence shows that the improvements in practice, both in teaching and assessing, would not have resulted from the introduction of traditional standardized tests alone, but depended on a wider approach with moderated teacher assessment at its core. (Gipps *et al.*, 1995, pp. 187–8)

In discussing these findings the authors raise several important questions concerning the future direction of teacher assessment (TA and ta) in the light of the subsequent changes in the national assessment programme which followed the Dearing review. Some of these will be taken up in the final section of this chapter.

Evaluation of Teacher Assessment (Maths and Science) at Key Stage 1

In 1994 SCAA commissioned the NFER to carry out an evaluation of National Curriculum teacher assessment in maths and science at Key Stage 1. When it was carried out there was already a shift in the national assessment arrangements towards Teacher Assessment although the Revised National Curriculum had not been put in place. The study used a nationally representative sample of schools in England and Wales, including Welsh medium schools. Questionnaires for the participating head teachers and Year 2 teachers were supplemented by interviews held in a random selection of case study schools. The study aimed to assess the teachers' level of confidence in their own assessments, the consistency of these assessments and difficulties encountered, and also looked at training and the use of support materials.

The study found that class teachers and head teachers were broadly confident in administering their assessments and confidence levels did not change over the period of the study (Sizmur *et al.*, 1995), In general teachers with previous experience of conducting Teacher Assessment or the SATs were the most confident. Assessment support materials in the form of optional tasks and standard tasks from previous years were a particularly useful means of support for Teacher Assessment. Nearly all schools had some form of school assessment policy in place, covering recording systems, individual portfolios of evidence and school porfolios of work, with the core subjects as the focus. Teachers based their final level judgments on a variety of sources of information including notes of their observations of children working, results of assessment tasks, marked or annotated work and statement of attainment records kept as part of school policy.

Consistency of assessment judgments was most commonly achieved by discussion of examples of work, often leading to the production of school or class portfolios. The researchers also found that the results of Teacher Assessment, including informal day to day information gathering, often informed both further teaching in the short term and curriculum and assessment policy in the longer term.

As in the Swansea University Impact Study the teachers were also asked what changes they anticipated in the way assessment would be carried out in the Revised National Curriculum. A reduction in workload was expected but there was uncertainty about the future of record keeping based on statements of attainment and about the amount of evidence that would need to be kept.

The authors concluded that the formative use of assessment is a key feature of teachers' work in the classroom. Looking ahead to the revised arrangements for National Curriculum assessment they stressed the need to clarify the relation between programmes of study, level descriptions and the assessments made against each. There is also a strong need for specific guidance for teachers in moving from the range of information they collect on a regular basis to their final holistic level judgments. Other recommendations include the further provision of assessment support materials designed to promote reflective formative practice, and the monitoring of schools' effectiveness in Teacher Assessment, given the dropping of formal arrangements for external audit moderation. Finally they point to the danger of schools according less importance to the assessment of those areas of the National Curriculum where formal reporting of Teacher Assessment is not required (currently in the non-core subjects at Key Stages 1 and 2), and urge SCAA to clarify its policy on the relation between curriculum and assessment and between tests and Teacher Assessment.

Conclusion from the Research Studies

The following main conclusions can be drawn from the research studies of National Curriculum assessment outlined above:

1   The imposition of a system of assessment and record keeping based upon explicit performance criteria and the recording of objective evidence posed

a major challenge to many Key Stage 1 teachers who had traditionally relied upon making intuitive, largely unrecorded assessments of their children's progress and attainments;

2   Teachers found the required National Curriculum assessment and record keeping very time consuming and their resentment was focused on the administrative workload, the perceived irrelevance of some aspects of the programme, and the lack of central or local guidance as to what forms of recording and evidence to keep in support of their subsequent judgments of children's performance levels;

3   Despite strong reservations teachers put a great deal of effort into making the assessments and keeping the evidence and records they thought were required;

4   Despite their concerns about the possible impact of formal assessment upon children aged 7 Year 2 teachers invested considerable effort into mastering the summative process required and, as a result, developed enhanced understanding and practice in assessment which beneficially fed into their ongoing teaching and into the assessment policies of their schools;

5   Teachers anticipated that, following the Dearing Report, the National Curriculum assessment procedures would be simplified with a significant reduction in the administrative burden of record and evidence keeping. There was some uncertainty about the future form that teacher assessment and record keeping would take given the move to end of key stage level descriptors.

National Curriculum Assessment Following the Dearing Review

In his final review report to the Secretary of State for education Sir Ron Dearing (1994) stated that common standards of National Curriculum (summative) assessment can be provided by national tests marked to nationally applied standards and/ or Teacher Assessment based upon clear statements and exemplar material to show what is required at each level and which is *subject to appropriate moderation and audit* (my emphasis). He advised that both systems of assessment, tests and Teacher Assessment, should be designed to be complementary. His main recommendations for assessment can be summarized as follows:

- simplifying national tests and reducing the time they require;
- providing materials to guide Teacher Assessment;
- restricting the requirement for statutory Teacher Assessment to the core subjects only in primary schools; and
- reducing the burden of record keeping in primary schools.

In Appendix 6 of the report guidance is offered to help schools develop recording systems which should be 'useful, manageable, easy to keep and easy to interpret'. As Dearing states, if such records do not provide a significant contribution to teaching and learning there is little point in maintaining them. Most importantly he also states that the workloads of teachers at the end of the key stage will be minimized if their judgments are supported by records made throughout the key stage. At the very least a record should be made annually as a basis for reporting to parents.

The changes to the National Curriculum assessment programme made by the government following the Dearing review and consultations have implemented most but not all of his recommendations. Since 1994 the SATs which were designed to reflect normal classroom activities and required a range of children's responses, not simply written ones, now have a lesser role in the Key Stage 1 and 2 programmes. For example, at the time of writing in 1996, there are two tasks for 7-year-olds in English (reading and writing), but only one in maths (at Level 1 only). The SATs have been partly replaced by 'simpler' standardized tests of the pencil and paper variety, which inevitably will appear more formal and test like to children no matter how teachers may try to disguise their purpose.

Teacher Assessment in the core subjects remains a statutory requirement at the end of Key Stage 1 and the government claims that it will have equal status with the tests/Tasks in that both sets of results are now included in the annual reports to parents. (In science Teacher Assessment is now the *only* form of national assessment at Key Stage 1.)

However, contrary to the Dearing recommendations, the statutory requirement for the external audit/moderation of Teacher Assessment has now been dropped, allegedly because of the 'increased consistency in Teacher Assessment that has been achieved in the previous years when the external moderation arrangements were in place' (SCAA/ACAC, 1994). Gipps *et al.*, 1995 deplore this decision which they argue will effectively downgrade the status of Teacher Assessment. Moreover they claim that only test results will be published in the forthcoming 'league tables' at Key Stage 2. (The results will be unpublished at Key Stage 1.) However a recent publication by SCAA (1996) re-affirmed that 'The judgments made by teachers at the end of a key stage have equal status with test results in all forms of public reporting.' (page 4)

The statutory arrangements for assessment and recording of National Curriculum and other attainments during Key Stage 1 remain largely unchanged. Schools are required to assess and record children's progress and attainments in all National Curriculum subjects and in other subjects and activities and to update these records at least once a year. *How* such progress and achievement is assessed and recorded is left entirely to teachers' professional judgment but, following the Dearing review, there is an affirmation that 'elaborate systems of recording will neither be required by the National Curriculum nor expected by inspectors operating within the statutory framework. Nor will voluminous evidence need to be kept to back up teachers' judgments, only samples of pupils' work which exemplify attainment at each level. (Her Majesty's Chief Inspector of Schools in Wales, 1994.) However teachers are urged to promote the quality of their assessments by using a range of strategies such as observation and listening to children, discussion and an occasional task or test. The evidence on which to base assessment judgments (presumably of levels of attainment) will be available to teachers in a range of forms including classroom work, marking comments and National Curriculum records. It is also recommended that teachers should keep a small annotated collection of work for each child as a resource for discussion and for consideration at the end of the key stage.

Level Descriptions

A major change in the revised National Curriculum Teacher Assessment framework was the replacement of the multiplicity of statements of attainments for the various attainment targets by the new level descriptions. These are designed to enable teachers to make 'snapshot', summative assessments of pupils' levels of attainment at the end of the key stage and they set out the standards of performance expected of the majority of pupils in relation to the attainment targets of all of the National Curriculum subjects at Key Stages 1 and 2 (except for art, music and physical education which have 'end of key stage descriptions'). For each attainment targets teachers are expected to use their knowledge of each child's work to judge which of the levels best fits his or her performance across a range of contexts. (The old ten-level scale has now been reduced to eight levels plus a description of 'exceptional performance' at Key Stages 1 to 3.)

Before the revised National Curriculum arrangements were put into place from September 1995 both SCAA in England and ACAC in Wales had mounted extensive consultations with teachers, schools and other bodies regarding the proposals. The reports subsequently published by these agencies (SCAA, 1994; Curriculum and Assessment Authority for Wales, 1994) stated that the planned replacement of the statements of attainments by the new level descriptors was broadly welcomed by those consulted. In particular, the idea of teachers using their professional judgment to decide which description best fits a pupil's performance was endorsed as a realistic approach to end of key stage assessment by teachers. However there was widespread concern over the need to ensure that teachers should interpret the descriptions consistently and, in response to this concern, both agencies have produced national benchmark exemplification materials which schools can use to help standardize their judgments (see, for example, SCAA, 1995).

Reporting to Parents

Schools are required to send parents at least one written report every school year which should include information about the pupils' progress in all of the National Curriculum subjects and in 'all other subjects and activities', together with the pupils' National Curriculum assessment results at the end of Key Stages 1 and 2. The reports should also show how each pupil's end of key stage assessment results compare with those of children of the same age in the school. In addition the report should include national comparative information about pupils' end of key stage performance. Where there are significant differences between a pupil's Teacher Assessment level judgment and the relevant test/task result an explanation should be offered along the following lines:

> Teacher assessment is based on a teacher's knowledge of a pupil formed over a period of time and covering the full programmes of study in the subject and the tests/tasks are short externally set standardised assessments covering a specific part of the subject, taken at the end of a key stage and yielding information which is directly comparable with that of other schools. (DFEE, 1996a, p. 7)

Future Developments in National Curriculum Assessment

As outlined in Chapter 7 assessment serves a range of purposes and it is vital that the government, schools, parents and the public at large should be clear what the different purposes are and by what means they can be best achieved. Since the introduction of the National Curriculum in 1989 we have seen a strong push from the government towards more explicit and objective assessment and recording in primary schools than prevailed previously, culminating in the high profile summative assessments in the core subjects (based upon both Teacher Assessment and tests/tasks) at the end of each key stage. Similarly, in the following chapter, Gill Harper Jones describes how the pressures are mounting upon early years practitioners to move toward more explicit and systematic 'baseline assessment' of 5-year-olds which may likewise serve the government's aim of making schools and other early years providers more 'accountable'.

Unfortunately, as Gipps (1995) stresses, it is not possible meaningfully to use one single form of assessment for a range of purposes, convenient as that would be. We can however, says Gipps, have an assessment programme which serves several purposes. Such programmes should form part of school assessment policies which should state the principles, aims and objectives of the assessment system. Such policies will obviously take account of the statutory requirements for National Curriculum assessment and reporting as well as non statutory guidance on the conduct of such assessment and recording. The basis of National Curriculum assessment programmes will continue to be teacher assessment (both ta and TA) and standardized assessments through tests/tasks and each have their own requirements and features.

Formative Teacher Assessment

The foundation of National Curriculum assessment carried out by Key Stage 1 teachers is ongoing formative assessment which is built into the planning and teaching process. For this kind of assessment, as Gipps (1995) points out, validity is the key requirement, i.e., that what is assessed and recorded is directly related to the aims and objectives of the teaching programme. Reliability, i.e., the consistency of assessment judgments, is relatively less important in this context but becomes a key requirement when ta becomes Teacher Assessment, i.e., is used as the basis for summative judgments at the national reporting level. To be effective formative assessment needs to be based upon a set of performance criteria to frame teachers' judgments. Gipps *et al.*, 1995 reported in their NAPS study that around one-fifth of the Year 2 teachers routinely used the National Curriculum statements of attainments as their criteria but others did not find them sufficiently detailed and had broken them down into further 'can do' lists and were assessing and recording against these. This raises the problem in formative assessment of over specificity leading to overload and fragmentation of teachers' judgments.

On the issue of judgment specificity Gipps (1995) raises questions about the use of the new level descriptors which form a key part of the simplified programmes of study. Will they form part of teachers' ongoing formative assessment or will they mainly be used as the basis for end of key stage judgments as officially recommended (see for example SCAA, 1994b)? If the latter what criteria will teachers use instead for their formative assessment? As discussed in Chapter 8 there is a strong case for using teaching objectives derived from the programmes of study for this purpose. In this way the teachers' formative assessment and record keeping will be built into the relevant schemes of work. It is also important that the valuable experience and expertise gained by Year 2 teachers from their national assessment experiences should feed into the development of well planned and effective day to day assessment and record keeping systems.

Standardized Assessment

There is little doubt that, whatever developments take place in the area of teacher assessment some form of externally devised national standardized assessment will continue to form a major plank in government policy for imposing public accountability on schools and raising educational standards. As mentioned earlier in this chapter the trend at Key Stages 1 and 2 has been to gradually replace the 'curriculum friendly' SATs with more conventional paper and pencil tests which carry with them the danger of causing teachers to narrow the focus of their teaching on the type of skills and knowledge reflected in the tests, a worry apparently shared by some parents as described in Chapter 4. Gipps *et al.*, 1995 strongly advocate the SAT approach to standardized assessment which fits much better into the ethos of early years education in that it samples curricular activities more broadly than do formal tests and is more likely to elicit the best performance from young children, especially slower learners and children with limited command of English.

Conclusion

At the time of writing the government has just produced a consultation document which looks ahead to the next five years of National Curriculum assessment and puts forward a set of proposals aimed at fine tuning the present system rather than introducing any major changes (DFEE, 1996b). In it the government accepts the recommendation made by SCAA in its recent review of National Curriculum assessment (SCAA, 1995), that both summative and formative assessment should continue to be the foundation of National Curriculum assessment, and that the curriculum and assessment agencies should provide further support to enhance teacher assessment in schools during each key stage, but especially at Key Stage 2.

The consultation document raises some of the issues discussed in this chapter and may provide teachers and educationists an opportunity so shape future government policy on national assessment. The possibility of restoring the external moderation of Teacher Assessment is raised but with the proviso that savings would have to be made elsewhere in the assessment programme to pay the costs of it.

There is no doubt that formative teacher assessment has a vital role to play in enhancing the quality of early years teaching and major gains have already been made by Key Stage 1 teachers in the quality of their assessment work under the impetus of the National Curriculum. These gains have been recorded in the research studies described earlier in this chapter (Pollard *et al.*, 1994; and Gipps *et al.*, 1995) and also in recent inspection reports. For example in Wales over 80 per cent of class teachers were judged to integrate assessment purposefully into their daily routines and to make good use of assessment data in planning new work (Welsh Office, 1996). In England also it was reported that many teachers, particularly at Key Stage 1, used a broad range of strategies to assess pupils' progress, although it was also commented that one-third of schools at this key stage had relatively weak records which failed to support pupils' progression and to inform teachers' judgments (OFSTED, 1996). These gains need to be built upon through further support, guidance and training for teachers in this vital aspect of their work. Clarke (1996) urges the government to provide firmer guidance to teachers on the conduct of their day to day formative assessments, especially through stating a set of principles and by providing models showing how these could be translated into practice.

Finally although the focus of this chapter has been on assessment at Key Stage 1 the wider implications of the issues raised for teachers working with under-5s also need to be considered. Gill Harper Jones looks at some of these in the following chapter on baseline assessment at ages 4 to 5 and Mary Drummond argues in Chapter 9 that this high quality assessment and recording should include children's learning through play.

To sum up, as Gipps (In Press) puts it:

> Assessment has a role in accountability and reporting; but the main role of assessment in the classroom must be to support learning. By developing teachers' skills in assessment and in feedback (to pupils) we can continue to build on good practice in primary assessment. (Gipps, In Press)

References

CURRICULUM AND ASSESSMENT AUTHORITY FOR WALES (ACAC) (1994) *The National Curriculum Proposals in Wales: Report on the Consultation, Summer 1994*, Cardiff, ACAC.

CLARKE, S. (1996) 'Search out the flaws to give stability', *Times Educational Supplement*, 26 April, p. 13.

DEARING, R. SIR (1994) *The National Curriculum and its Assessment: Final Report*, London, SCAA.

DEPARTMENT FOR EDUCATION AND EMPLOYMENT (DFEE) (1996a) *Circular Number 2/96, Reports on Pupils' Achievements in Primary Schools in 1995/96*, London, DFEE.

DEPARTMENT FOR EDUCATION AND EMPLOYMENT (DFEE) (1996b) *Review of Assessment and testing: Consultation Paper, 25 January 1996*, London, DFEE.

DEPARTMENT FOR EDUCATION AND SCIENCE (DES) (1988) *National Curriculum Task Group on Assessment and Testing: A Report (The TGAT Report)*, London, HMSO.

GIPPS, C. (1995) 'Teacher assessment and teacher development in primary schools', *Education 3–13*, pp. 8–12.

GIPPS, C. (In Press) *Assessment in Primary Schools*, London, The Curriculum Association.

GIPPS, C., BROWN, M., McCALLUM, B. and McALLISTER, S. (1995) *Intuition or Evidence?: Teachers and National Curriculum Assessment of Seven-Year-Olds*, Buckingham, Open University Press.

GIPPS, C.V., STEADMAN, S., GOLDSTEIN, H. and SHERER, B. (1983) *Testing Children: Standardised Testing in Schools and LEAs*, London, Heinemann.

HER MAJESTY'S CHIEF INSPECTOR OF SCHOOLS IN WALES (1994) 'Review of the National Curriculum and its assessment', in Curriculum and Assessment Authority for Wales (ACAC) (1995) *Overview of the Revised National Curriculum in Wales*, Cardiff, ACAC.

OFFICE FOR STANDARDS IN EDUCATION (OFSTED) (1996) *Subjects and Standards: Issues for School Development Arising from OFSTED Inspection Findings 1994–5, Key Stages 1 and 2, A Report from the Office of Her Majesty's Chief Inspector of Schools*, London, HMSO.

POLLARD, A., BROADFOOT, P., CROLL, P., OSBORN, M. and ABBOTT, D. (1994) *Changing English primary Schools?: The Impact of the ERA at Key Stage One*, London, Cassell.

SCHOOL CURRICULUM AND ASSESSMENT AUTHORITY (SCAA) (1994a) *A Report on the 1994 Consultation*, London, SCAA.

SCHOOL CURRICULUM AND ASSESSMENT AUTHORITY (SCAA) (1994b) *An Introduction to the Revised National Curriculum*, London, SCAA.

SCHOOL CURRICULUM AND ASSESSMENT AUTHORITY (SCAA) (1995) *Consistency in Teacher Assessment: Guidance for Schools, Key Stages 1–3*, London, SCAA.

SCHOOL CURRICULUM AND ASSESSMENT AUTHORITY (SCAA) (1996) *Review of Assessment and Testing: Report from the SCAA to the Secretary of State for Education and Employment, December 1995*, London, SCAA.

SCHOOL CURRICULUM AND ASSESSMENT AUTHORITY (SCAA)/CURRICULUM AND ASSESSMENT AUTHORITY FOR WALES (ACAC) (1994) *Key Stage 1 Assessment Arrangements 1995*, DFE/Welsh Office, London, HMSO.

SCHOOL EXAMINATIONS AND ASSESSMENT COUNCIL (SEAC) (1993) *School Assessment Folder 1993, Key Stage 1*, London, SEAC.

Sizmur, S., Sainsbury, M., Ashby, J., Hargreaves, E. with Jones, E. (1995) *Teacher Assessment 1994 Key Stage 1 Evaluation (Mathematics and Science), Final Report*, London, SCAA.

Welsh Office Education Department (1996) *Review of Educational Provision in Wales 1994–5, Report of Her Majesty's Chief Inspector of Schools in Wales*, Office of HM Chief Inspector of Schools in Wales (OHMCI), Cardiff, Welsh Office.

7 Assessment Issues and the National Curriculum II: Baseline Assessment

Gill Harper Jones

This chapter discusses baseline assessment in terms of its political and educational context. It aims to give an overview of some of the issues surrounding this contentious topic and provides some pointers for teachers who currently may be considering developing such assessment in their own schools.

The Context: What Has Triggered the Push for Baseline Assessment?

There has been increasing interest over the last few years in establishing some kind of baseline assessment on entry to school at age 5. Baseline assessment is only the latest in a long line of assessments that have been introduced into education during the last decade, most of which can be traced back to the early 1980s, when the escalating costs of education in many areas of the world came under increased scrutiny and there were calls for greater accountability (Carr and Claxton, 1989). In the United Kingdom, this led to the introduction of the National Curriculum, and its associated assessment procedures, which were established by the wide ranging powers of the Education Reform Act (1988). It has been argued (Hargreaves, 1989) that the whole thrust of educational reform in the 1980s was driven not by curriculum or pedagogy, but assessment, which became 'the prime focal point for educational change'.

Since the 1988 Education Reform Act, it has been a statutory requirement, in England and Wales, for teachers to assess their pupils at the end of each of the four key stages of education (i.e., at the ages of 7, 11, 14 and 16 years) and since 1993, the government has published schools' and colleges' GCSE and 'A' level exam results. These initiatives are part of an overt political agenda aimed both at raising educational standards and giving parents more information on which to base their choice of schools for their children. The publication of raw examination scores in the form of 'league tables' has caused disquiet amongst educationalists at all levels, not least because the tables take no account of the entering characteristics of individual schools' pupils, making it impossible to judge accurately the educational 'value' which a school has 'added'.

At the secondary level of schooling serious attempts are being made to address this issue, with researchers using sophisticated statistical techniques, such as multilevel modelling, to re-evaluate the raw data of results tables in order to determine how well a school is doing relative to the national average or other schools in the same area. It is possible in these calculations to take a range of variables into account, including socio-economic data, but a consensus appears to be emerging that prior attainment constitutes the most important factor. For example, Fitz-Gibbon (1994), writing in the *Times Educational Supplement*, reckoned that home background accounts for no more than 9 per cent of the variance in exam result, whereas measures of prior achievement account for at least 36 per cent. Secondary schools often have at their disposal, the results of a number of locally administered measures, such as LEA reading test scores for 11-year-olds, and these are commonly used as a baseline against which to judge children's later performance. With the advent of National Curriculum testing for this age group, it will soon be possible for schools to use the scores from the national reading, mathematics and spelling tests as part of their baseline assessments.

It has always been the government's stated intention to encourage the publication of the results of national curriculum assessments carried out in primary schools. However, the teachers' boycott of the tests in 1993 and 1994 had thus far prevented this, so that 1995 is the first year for which a complete set of results is available for scrutiny. The media reports accompanying the publication of the results of the 1995 National Curriculum assessments have been extremely critical of primary teachers and teaching methods and this has been compounded by the annual report of the Chief Inspector of Schools (OFSTED, 1996) which, for the first time, lists failing schools at both primary and secondary levels. It has been made clear that, from 1996 (from 1997 in Wales), the results of National Curriculum assessments at primary level will be published in the form of league tables, just as they have been at secondary level.

For primary head teachers this raises all the same concerns that surrounded the publication of raw score league tables at secondary level. How fair will the comparisons that parents and other interested parties make if no account is taken of the entering characteristics of the intake of the school and the value added by it? (i.e., how much progress children make relative to their starting point or baseline) Is it fair, for example, to compare the results of School A, situated in a leafy, middle class suburb with School Z based in an inner city with 50 per cent of the intake having English as a second language, when the starting points of both groups of children may be very different? Even though School A's scores may be better than School Z's, it is possible that in School A, children are making less progress than might be expected, whereas in School Z, children are achieving well beyond that which might be expected, relative to their starting points. Which school then is doing the better job? Raw assessment scores do not allow this kind of comparison to be made and it is only by having some kind of quantitative baseline measure that children's progress and the value added by the school can be calculated.

Whilst scores from the National Curriculum tests at the end of Key Stage 2 (children aged 11 years) will, as we have seen, provide a baseline for measuring secondary school performance, there is, at present, no comparable baseline against which to measure attainment at Key Stages 1 and 2. Arguably, the level scores from the national curriculum assessment at the end of Key Stage 1 (children aged 7 years) could be used as a baseline for attainment at Level 2, but this does seem a very crude measure involving, as it will, only three, or at most, four levels. Neither does it solve the problem of how progress and attainment at the end of Key Stage 1 can be fairly assessed without some notion of the children's starting point two or three years earlier. Hence the argument for a quantitative baseline of entering characteristics to be established at 5 years of age, so that assessment results at 7 years might be used to determine the value added by the school, rather than merely comparing a school's raw results with the national standard.

It is not surprising, therefore, that head teachers, particularly of schools in areas of socio-economic disadvantage, are keen to develop baseline assessments which will allow them to measure their school's effectiveness relative to the prior ability of their intake. Head teachers hope that the use of value-added measures will prevent invidious comparisons with schools in more privileged catchment areas and will also assist them in bidding for a fair share of the economic cake.

How Are Schools Responding to the Downward Push of Assessment?

There is disturbing evidence (Stierer, 1990) that some schools have begun to use the National Curriculum levels of attainment as the 'main units of measurement' in their baseline profiles of rising 5s. Often these consist of little more than a record of which Level 1 statements children are able to satisfy by their fifth birthday. (No doubt based on the logical, but flawed, reasoning that if each level of the attainment targets represents roughly two chronological years of educational growth and the average 7-year-old can be expected to achieve Level 2, then Level 1 ought to be the baseline for the average 5-year-old). Other schools have pursued this line of reasoning even further, and have invented a Level 0 for those children who do not achieve Level 1 on entry to school (but see Chapter 8).

It is difficult not to be struck by the irony of a situation in which primary teachers, whose vociferous arguments that a ten-level, ten-subject National Curriculum was inappropriate for the early years went unheard in 1989, are now applying those self-same criteria to the youngest children in the school system in what has been described as the 'downward spiral of assessment' (Stierer, 1990).

But, it could be argued that this inappropriate use of the National Curriculum attainment targets has more to do with 'teacher protection than child development' (Blenkin and Kelly, 1992) and that reception and nursery teachers are being forced to compromise their principles as the 'accountability buck' is passed further and further down the line. These top–down pressures for the 'effective delivery' of, what has proved to be, an unworkable national curriculum have led to feelings of defeat and disempowerment amongst many early years teachers and these are compounded by continued, and often vitriolic, attacks regarding reading standards and teaching and organizational methods (Siraj-Blatchford, 1993).

Although early years teachers may have the responsibility of carrying out baseline assessments, the initiative for developing these measures has not sprung from them, but rather from head teachers feeling the pressures of public account-ability to governors, the Local Education Authority, OFSTED inspectors, and par-ents. It is hardly surprising, therefore, to find that one of the largest research projects currently developing and piloting baseline assessment and based at the University of Newcastle upon Tyne, is being funded by the National Association of Head Teachers (Performance Indicators in Primary School [Tymms, 1995]).

According to a recent survey carried out by the National Foundation for Edu-cational Research (NFER) (Hill, 1994), only two LEAs, Avon and Wandsworth, have implemented wide-scale baseline assessment of 5-year-olds with a clearly stated intention of carrying out value added analyses. Both LEAs have been col-lecting baseline data since 1993 and are due to carry out the value added analysis of the first cohorts to have completed Key Stage 1 in the Summer of 1995. Other LEAs are proceeding in more piecemeal fashion. In Birmingham, for example, in 1994, 43 per cent of primary schools took part voluntarily in baseline assessments and in 1995 the proportion rose to 67 per cent with more expected to join in 1996 (*Guardian*, 23 May 1995). Sheffield Education Department (1991), on the other hand, has developed a baseline assessment for under-5s, designed to be used in *all* early childhood settings, including starting school, but which is clearly unsuitable for completing value added calculations.

The beginning of 1996 saw the publication of *Desirable Outcomes for Chil-dren's Learning on Entering Compulsory Education* (DFEE/SCAA, 1996) which are part of the quality assurance and inspection arrangements linked to the govern-ment's nursery voucher scheme in England and Wales (which will have separate arrangements). It will be a requirement that those nursery providers seeking vali-dation under the scheme must work towards these learning outcomes and agree to be inspected against them. The desirable outcomes are presented as goals for learn-ing by the time children enter compulsory education. The outcome measures are broken down into six areas: early literacy, numeracy, personal and social skills, physical development, creative development and knowledge and understanding of the world, which are expected to provide a foundation for later achievement. The accompanying documentation includes charts which explicitly link the outcomes to level and end of key stage descriptions in various national curriculum subjects. These learning outcomes effectively provide schools with a national curriculum Level '0', which could serve as the starting point for baseline assessment on entry to formal schooling. However, the government has also instructed School Curric-ulum and Assessment Authority (SCAA) to investigate how schools are testing their 5-year-olds and draw up proposals for formal consultation on this baseline assessment later in the year. On the basis of this consultation it will then be decided whether to introduce a voluntary system of assessment using national materials or whether a statutory national system is needed to ensure consistency and quality (*T.E.S.* 12 January 1996).[1] In the same article, Vicky Hurst, a member of the Early Years Curriculum Group and a contributor to this book, expressed disquiet at all these measures seeing them as an insidious 'trickle down' effect of the National Curriculum which was forcing an inappropriate curriculum on pre-schools.

Traditionally, the early education lobby has held very different views of the assessment of young children on entry to school and it is to these we now turn.

Issues in Early Years Baseline Assessment

Purposes of Assessment

Despite Drummond's (1993) assertion that questions of what, when, where and how to assess are of secondary importance besides the more searching question of 'Why assess?', it certainly appears from the literature on early years assessment, that much more attention is given to the former than to the latter. Interestingly, *Making Assessment Work*, a book co-authored by Drummond (Drummond, Rouse and Pugh, 1992), whilst long on principles, feelings and values, is distinctly short on any comprehensive discussion of purposes. Many of the aims listed in the pack are circular, and appear to be more concerned with informing teachers about assessment so they may become better assessors, rather than better teachers!

Whilst individual writers tend to emphasize different purposes in line with their personal philosophies, the aims of assessment in the early years seem little differentiated from those of later stages and share many points of similarity. Perhaps the best summary of the purposes of assessment appear in the guidelines of the American National Association for the Education of Young Children (NAEYC) (Bredekamp and Rosegrant, 1992) which declare that assessment provides information necessary for making important educational decisions that affect the child including:

- instructional planning;
- communicating with parents;
- identification of special needs; and
- programme evaluation and accountability.

British educationalists tend to take a softer line with regard to accountability and so we find terminology such as 'reviewing provision' (Stierer *et al.*, 1993), 'informing curriculum planning and evaluating provision' (Lally, 1991), 'helping the teacher evaluate curriculum provision' (Dorset Education Authority, 1990) and 'to review provision as a whole' (Drummond, Rouse and Pugh, 1992).

Only Stierer *et al.* (1990), Stierer *et al.* (1993) and Blatchford and Cline (1992) include explicit reference to the aim of using entry assessments as a basis for measuring future progress, but hold different views on how this could best be achieved as well as the uses to which the information might be put. By far the majority of aims in the recent literature might be termed 'child-centred', and are associated with getting to know the individual child's strengths as a starting point for improved teaching and learning. Drummond *et al.* (1992) add an equal opportunities dimension, insisting that assessment should benefit all children regardless of special needs, ability, ethnicity, culture and heritage.

The whole question of collecting and using baseline data as part of a larger accountability exercise is an issue that, so far, has been little exercised at primary and early years level and as a consequence, there is no substantial research literature of a theoretical or technical kind. It is apparent, however, that moves towards baseline assessments geared towards value added calculations will bring a much harder edge to questions of accountability, particularly in the case of unfavourable value-added scores. Early results from Wandsworth (Wandsworth Research and Evaluation Division, 1994) and Birmingham (*Guardian*, 23 May 1995) are hopeful, in that they indicate the positive effect of nursery education on pupils' performance and this is particularly marked for children whose first language is not English or who come from disadvantaged backgrounds. For example, the Wandsworth results for 1992/3 and 1993/4 clearly indicate that children who attended nursery school had significantly higher scores on the baseline assessment than those who had not attended. Children entitled to free school meals, or whose first language was not English, achieved significantly lower scores than children from less disadvantaged backgrounds or whose home language was English. However, the scores of both these groups were raised by nursery attendance, with those attending three terms or more showing most improvement. The results from Birmingham echo the findings from Wandsworth, clearly showing that children whose first language is not English and who have not been to nursery school do significantly worse in baseline assessments than those who have.

What Should Be Assessed and How?

It is immediately apparent, both from examining published examples of early years assessment materials and from reading the literature, that there is a deep divide between child-centred practitioners, who advocate qualitative forms of assessment which encompass the 'whole child', and a more hard-nosed, psychometric camp promoting quantitative approaches, which are often narrower in focus and stress skills and knowledge. Although it is beyond the scope of this paper to rehearse the different philosophies underlying this distinction, the question of whether some form of rapprochement is possible will be returned to later on.

Qualitative, Observational Approaches

Traditionally, early years practitioners have maintained, from the outset, descriptive records of children which are longitudinal, cumulative, based on close observation and a knowledge of child development. Although generally formative in nature, the collected data can be used as the basis of summative reports. Blenkin and Kelly provide a neat summary:

> Assessment has always been a major feature of education in the early years. It has been a planning tool, employed internally by the schools and teachers to develop forms of curriculum appropriate to pupils' needs. It

has been formative rather than summative, judgemental rather than statistical, holistic rather than identifying weaknesses. (Blenkin and Kelly, 1992: back cover of 'Assessment in Early Childhood Education')

Various frameworks for recording such information have been produced, often by teachers themselves, through INSET courses (Mid- Glamorgan County Council, 1991), in collaboration with HE institutions and research projects (Target Child Observation Method — Sylva *et al.*, 1980). Some are commercially produced, such as 'PROCESS' (Stierer *et al.*, 1993), but many are local initiatives with limited availability.

The categories represented in these frameworks vary, but commonly these cover aspects of social, emotional, physical and cognitive development with differing degrees of emphasis. Thus the 'High Scope Record of Key Experiences' (High Scope, 1991) includes sections for recording social and emotional development, movement and physical development, and cognitive development incorporating representation, language, classification, seriation, number, space and time. The 'PROCESS' record (Stierer *et al.*, 1993), on the other hand, is called a 'classroom observation notebook' and has a cognitive emphasis, which also stresses children's attitudes to their own learning. The headings used are interaction, attitudes, investigating/problem-solving, communicating/representing/interpreting, and individual needs/special educational needs (SEN).

In addition, records often contain a section devoted to life history, which may include information about position in family, health problems, hospitalization, eating habits, and details of previous pre-school experiences, all of which are usually gathered during parental consultations on entry.

The protocols accompanying these frameworks and early years assessment manuals usually stress regular, planned, targeted observations of individual children, with an average duration of ten to fifteen minutes a day. Often a rota system, with a set number of children observed per day/week/half-term, is suggested as a means of ensuring that all children receive equal attention. The essence of qualitative, observational approaches lies in using the collected observations to build up a picture of the 'whole child' over a period of time and crucially, deferring judgments until sufficient evidence has been accumulated. The emphasis, common to all assessments of this type, is essentially a positive one, in which the 'strengths, interests, and experiences of young children are identified as leading points for learning' (Hurst and Lally, 1992).

Descriptive information gathered in this way can be used as the basis for a summative record when reporting to parents or to other colleagues, such as when a child moves from nursery to reception class or begins full-time school. Arguably, the more regularly detailed observations have been recorded, the more informative and valid the summative record will be (Stierer, 1990).

As Blatchford and Cline (1992) point out, whilst such information may well be helpful in obtaining a picture of the child, it is important to recognize that it will not provide the kind of baseline which will allow the linear measurement of progress and which is necessary if value-added calculations are to be made.

Quantitative Approaches

These methods of assessing young children have most usually been developed by psychologists and are widely available from publishers and testing agencies, such as the National Foundation for Educational Research.

A variety of formats is used to gather information, including rating scales (Infant Rating Scales, Lindsay, 1981; The Infant Index, Desforges and Lindsay, 1995.), checklists (Keele Pre-school Assessment Guide, Tyler, 1980), and performance measures (Bury Infant Check, Pearson and Quinn, 1986, and Early Years Easy Screen, Clerehugh *et al.*, 1993). Many of these types of assessment are skills based and include categories such as memory skills, oral language skills, number skills, perceptual-motor skills, auditory reading skills, visual reading skills and active body skills.

Assessing a young child's performance on tasks devised expressly for a test can be misleading, particularly if they are outside that child's experience, so test constructors usually try to ensure that performances can be measured during activities that are part of the normal classroom context and are thus familiar.

All these approaches allow some form of quantitative measurement to be made, often involving either subtest scores, total scores, profiles (or combinations of all three) which can be compared with the cumulative scores of the standardization sample.

Some of these instruments were developed in the 1980s as a response to the 1981 Education Act and are commonly employed by schools and educational psychologists as screening devices, with the aim of identifying children with special educational needs at an early stage in their school career. They are now attracting renewed interest as 'off-the-shelf' baseline assessments for use in value-added calculations at the end of Key Stages 1 and 2.

Although all these instruments are based, implicitly or explicitly, on skills that are considered important for future progress at school, there may prove to be very weak correlations between some of these items and later attainment at 7 years (Blatchford and Cline, 1992). In Tizard *et al.*'s, 1988 study of young children in inner city schools, for example, the strongest predictor of attainment at 7 was the amount of 3R knowledge the children had before they started school and specifically, the number of letters they could identify at age 4. Other items with apparent face validity, such as word matching and concepts about print were relatively weak predictors. Care needs to be taken, therefore, in ensuring that the selection of items in a baseline assessment is grounded in thorough preparatory empirical work, with an explicit rationale and adequate sampling procedures.

Who Should Be Involved in Baseline Assessment?

There is widespread support in the United Kingdom (Lally and Hurst, 1992; Dowling, 1988; Drummond, Rouse and Pugh, 1992; Stierer *et al.*, 1993; Wolfendale, 1993) for the argument that any assessment of very young children, whether carried out by playgroup, nursery or school staff, should include the views of parents, whose intimate knowledge of their children places them in the best position to report upon their progress and development.

Some schemes, such as the checklist *All About Me* (Wolfendale, 1990) have been designed specifically as a record for parents to complete. The manual even suggests that parents should involve the child in the task of filling in the booklet, so that it represents both the child's as well as the adult's views and feelings. To this end all the statements in the checklist are couched in the first person, for example, 'I am old enough now to go to the toilet by myself' to be checked either 'yes' or 'not yet'. The resultant record is intended to give parents a basis on which to discuss their child's progress with nursery and infant teachers or playgroup leaders.

There are others, such as the PROCESS pack (Stierer *et al.*, 1993) and the Mid Glamorgan Foundation Profile, (Mid-Glamorgan County Council, 1991), which recognize the value and significance of the parents' contribution, by including sections to be completed in discussion with them, but without handing over the entire procedure. This is by far the most common approach, incorporating notions both of starting 'where the child is' and actively involving parents very early on in their child's educational life and progress. This explicit involvement of parents in the assessment of their young children is in direct contrast to the approach advocated by the American NAEYC (Bredekamp and Rosegrant, 1992), where parents are seen as the main audience for assessment information rather than contributors.

Where the assessment is observational, ongoing and formative, a good case is often made for involving other adults and professionals with whom the child comes into contact during the nursery or school day (including nursery nurses, student teachers, parent helpers and nursery nurses in training), either directly, by making their own records of selected children or activities, or by relieving the teacher in order that he or she might do so (Dowling, 1988; Lally, 1991; Lally and Hurst, 1992). However, the teacher is seen as having primary responsibility not only for integrating and organizing the information collected by others, but also for summative recording and reporting.

The same arguments could be applied to more quantitative forms of assessment, with the teacher taking the major role in recording and reporting, but being supported and informed by other adults working alongside.

When Should Baseline Assessments Be Carried Out?

Traditionally, information concerning developmental milestones, likes, dislikes and self-help skills is gathered and recorded in consultation with parents either before or shortly after young children join nursery or reception classes. Generally, nursery and reception teachers assess and record in a formative way throughout the year, using this longitudinal evidence as the basis of a summative report for parents and/or the next class teacher at the end of the year. Because both nursery and reception age children fall outside the scope of the National Curriculum assessment and reporting requirements, some schools and LEAs have devised assessment systems which are designed to be used from the beginning of nursery through to the end of the reception class, with built-in opportunities for summative reporting at key points (e.g., Mid-Glamorgan Foundation Profile).

The question of timing is much more crucial with regard to baseline assessments. In the United Kingdom, it could be argued that the obvious and most appropriate time for a baseline to be completed is on entry to formal schooling at age 5. But this is not quite so straightforward as it might first appear, as in some LEAs children are admitted into reception classes as 4-year-olds, some admit rising-5s and some wait until the term after the child's fifth birthday.

The picture is further complicated by the fact that in some areas of the country, South Wales, for example, LEA preschool provision is widespread, and some 5-year-olds entering reception classes may already have had two years of part-time nursery education (if their birthday falls in September, for example, as entry is often linked to birth date). This raises the issue of whether the baseline assessment for such children should be moved back two years to when they first enter preschool. Whether baseline assessments of 3-year-old children can ever be sufficiently reliable or accurate enough to form the basis of value added calculations, or whether they should even be attempted, is a debatable point, the not so hidden agenda of which can only be fully appreciated by a minor digression into politics.

Preschool education in the United Kingdom is at present voluntary and far from universal. Currently, there is a powerful lobby from parents, teachers and educationalists to make preschool provision available to all 3- and 4-year-olds, such that the government has publicly stated its commitment to extending provision within the lifetime of the present parliament. Whereas parents and teachers were keen that decisions should be made in terms of long term educational gains for children, it is, in fact, short term economic considerations which have prevailed.

Despite the accumulating research evidence, (not least that provided by early data from baseline assessments in Wandsworth and Birmingham) that LEA-run nursery classes and schools are having positive effects on educational performance, they are expensive both to set up and run. On the supposed grounds of 'choice and diversity' the DFEE has proposed instead a voucher scheme, under which eventually, all parents of 4-year-olds will be given £1,000 to spend on their preferred form of preschooling. Four local authorities, Norfolk, Westminster, Kensington and Chelsea and Wandsworth, will be piloting the government's scheme from April, 1996 onwards. Under the scheme, parents of 4-year-olds can apply to the Child Benefit Centre in Durham for nursery vouchers, which are issued termly, and can be exchanged at maintained or private nurseries. However, being issued with a voucher is no guarantee of a place in either state or maintained nurseries, and in any case, not all parents will be able to afford to 'top up' the subsidy to pay for a place in private school even if one were available.

Such a scheme will mainly benefit parents in urban areas, where there is already a greater choice of state and private nurseries and playgroups than in rural counties. However, the amount of money available is insufficient to fund widespread new provision and as much of it is being found from current LEA grants it may possibly result in cut backs in current LEA provision. Equally, local education authorities without provision are unlikely to be tempted into setting up nursery classes or schools on the basis of this kind of funding, as capital expenditure, running costs and teachers' salaries could not be guaranteed. Norfolk, one of the four local authorities taking part in the nursery voucher pilot scheme, joined only after securing the government's agreement that it could pay for the new places by increasing its capital borrowing and servicing the loan out of voucher income. The DFEE has also agreed in this instance to let parents take their vouchers to the local authority for allocation under its local management scheme, rather than directly to the nursery providers. In this way, Norfolk has maintained some overall control of how best the money shall be spent, rather than being entirely at the whim of market forces, which would make long term planning difficult. (*TES*, 19 January 1996.)

It is questionable just who will benefit under this scheme, as the funding is only for 4-year-olds (not 3-year-olds, as first promised), many of whom are already in full time schooling in reception classes. Local authorities which already offer good nursery provision for 3-year-olds are worried about the skewing effect this money aimed at 4-year-olds will have upon the system. Playgroups, along with all other nursery providers, will only receive validation (and hence voucher payment) if they can demonstrate, through inspection, that they are achieving the educational aims laid down in the 'Desirable Outcomes' document (DFEE, 1996). It was originally thought that playgroups might be net gainers under the voucher scheme, given that staffing is often by volunteers and children's attendance is sometimes only three morning or afternoon sessions a week. However, given also that many playgroups have avowedly social rather than educational aims, it is unlikely that the government's criteria will be met in all cases.

For political reasons therefore, state sector nursery teachers are keen to be seen providing an effective service and head teachers are keen to promote preschool education as value for money. Baseline assessments for 3-year-olds are viewed, particularly by head teachers, as a useful tool in calculating the value-added by preschool education, which subsequently can be used as a weapon in the battle with local administrators and in the war with central government to justify, maintain and expand preschool provision. Preschool teachers, whose personal philosophies of early childhood education might be expected to be at odds with baseline assessments and value added calculations, are having to grasp the nettle in order to safeguard jobs and continued funding.

The, as yet, untested assumption that preschooling will demonstrably add value to children's educational progress is being taken for granted by both parties, although as we have seen, first indications from Birmingham and Wandsworth are good.

Developing Effective and Appropriate Baseline Assessment Procedures

As is now apparent, the picture that emerges from the literature is a paradoxical one. Early years teachers, as we have seen, are happiest with qualitative forms of assessment which are longitudinal and descriptive and take into account 'the whole child'. The push for baseline assessment, on the other hand, appears to run directly counter to the child-centred culture and philosophy that permeates early years education, requiring, as it does, quantitative information collected about children possibly as young as 3-years-old.

Theoretically, it ought to be possible to develop a form of baseline assessment which is rigorous, and meets the needs of the value-added lobby, without violating the sensibilities of early years teachers. Wolfendale (1993), in a review of current practices in baseline assessment, argues cogently that it is educationally desirable to have a system of assessment on entry to school which should be sound, robust and reflectively applied, as opposed to *ad hoc* approaches which have no theoretical foundations and which have not been empirically tested. She also provides guidelines to support teachers and schools in making decisions about which forms of assessment may be suitable for their purposes. The guidelines fall under the following headings:

- Principles (issues concerned with the rights of children and parents);
- Who wants and needs the information? (purposes of baseline assessment and who benefits from the information);
- Criteria (for determining quality and effectiveness of assessment materials); and
- A dynamic process of decision-making (a flow chart which clarifies the steps for reviewing baseline assessment procedures).

These embody Wolfendale's advocacy for baseline assessment practice that is 'sound and just — on behalf of all the children'.

Blatchford and Cline (1992) share a similar viewpoint and also argue for baseline assessment to be put on a more formal footing in order to ensure greater fairness, through being more systematic and open, and having greater relevance, by being carefully related to the school's curriculum and teaching arrangements. They set out a list of criteria for evaluating baseline assessment schemes, which includes questions about theoretical integrity, practical efficacy, equity and accountability.

So what issues should school staff be considering when either reviewing current assessment procedures or devising new ones? Set out below are some questions that might serve as useful starting points, although readers should refer to Wolfendale (1993) and Blatchford and Cline (1992) for a fuller discussion of these concerns:

- What is the purpose of developing a baseline assessment? Is it to provide information for measuring future progress; to get an overall picture of the new intake; to begin the process of gathering information for an individual pupil profile; to identify pupils who may have special needs or a combination of any or all of these? What effects/constraints might different purposes have on the form the assessment takes? Is it possible, for example, to devise a baseline assessment that is both developmentally appropriate and capable of providing a sound basis for value added measurements?

- Will the baseline assessment be the start of a record of achievement or built into a form of ongoing assessment and record keeping or will it be free-standing and simply for comparison at the end of Key Stage 1?
- At what point is the baseline assessment to be made — on entry to nursery or entry to the reception class? What is the most effective time for administering an assessment like this? Will it be after a term or around the fourth or fifth birthday regardless of where in the school year this falls? Will assessments be completed for the wholes class at the same time or will they be ongoing?
- Will the information recorded be accurate and reliable? Is it possible to make robust and reliable assessments of children as young as 3-years-old? Will the assessment be based on sound models of child development and learning processes? Will the assessment provide practical information to guide teaching?
- What information is it important to record in nursery and reception classes? Will the assessment and recording categories be different in these two settings? Is it possible to ensure that assessment carried out at nursery or reception will relate to the National Curriculum assessments at the end of Key Stage 1?
- How will the baseline assessment be carried out? Will it be through observation, questioning, testing techniques or a combination? Will it be carried out by school staff or will parents be involved, through interviews or home visits? Will the assessment operate fairly with respect to gender, social class, ethnicity, language and religion?
- Will the results of baseline assessments be made public and if so in what form?
- Will the administrative burden of completing baseline assessments interfere with the process of teachers building sympathetic relationships with newly arrived children?

The whole review process connected with baseline assessment will involve staff in wide ranging discussions with the aim of finding answers to questions like these and should prove valuable in the professional development of teachers. The actual process of carrying out systematic assessment should prove equally useful, as it will allow teachers to evaluate their own work and gain access to new thinking (DES, 1989). As Blatchford and Cline point out:

> Given the more defensive uses that may well be made of assessment on entry — for example to off-set the possibility of relatively poor summative scores at the end of Key Stage 1 — it seems especially important to stress this more positive role. (Blatchford and Cline, 1992, p. 266)

Evidence from research into Key Stage 1 National Curriculum assessment procedures (Gipps *et al.*, 1995) would seem to bear this out. A group of Year 2 teachers, whose assessment practice was followed over a period of four years, were found to take greater care in planning and in close observation of children. They also had a more detailed understanding of individual children's progress and were working more collegially with staff at both Key Stage 1 and Key Stage 2. Many of the teachers in the sample moved away from intuitive approaches to assessment toward more systematic, evidence based techniques, which, the researchers claim, led to improvements both in teaching and assessing (see Chapter 6).

Note

1 Since this chapter was written the Government has announced plans to introduce a statutory framework for the assessment of five year olds, on entry to compulsory education, against approved criteria, from September 1997. This will be accredited by the curriculum and assessment agencies (SCAA and ACAC).

References

BLATCHFORD, P. and CLINE, T. (1992) 'Baseline assessments for school entrants', *Research Papers in Education*, **7**, pp. 247–69.

BLENKIN, G. and KELLY, V. (Eds) (1992) *Assessment in Early Childhood Education*. London, Paul Chapman.

BREDEKAMP, S. and ROSEGRANT, T. (Eds) (1992) *Reaching Potentials: Appropriate Curriculum Assessment for Young Children*. Washington, D.C., National Association for the Education of Young Children.

CARR, M. and CLAXTON, G. (1989) 'The costs of calculation', *New Zealand Journal of Educational Studies*, **24**, pp. 129–39.

CLEREHUGH, J., HART, K., PITHER, R., RIDER, K. and TURNER, K. (1993) *Early Years Easy Screen*, Windsor, NFER/Nelson.

DEPARTMENT FOR EDUCATION AND EMPLOYMENT (DFEE)/SCHOOL CURRICULUM AND ASSESSMENT AUTHORITY (SCAA) (1996) *Nursery Education Scheme: The Next Steps and Desirable Outcomes* for Children's Learning, London, DFEE/SCAA.

DEPARTMENT FOR EDUCATION AND SCIENCE (DES) (1989) *National Curriculum: From Policy to Practice*, London, HMSO.

DESFORGES, M. and LINDSAY, G. (1995) *Infant Index*, London, Hodder and Stoughton.

DORSET EDUCATION AUTHORITY (1990) *Starting Out: Working Together Developing Early Years Assessment Procedures*, Dorchester, Dorset County Council.

DOWLING, M. (1988) *Education 3–5: A Teachers' Handbook*, London, Paul Chapman.

DRUMMOND, M. (1993) *Assessing Children Learning*, London, David Fulton.

DRUMMOND, M., ROUSE, D. and PUGH, G. (1992) *Making Assessment Work: Values and Principles in Assessing Young Children's Learning*, Nottingham, NESArnold/National Children's Bureau.

FITZ-GIBBON, C. (1994) 'Three routes to the wrong answer', *Times Educational Supplement*, 9 November, p. 11.

GIPPS, C., BROWN, M., McCALLUM, B. and McALISTER, S. (1995) *Intuition or Evidence: Teachers and National Assessment of Seven Year Olds*, Buckingham, Open University Press.

GUARDIAN (1995) *Early learning*, 23 May (pages 2 and 3).

HARGREAVES, A. (1989) *Curriculum and Assessment Reform*, Milton Keynes, Open University Press.

HIGH SCOPE (1991) High Scope Key Experiences for Children Age 3–5 in DRUMMOND, M.J. *et al. Making Assessment Work*, Nottingham, New Arnold/National Children's Bureau.

HILL, L. (1994) *Value Added Analysis: Current Practice in Local Education Authorities*, Slough, Education Management Information Exchange.

HURST, V. and LALLY, M. (1992) 'Assessment and the nursery curriculum', in BLENKIN, G. and KELLY, V. (Eds) *Assessment in Early Childhood Education*, London, Paul Chapman.

LALLY, M. (1991) *The Nursery Teacher in Action*, London, Paul Chapman.

LALLY, M. and HURST, V. (1992) 'Assessment in nursery education: A review of approaches', in BLENKIN, G. and KELLY, V. (Eds) *Assessment in Early Childhood Education*, London, Paul Chapman.

LINDSAY, G. (1981) *The Infant Rating Scales*, London, Hodder and Stoughton.

MID-GLAMORGAN COUNTY COUNCIL (1991) *Quality Living and Learning: Mid-Glamorgan Foundation Profile*, Porth, Mid Glamorgan, Mid Glamorgan County Council Education Department.

OFFICE FOR STANDARDS IN EDUCATION (OFSTED) (1996) *The Annual Report of Her Majesty's Chief Inspector of Schools: Standards and Quality in Education*, 1994–5, London, HMSO.

PEARSON, L. and QUINN, J. (1986) *The Bury Infant Check*, Windsor, NFER/Nelson.

SHEFFIELD EDUCATION DEPARTMENT (1991) *Record Keeping for Children under Five in All Settings*, Sheffield, City of Sheffield Education Department.

SIRAJ-BLATCHFORD, I. (1993) 'The professional identity of early years teachers: Challenges and constraints', in GAMMAGE, P. and MEIGHAN, J. (Eds) *Early Childhood Education: Taking Stock*, Ticknall, Derbyshire, Education Now Publishing Co-operative.

STIERER, B. (1990) 'Assessing children at the start of school: Issues, dilemmas and developments', *Curriculum Journal*, **1**, pp. 155–69.

STIERER, B., DEVEREUX, J., GIFFORD, S., LAYCOCK, E., and YERBURY, J. (1993) *Profiling, Recording and Observing*, London, Routledge.

SYLVA, K., ROY, C. and PAINTER, M. (1980) *Childwatching at Playgroup and Nursery*, London, Grant McIntyre.

TIMES EDUCATIONAL SUPPLEMENT (1996) 12 January, 'National tests loom for five-year-olds' (page 2).

TIMES EDUCATIONAL SUPPLEMENT (1996) 19 January, 'Nursery pilot cleared for take off' (page 6).

TIZARD, B., BLATCHFORD, P., BURKE, J., FARQUHAR, C. and PLEWIS, I. (1988) *Young Children at School in the Inner City*. Hove, Lawrence Erlbaum Associates.

TYLER, S. (1980) *Keele Pre-school Assessment Guide*, Windsor, NFER/Nelson.

TYMMS, P. (1995) *Performance Indicators in Primary Schools*, University of Newcastle upon Tyne, Project Newsletter.

WANDSWORTH RESEARCH AND EVALUATION DIVISION (1994) *Wandsworth Baseline Assessment 1993/4 REU 39/94*, London, Wandsworth Education Department.

WOLFENDALE, S. (1990) *All About Me*, Nottingham, NEW Arnold.

WOLFENDALE, S. (1993) *Baseline Assessment: A Review of Current Practice, Issues and Strategies for Effective Implementation*, Burton upon Trent, Trentham Books.

8   The National Curriculum and Children's Special Educational Needs in the Early Years

Theo Cox

The aim of this chapter is to discuss the problems and challenges of teaching children with Special Educational Needs (SEN) within the framework of the National Curriculum during the early years and how they may be met. The emphasis will be upon children with mild or moderate difficulties who do not require the issue of a statement under the 1993 Education Act, i.e., the majority of the 20 per cent of children who, according to the Warnock Report (DES, 1978), can be expected to develop a special need at some time during their school careers. The focus will be upon curriculum and teaching issues at the classroom and school level, rather than on wider issues of LEA and government policy and practice which are well covered elsewhere (see for example Lewis, 1995a.)

After presenting an outline of two major developments with regard to the teaching of children with SEN, namely the Government's Code of Practice and the introduction of the Revised National Curriculum, the chapter will bring together findings from research and other reports of the impact of the National Curriculum upon these children, including the Swansea University Impact Study, and discuss their implications. Some conclusions are drawn and key challenges for early years teachers with regard to children's SEN are stated.

Introduction

It is important to realize that, as pointed out in a booklet on SEN in the National Curriculum produced by the former National Curriculum Council (NCC, 1989), special educational needs are not just a reflection of pupils' inherent difficulties; they are often related to factors within schools which can prevent or exacerbate some problems. The interaction between the pupil and the school, including its curriculum, can also lead to learning difficulties.

The Code of Practice

The Code of Practice (referred to as 'the Code' in the rest of this chapter), was issued by the Secretary of State, as required by the 1993 Education Act, with the aim of 'giving practical guidance to LEAs and governing bodies of all maintained schools on their responsibilities towards all children with SEN'. (DFE, 1994, p. i.) Since it is essentially a guidance document it does not in itself have statutory force but all those to whom the Code applies have a statutory duty to 'have regard to it' when exercising their duties and responsibilities under the 1993 Act and its Regulations.

The fundamental principles of the Code emphasize that there is a continuum of SEN and a continuum of special educational provision, and that the needs of most pupils with SEN will be met in the mainstream of ordinary schools and without a statutory assessment or statement. Such pupils should have the greatest possible access to a broad and balanced education, including the National Curriculum.

Regarding identification, assessment and educational provision for children with SEN the core of the Code is the five-stage model designed to help schools and LEAs to match special educational provision to each child's needs. In this the responsibility for pupils lies with the school for stages 1–3 (with close involvement of the LEA at stage 3), and jointly with the LEA and the school for stages 4 and 5 which involve a statutory assessment of a child's SEN, possibly leading to a formal statement of need and provision. The model is based upon the premise that the SEN of the great majority of children can be met by the schools, either under their own resources (stages 1 and 2), or with guidance and support from the LEA or other outside services (stage 3). Only a small minority of children are expected to have SEN of such severity and complexity that they can only be met through additional or alternative provision resourced by the LEA and secured by a statement, and these children would normally have passed through stages 1–3.

The school's procedures for identifying and meeting the needs of its pupils with SEN have to be spelled out in its SEN policy, the statement of which is a statutory requirement under the 1993 Education Act. Overall responsibility for this policy lies with the governing body and the head teacher, although the whole school should be involved in its development.

The Code can be viewed as a move by government to clarify the balance of responsibilities for SEN between the school and the LEA and to encourage the early identification and provision for such need at the school level (Vincent *et al.*, 1995). This move may have been partly driven by its desire to reduce the unwieldy numbers of children for whom many LEAs were producing statements by improving the quality of school based identification and provision (Lewis, 1995a). Unfortunately, although such a reduction would save money, since statutory assessment and statementing are very expensive processes, the government has not provided additional funding to schools in order to implement the Code. This raises questions about the feasibility of the full implementation of the Code in ordinary schools, particularly with regard to providing adequate support and resources for the school's special educational needs coordinating officer (SENCO), as will be discussed later in this chapter.

The Code of Practice and the Early Years (3–5)

The Code rightly underlines the importance of the early identification, assessment and provision for every child who may have SEN. The widespread introduction in primary and first schools of some form of 'baseline assessment' of children aged 5 or even younger (see Chapter 7) should increase the likelihood that children with actual or potential SEN will be identified by schools as early as possible and suitable forms of intervention undertaken. It is also vital that early parental concerns about any aspect of a child's development should be responded to promptly and sympathetically by the school, and acted upon if justified by further investigation.

The Code states that those responsible for the governance of schools in both the maintained and private sectors are required by law to do all that they can to secure that appropriate SEN provision is made for all registered pupils with learning difficulties. It adds that an LEA may expect a maintained nursery class or school to follow broadly the same procedure for identifying the SEN of children under 5 as the Code requires for children of compulsory school age. It goes on to recommend a series of steps that a school should take if a child enters the compulsory school age with an identified or potential SEN. These include:

- identifying and focusing attention on the child's skills and highlighting areas for early activity to support the child within the class; and
- involving parents in developing and implementing educational programmes at home and at school.

The Code states that the observations of a wide range of early service providers, e.g., playgroups, will be invaluable in ensuring that schools can prepare an entry profile for children who may experience difficulties. Unfortunately there is some evidence that teachers at Key Stage 1 have tended to make little use of assessment information passed on by staff in preschool settings (Blyth and Wallace, 1988).

The Revised National Curriculum and SEN

The Revised National Curriculum which came into operation in primary schools in September 1995 has a greater flexibility than before to enable teachers to meet the learning needs of both pupils with SEN and of more able pupils. This is partly achieved through its Access provision in the Common Requirements section which forms part of each new subject Order. This allows teachers to select material from earlier or later key stages where this is necessary to enable pupils to progress and demonstrate achievement. (Previously it was necessary for a formal statement to be written modifying the National Curriculum for an individual child to have access to programmes of study appropriate to an earlier or later key stage.) The Access statement also requires schools to make appropriate provision for pupils experiencing difficulties in responding to oral or written language, such as the use of technological and computer aids and signing and symbolic communication systems.

A report on the 1994 consultation preceding the introduction of the Revised National Curriculum stated that there was widespread approval by the teachers and professional associations consulted that special educational needs had been considered in the curriculum review (SCAA, 1994). It was recognized that the proposals reflected input from teachers of pupils with SEN on subject advisory groups and the majority of teachers at each key stage felt that the proposals were helpful for planning the curriculum and assessment. Those consulted also felt that the statements supporting access to the National Curriculum would help teachers in planning appropriate work for pupils with SEN, and the flexibility to supplement content by using material from earlier key stage programmes was widely welcomed. There was also a welcome from teachers consulted for the flexible programming provision for able pupils.

In addition to improved flexibility regarding access the programmes of study in the revised National Curriculum have been simplified and clarified and given central prominence, replacing the previous emphasis upon attainment targets. Also the amount to be covered in the non-core subjects has been reduced and the attainment targets adjusted accordingly. These changes, coupled with the reduction in teacher assessment and record keeping, should reduce the burden of national curriculum implementation for teachers, and, as discussed later in this chapter, increase their scope for planning to meet the individual learning needs of children with SEN.

SEN in the Early Years

Virtually all primary and first schools will have children under 5 attending nursery, reception or mixed age classes who will fall within the ambit of the school's SEN policy. While the National Curriculum strictly only applies to children from age 5 upwards it has been shown to have knock-on effects upon children under 5 (see Chapters 1, 2 and 11) so that some of the benefits from the Revised National Curriculum discussed above should extend to younger children with learning difficulties. The unlinking of key stage programmes of study and chronological age seems unlikely to bring any benefit to children with learning difficulties in Years 1 and 2 of the National Curriculum since they will be working within Key Stage 1 anyway but it should bring benefits to more able children in these years since they could be given access to programmes of study at Key Stage 2.

Access to the National Curriculum for Children with SEN

Since access to the National Curriculum is a statutory entitlement for all pupils regardless of ability it is important to establish whether such children do indeed enjoy such access. The relevant findings from the Swansea University Impact Study will be presented first and then related to other findings on this question.

The Swansea University Impact Study

Just under half (eleven) of the head teachers reported no significant problems regarding access to the full National Curriculum for their slower learning pupils, including those with special educational needs. Seven gave qualified responses and five reported particular concerns.

Reporting full access for these pupils one head teacher stressed that the curriculum tasks were differentiated for them and they progressed more slowly through the curriculum. The same teacher commented that even though there was an emphasis on ensuring that the children gained competence in the basic skills they were not presented with a narrow curriculum. To quote:

> It is important that their experience is widened and that activities are offered which arouse their interest and imagination.

In contrast some of the head teachers giving a qualified response to the question on access felt that the ability of children with SEN to cope with the demands of the full National Curriculum was significantly impaired by their limited basic skills. In their view the requirement to give them full access to the whole National Curriculum conflicted with the need to concentrate on their weaknesses in this area

> Because of the demands of the National Curriculum children lacking in basic skills can't take full advantage of opportunities in the National Curriculum, for example in researching history. More time should be spent on their basic learning needs. They have access to the whole curriculum but this is a bit false.

Two head teachers commented that the sheer scale and depth of coverage of the full National Curriculum was beyond the capacity of pupils with SEN to contend with, especially when this was coupled with limited basic skills.

The particular problems of access reported were focused upon children with physical disabilities, such as a child with motor impairment finding problems with technology, or a child with epilepsy needing one to one mainstream support because of difficulties in concentrating.

Other Studies

A survey of special needs provision of nearly 300 mainstream primary schools was carried out by Lewis (1995b) at the University of Warwick. She found that the majority of the children with SEN had access to the full National Curriculum. A national survey of the provision for, and educational achievement of, pupils with SEN in mainstream primary and secondary schools in England also found that these pupils had access to the full National Curriculum (OFSTED, 1996a). Had it been otherwise any of these children excluded from any parts of the National Curriculum should have been the subject of formal modification or disapplication orders under the 1993 Education Act.

It appears then that the majority of pupils with SEN are gaining access to the full National Curriculum, albeit in a differentiated fashion which takes account of their learning difficulties. As discussed earlier in this chapter the inclusion of standard access statements in all subject orders in the Revised National Curriculum is intended to improve the flexibility of the National Curriculum so that the use of formal modifiaction and disapplication procedures should become quite exceptional.

Impact of the National Curriculum upon Children with SEN

Given that the great majority of pupils with SEN appear to have access to the full National Curriculum what benefits does this bring to them and are there any disadvantages for them?

The Swansea University Impact Study

Impact on Slower Learning Children and Children with SEN

In response to the question asked at interview concerning the effect of the introduction of the National Curriculum upon slower learners, including children with SEN, over half of the head teachers (twelve) and of the Year 1 class teachers (seventeen) felt that these children had suffered some disadvantage. Of the remaining teachers some reported a mixture of benefits and disadvantages and a few felt that there were no discernible effects either way. By far the main concern was over the reduction in the time available for teachers to consolidate the children's learning in the basic skills as a consequence of the requirement for them to be given access to the full National Curriculum. As one class teacher put it:

> Although slower learning children and children with SEN are now guaranteed a learning experience which covers a variety of subjects I do feel at times that quantity is the driving force, not quality with these children. Of course they need the variety of learning experiences of more able children but at times, because of the amount of attainment targets to cover the time needed for them to develop basic concepts has gone.

Some of the teachers expressing such views clearly felt under pressure to push the slower learning children to reach the generally expected levels of achievement in the basic skills. This could mean pushing the children beyond Level 1 before they were ready.

Several class teachers reported that, in addition to their difficulties in learning basic skills, slower learning children also experienced some difficulties in learning aspects of the wider curriculum. For example one teacher felt that the variety of subjects and the quantity of oral and written work required of the children, e.g., in history and geography, posed great difficulties for them. They were being required to think for themselves but were hampered by their limited concepts of time and space and needed a great deal of teacher direction. Two other teachers commented that the breadth of the curriculum was too much for slow learners who were being hurried through the curriculum at the expense of their concentration and understanding.

On the positive side a small number of both head and class teachers reported some benefits to slower learners from experiencing the National Curriculum. These stemmed from the helpful planning structure provided by the programmes of study for teachers which helped them in teaching these children and also from the broadening of the curriculum now available to them.

> The National Curriculum has widened their experience and boosted their confidence and given them more varied practical experiences. All children now have to do more things for themselves. (Head teacher)

Impact on More Able Children

Although more able and gifted children are not officially designated as having SEN, unless they have accompanying social or emotional or other diffficulties, some teachers in the study considered that they too had special needs. Moreover more able children and slower learners represent two poles of the wide spectrum of scholastic abilities. The teachers in the study were therefore also asked about the impact of the National Curriculum upon their more able pupils. In contrast to their views regarding the effects upon slower learners over half of the head teachers and two-thirds of the Year 1 class teachers reported mainly benefits for more able children. These were, firstly, the broadening of the curriculum, with a wider range of content and activities than before, and, secondly the support provided by the National Curriculum for teachers in planning the work for more able children in order to challenge them and extend their learning.

Other Studies

In the national survey carried out in England by Lewis (1995b) 37 per cent of the primary teachers responding concluded that, on balance, the National Curriculum was a good thing for children with SEN, 14 per cent said that it was not a good thing and 46 per cent said that it was partly a good thing. Lewis comments that this ambivalence was reflected in the wider picture of perceived strengths and weaknesses in the implementation of the National Curriculum for these children. The three most frequently cited benefits were: the provision of the same basic entitlement for all children, a clear curricular framework and a structure within which to differentiate learning for pupils with SEN. The most frequently cited disadvantages of the National Curriculum for children with SEN were: problems in effectively differentiating the curriculum, providing the breadth without sacrificing the depth and having inadequate resources to fulfil curricular demands.

It will be seen that there was some agreement between the views of the teachers in the two studies as to the advantages and disadvantages of giving children with SEN access to the full National Curriculum, although concern about the adverse effects upon the quality of the children's learning of the basic skills was much more explicit among the teachers in the Swansea University study. The *principle* of access to the full National Curriculum for all children with SEN seemed to be widely accepted by the teachers despite their concerns about the practical difficulties.

Differentiating the National Curriculum

Clearly the extent to which children with SEN can gain meaningful access to the range of experiences embraced in the National Curriculum programmes of study will depend crucially upon the ability of their class teachers to differentiate the curriculum according to their individual learning needs. According to Lewis (1995b) the National Curriculum has been associated with an increase in teachers' awareness of the need for such differentiation but some of the teachers in her survey perceived this as a source of difficulty rather than a benefit. Adapting the National Curriculum to meet a wide range of children's learning needs, including both children with SEN and more able children, is probably the greatest challenge facing primary teachers at Key Stages 1 and 2 but especially the latter, and their need for adequate support, training and resources to help them achieve this goal is very great. In its report on special needs and the National Curriculum OFSTED (1993) stated that a persistently reported weakness in INSET was its failure to address adequately the question of how best to match work to pupils' different learning abilities, particularly in classes where the ability range was wide.

A very useful discussion of the various aspects of differentiation, e.g., of teaching goals and teaching methods, is provided by Lewis (1995b). She also provides helpful practical guidelines for the teacher in carrying out both kinds of differentiation. Another useful guide to this topic is provided by Webster 1995 as part of a compendium on meeting children's SEN.

Assessment and Recording

The key to successful differentiation lies in the skillful assessment of children's individual learning difficulties and needs. As the OFSTED (1993) report on special needs and the National Curriculum puts it,

> Teachers can hardly expect to plan and provide a good match of work to ability and special needs in the absence of an assesssment of pupils' performance which adequately pinpoints their strengths and weaknesses. (OFSTED, 1993, p. 22)

The report observed that assessment remained the weak link in many schools and needed to be urgently addressed in their planning for INSET. In similar vein the annual report of the Chief Inspector for Wales for 1994–5 (Welsh Office,

1996a) commented that the production and, in particular, the consistent implementation of individual education plans (IEPs) were proving to be challenging tasks in many schools, more so than the procedural aspects of the Code.

Although there are several alternative frameworks for curriculum assessment and planning (see Lewis, 1995b for a discussion of these) the most suitable for the class teacher is provided by the National Curriculum Programmes of Study, particularly in its revised version which gives much greater prominence to these. This is a strong recommendation of the 'Small Steps' study carried out by the NFER for SCAA (Lee and Fletcher-Campbell, 1995). The aim of this study was to carry out research into effective practice in assessing, recording and accrediting the achievements of pupils making small steps of progress in the National Curriculum. The target group of pupils included those working at Levels 1, 2 or 3 for several years. A variety of formative and diagnostic methods was found to be in use in schools, including observation and assessment within learning activities, specific assessment tasks and externally provided tests or tasks. Some schools and LEAs had produced small step 'schemes' which listed statements supplementing those provided in the National Curriculum attainment targets. However the authors of the study concluded that the process of devising small steps was more appropriately based on an analysis of the revised programmes of study and planning how elements might be taught and assessed according to the needs of individuals or groups of pupils in class. Publishers and specialists in learning difficulties had a part to play in the development of this approach.

For early years teachers of course the focus will be upon children working towards and within Level 1. Several teachers in the Swansea University study referred to the need for more finely graded steps between the levels and within Level 1 if children with SEN were not to get discouraged. They also sought recognition for the learning that had taken place *prior* to Level 1. Lewis (1995b) argues that Level 1 should be regarded as a broad initial level within which children can be seen to be working rather than as a cut-off stage below which children are regarded as falling outside the National Curriculum.

Unfortunately, as Lewis discusses in some detail, the official criterion for judging whether Level 1 has been achieved seems to be stricter than those for reaching judgments about attainment of Levels 2 and above. In the latter case, teachers judge which level description best fits the child's current level of performance relating to the given attainment target (i.e., it is an holistic judgment). In the case of Level 1 however teachers are instructed that where a child is working toward Level 1 in an attainment target this should be represented by zero (DFEE/SCAA, 1995). As Lewis points out, for children with learning difficulties this could have the demoralizing effect of keeping them at Level 0 for a long time for reporting and assessment purposes.

The satisfactory matching of curricular tasks to individual learning needs also requires that teachers have an adequate depth of knowledge of the various subjects of the National Curriculum in order to be able to diagnose each child's learning needs. While this applies equally strongly to both core and non-core subjects it is in the latter that primary teachers appear to feel less well equipped (see Chapters

1 and 5). Failure to make such a match can result in frustration and loss of confidence by children with SEN, which, if prolonged, could in some cases lead to them developing emotional and behavioural difficulties (EBD).

Achieving Competence in the Basic Skills

A major concern expressed by the teachers in the Swansea University study regarding the effects of the National Curriculum upon slower learning children, including those with SEN, was that its overloaded content threatened the quality of their learning of the basic skills (i.e., reading, writing and number). We need to ask whether this concern is borne out by the latest evidence about standards of achievement in the basic skills at Key Stage 1.

Standards of Achievement

Evidence from National Assessments

Results of the national tests at Key Stage 1 in 1995 in England (DFEE, 1996) and Wales (Welsh Office, 1996b) show that in English, mathematics and science approximately 80 per cent of children achieved the 'target level' of Level 2, i.e., the level expected to be typical of 7-year-olds. Within English the breakdown for the component skills showed an uneven breakdown with the best result in speaking and listening and the worst result in spelling, where the percentage of pupils achieving Level 2 dropped to below 70 in both tests and teacher assessment.

Since many of the children with SEN at Key Stage 1 are likely to be working within or toward Level 1 it is important to examine the national results in this respect. These show that the number of children working towards or achieving this level ranged from around 16 per cent (speaking and listening) to approximately one-third for spelling. In all aspects of English more boys than girls were found to be operating at this level, with percentages ranging from around 20 per cent (speaking and listening), through 24 and 30 per cent in reading and writing respectively, to nearly 40 per cent in spelling. These are worrying figures and to some extent support the concerns of teachers in the Swansea University study. Moreover the raising of the standard of performance needed to satisfy the new Level 1 criteria in reading and writing may well exacerbate this situation.

Evidence from School Inspections and Surveys

National reports of school inspections and surveys provide a further important source of evidence about standards of achievement. In England the report from the Chief Inspector of Schools (OFSTED, 1996b) for 1994–5 stated that in all key stages (but especially Key Stage 2), standards in writing were below those in the other aspects of English and standards in speaking and listening were generally better than in reading. At Key Stage 1 standards of reading were described as needing considerable improvement in at least one school in twenty. The report expressed concern about the under performance of children in the majority of schools serving socially disadvantaged areas, where standards of reading and writing remained well below national norms. The report urged the direct teaching of phonic and other word recognition skills in early literacy programmes.

A report for the same year by HMI on standards of English in primary schools in Wales (OHMCI, 1996) reached the somewhat different conclusion that standards in reading were generally better than standards in speaking, listening and writing. Standards of reading had improved during the past two years and were at least satisfactory in about 85 per cent of classes at Key Stage 1. Where standards of reading were unsatisfactory this was largely because there was insufficient direct teaching of the skills needed to tackle unfamiliar words and too few opportunities for children to discuss their reading experiences. More generally there was an inadequate appreciation of oral language in laying the foundations of literacy. The report also urged schools to provide children with challenging opportunities to apply their literary skills across the curriculum and to develop closer links with parents through home–school reading links.

A survey of provision for pupils with SEN in mainstream primary schools in England during 1994 (OFSTED, 1996) reported that overall standards of achievement by pupils with SEN were 'generally sound' and better at nursery and Key Stages 1 and 2 than at stages 3 and 4. However no further details of the children's performance were provided. The report added that the quality of teaching and learning and standards achieved by SEN pupils were frequently too variable both within and between schools.

Time Devoted to Teaching Basic Skills

Many of the teachers in the Swansea University study felt that, due to the need to cover the whole curriculum, there was insufficient time to devote to the consolidation of basic skills, particularly in reading, for slower learners. However official reports based upon school inspections and surveys have not tended to support this view (see Cox and Sanders, 1994, for example). As mentioned in Chapter 1 the latest report on subjects and standards based on school inspectors' findings (OFSTED, 1996a) has criticized primary schools for concentrating on the basics at the expense of some of the non-core subjects. Lewis (1995b) points out that the only legal requirement is that schools should spend a 'reasonable time' on the latter in order to carry out worthwhile work and she refers to a very strong tendency for primary schools to spend about 50 per cent of the available time on English and mathematics, a tradition which may be difficult to change.

Since September 1995 the Revised National Curriculum has come into operation and, in theory at least, it should only occupy 80 to 85 per cent of teaching time at Key Stage 1. If this proves to be the case it will increase the class teacher's scope and flexibility of planning to meet the basic learning needs of children with SEN, especially when taken in combination with the simplification and clarification of the programmes of study and the reduction in assessment and record keeping.

However a case could be made out for reducing even further the amount of time that should be devoted to coverage of the National Curriculum for children with SEN. According to Lewis (1995b) the figure of 70 per cent was put forward in a series of regional conferences on possible revisions to the National Curriculum. Given that the National Curriculum should not constitute the whole of the curriculum and, given the particular importance of fostering the personal, social and spiritual development of children with SEN, such a proposal is not unrealistic.

It will be important for schools to ensure that children with SEN receive adequate exposure to the foundation (non-core) as well as the core subjects, not only because it is their entitlement but because it offers them important opportunities to exercise their developing basic skills in wider learning contexts. As Lewis (1995b) points out, the reduction in the content of subject orders in the Revised National Curriculum should mean that children with learning difficulties will not be pushed hastily through the curriculum, which should lead to an improved quality in their learning. Lewis makes out a convincing case for children with SEN to be exposed to the kind of broad cross-curricular approach to learning that has characterized the primary early years phase. However, as discussed in Chapter 1, there is a real danger that the reduction in the prescribed content of the non-core curriculum, coupled with the government's emphasis upon the teaching of the basic skills, will threaten this desirable breadth of curricular coverage.

School SEN Policies

The principle of full access to the National Curriculum and the school's wider curriculum needs to be firmly enshrined in the school's SEN policy which is now a statutory requirement. Among other things this policy should include information on the allocation of resources to pupils with SEN, arrangements for INSET and arrangements for partnership with parents. The recent OFSTED report on provision for pupils with SEN in England (OFSTED, 1996a) sets out key features of school policies in promoting high achievement in such children. These include the recognition of SEN within all other school policies and within the school's development plan, and a commitment to SEN provision that permeates the whole of the school. The role of the SENCO in the implementation of the school's SEN policy is central.

The Role of the Special Educational Needs Coordinator (SENCO)

The key role of the SENCO in policy implementation was emphasized by a number of head teachers in the Swansea University study. One head of a large primary school serving a socially disadvantaged area put it as follows:

> The school is currently developing a policy and system based on staged referral, curriculum differentiation and a lot of in-service training. It was developed by the SENCO who keeps an overall record of individual cases

of children with SEN and the provision for them, and provides a resource pack of different activities. We have a policy of raising teachers' awareness, improving the quality of teaching and monitoring and evaluation of the provision.

The OFSTED (1996a) report on SEN provision in mainstream schools found that the best practice promoting achievement for SEN pupils was when the SENCO had sufficient time to liaise, coordinate and support staff in school, *usually in excess of one day per week* (my emphasis). At the same time the survey found that SENCOs frequently felt frustrated at having insufficient time and the necessary skills to engage in a thorough process of monitoring and evaluating the school's SEN provision. It identifies key features of monitoring procedures which include regular joint meetings between the SENCO, class teachers and other support staff and the involvement of parents in the learning process. In her national study of special needs provision in primary schools Lewis (1995b) found that the vast majority of the school SENCOs had additional responsibilities as well as special needs, and two-thirds of them had no time or less than one hour weekly to develop and coordinate SEN provision. Not surprisingly Lewis comments that, as things stand, most of the teachers currently acting as SENCOs will find it very difficult to fulfil the range of demands embodied in the Code.

A very important aspect of the work of the SENCO is to try to ensure the best coordination of effort between class teachers and special support teachers or assistants, a point that has emerged very clearly from several official reports (OHMCI, 1996; OFSTED, 1996a). The OFSTED (1996a) report for example found that at all key stages the most influential factor in the effectiveness of within-class teaching support was the quality of joint planning of the work between the class teacher and the support teacher. This often had spin-off benefits to a wider range of pupils. The issue of whether or when to withdraw pupils from the classroom for special help is also an important issue which needs to be addressed in the school's SEN policy, particularly bearing in mind the importance of maintaining full access of pupils with SEN to the National Curriculum.

Conclusions

The following conclusions can be drawn from this review of the teaching of children with SEN in the light of the Code and of developments in the National Curriculum:

1   The Code enables schools to develop SEN policies which can provide an effective framework for their work in identifying, assessing and making provision for children with SEN. The Revised National Curriculum gives teachers greater flexibility than before in adapting the programmes of study to meet individual learning needs and it provides teachers with a clear curriculum framework and structure within which to differentiate learning for these children;

2   The majority of children with SEN appear to be gaining access to the full National Curriculum but some teachers feel that this is at the expense of the time they need to consolidate their learning of the basic skills of literacy and numeracy. Recent inspection reports indicate than some schools are concentrating on teaching the latter at the expense of covering the wider curriculum;

3   The systematic assessment of children's learning strengths and difficulties, upon which to base teaching programmes matched to individual need, is probably the greatest challenge facing class teachers and the area where most help is needed;

4   Recent school inspection and survey reports indicate that standards of reading and related skills were generally satisfactory in the majority of schools at Key Stage 1 but the results of last year's National Curriculum assessments reveal that substantial proportions of children failed to reach Level 2 at the end of this stage;

5   Inspection reports suggest that while the teaching of reading and other literacy skills is sound in the majority of schools at Key Stage 1, in general there is a need for more direct teaching of these skills and for children to be given more opportunity to apply them across the wider curriculum.

Early years teachers face the following important challenges in trying to meet the needs of young children with SEN in their classes:

1   To develop the appropriate skills of observation and diagnosis of their learning difficulties and to adapt or differentiate the relevant National Curriculum programmes of study and their methods of teaching to over-come these;

2   To ensure that they spend sufficient time on the direct teaching of the basic skills of literacy and numeracy to ensure their consolidation in children experiencing learning difficulties in this area, but without unduly restrict-ing these children's access to the wider curriculum, including the non-core subjects. Allocation of curriculum time will not in itself be sufficient to ensure successful teaching; equally important is the quality of that teaching;

3   To manage the transition from children's informal exploratory learning through play and practical experience to more formal, teacher directed learning, taking into account the individual child's level of educational development. As Vicky Hurst points out in Chapter 12 this means helping children to make confident links between their personal experiences, par-ticularly through play and practical activities, and the formalized expres-sions of learning, so that their confidence and enjoyment of learning is enhanced;

4   To facilitate the active support of parents/care givers in helping to meet the educational needs of children with SEN, through personal contacts and through more systematic home–school links such as those described by Topping and Wolfendale (1985) and Wolfendale (1989).

To help them to meet these challenges teachers need to be given adequate resources, support and training, including the guidance of a clear school policy for SEN provision and the support of a well qualified SENCO with sufficient time to work closely with class teachers. Each school should carry out a thorough audit of its SEN provision (OFSTED, 1996a). The government's establishment of a national network of regional literacy centres, which will encourage good practice based upon teaching methods of demonstrated effectiveness, may also have an important part to play in the raising of teachers' expertise in the teaching of basic literacy skills. Teachers will also need the back-up provision of specialist teaching and guidance services and programmes, such as Reading recovery (Sylva and Hurry, 1995) for those children who fail to make sufficient progress through the provision made by the school.

Finally the provision of high quality early years teaching, based upon sound developmental principles, particularly during the pre-compulsory school years will minimize the number of children entering Key Stage 1 with actual or potential learning or behavioural difficulties. The essential features of such teaching is the theme of Part 3 of this book.

References

BLYTH, C.A. and WALLACE, F.M.S. (1988) 'An investigation into the difficulties of transferring written records from the nursery school to the primary school', *Educational Research*, **30**, pp. 219–23.

COX, T. and SANDERS, S. (1994) *The Impact of the National Curriculum on the Teaching of Five-Year-Olds*, London, Falmer Press.

DEPARTMENT FOR EDUCATION (DFE) (1994) *Code of Practice on the Identification and Assessment of Special Educational Needs*, London, DFE.

DEPARTMENT FOR EDUCATION AND EMPLOYMENT (DFEE) (1996) *Assessments of 7-Year-Olds in England*, London, DFEE.

DEPARTMENT FOR EDUCATION AND EMPLOYMENT (DFEE)/SCHOOL CURRICULUM AND ASSESSMENT AUTHORITY (SCAA) (1995) *Assessment Arrangements 1996*, London, HMSO.

DEPARTMENT OF EDUCATION AND SCIENCE (DES) (1978) *Special Educational Needs: Report of the Committee of Enquiry into the Education of Handicapped Children and Young People, (The Warnock Report)* London, HMSO.

LEE, B. and FLETCHER-CAMPBELL, F. (1995) *Small Steps of Progress in the National Curriculum: Final Report Executive Summary*, Slough, NFER.

LEWIS, A. (1995a) 'Policy shifts concerning special needs provision in mainstream primary schools, *British Journal of Educational Studies*, **43**, pp. 318–32.

LEWIS, A. (1995b) *Primary Special Needs and the National Curriculum, Second Edition*, London, Routledge.

NATIONAL CURRICULUM COUNCIL (NCC) (1989) *Curriculum Guidance Two: A Curriculum for All. Special Educational Needs in the National Curriculum*, London, NCC.

OFFICE FOR STANDARDS IN EDUCATION (OFSTED) (1993) *Special Needs and the National Curriculum 1991–2 The Implementation of the Curricular Requirements of the ERA, A Report from the Office of Her Majesty's Chief Inspector of Schools*, London, HMSO.

OFFICE FOR STANDARDS IN EDUCATION (OFSTED) (1996a) *Promoting High Achievement for Pupils with SEN in Mainstream Schools, A Report from the Office of Her Majesty's Chief Inspector of Schools*, London, HMSO.

OFFICE FOR STANDARDS IN EDUCATION (OFSTED) (1996b) *The Annual Report of Her Majesty's Chief Inspector of Schools: Standards and Quality in Education, 1994–5*, London, HMSO.

OFFICE OF HER MAJESTY'S CHIEF INSPECTOR FOR WALES (OHMCI) (1996) Report by HM Inspectors, Standards and Quality in Primary Schools: Literacy and English 1994–5, Cardiff, OHMCI.

SCHOOL CURRICULUM AND ASSESSMENT AUTHORITY (SCAA) (1994) *A Report on the 1994 Consultation*, London, SCAA.

SYLVA, K. and HURRY, J. (1995) *Early Intervention in Children with Reading Difficulties: SCAA Discussion Papers Number 2*, London, SCAA.

TOPPING, K. and WOLFENDALE, S. (1985) *Parental Involvement in Children's Reading*, London, Croom Helm.

VINCENT, C., EVANS. J., LUNT, I. and YOUNG, P. (1995) 'Policy and practice: The changing nature of special educational provision in schools', *British Journal of Special Education*, **2**, pp. 4–11.

WEBSTER, A. (1995) 'Differentiation', in MOSS, G. (Ed) *The Basics of Special Needs*, London, Routledge.

WELSH OFFICE EDUCATION DEPARTMENT (1996a) *Review of Educational Provision in Wales, 1994–5: Report of Chief Inspector of Schools in Wales*, Office of Her Majesty's Chief Inspector of Schools in Wales, Cardiff, Welsh Office.

WELSH OFFICE EDUCATION DEPARTMENT (1996b) *National Curriculum Assessment results in Wales 1995: Primary Schools, Key Stages 1 and 2*, Cardiff, Welsh Office.

WOFENDALE, S. (1989) *All About Me*, London, Polytechnic of North London/National Children's Bureau.

Part 3

Achieving High Quality Education in the Early Years

9   Play, Learning and the National Curriculum: Some Possibilities

Mary Jane Drummond

This chapter is based on the premise that the statutory forms of the National Curriculum cannot and will not prevent teachers from thinking for themselves about the whole enterprise of teaching and learning in the early years. Thinking about play is one aspect of this enterprise. It is not enough to provide for play, or to organize opportunities for play. It is also essential to place a proper value on play, a value that can be articulated and justified to others. Some current approaches to the early years curriculum (from New Zealand and from Reggio Emilia, Italy) are described; these approaches suggest some possibilities for ways in which educators in this country could learn to make a more effective case for play.

Introduction: Thinking about Play

At a conference in 1988, at a time when teachers and other educators were just beginning to think seriously about the implications of the Education Reform Act, I listened to a lecture by John Stannard, HMI. He told his audience that in the years ahead, as we settled into the new order, we should clearly distinguish between three aspects of primary education: the National Curriculum, the delivered curriculum and the received curriculum. Furthermore, he urged us, the focus of our professional attention should not be the National Curriculum, which would, from now on, be the province of the National Curriculum Council (NCC); nor need we concern ourselves with the received curriculum, which would be looked after by the Schools Examination and Assessment Council (SEAC). Teachers' energies, said HMI Stannard, should be devoted to the delivered curriculum, no more, no less. The other elements of the three-part division were, henceforth, outside our scope.

His words were received with alarm, incredulity and resentment. After the first gasps of astonishment came a stream of passionate contributions from conference delegates, vigorously rejecting Stannard's recommendations. The debate that followed was remarkable more for its intensity than for clarity of thought or level of argument, but there was one common thread running through every practitioner's attempt to set the record straight. Although the teachers in the room did not speak with one voice, they all claimed, each in their own way, their inviolable right to go on thinking for themselves, however tightly drawn the statutory orders covering the new curriculum might be. And this thinking, this exercise of professional independence, would continue to be done on teachers' own terms. No amount of legislation could rob the profession of the responsibility to think about curriculum *and* teaching *and* learning, in ways of their own invention.

Eight years have passed since that memorable conference, and successive versions of the National Curriculum have come and gone; early years educators have not perished on the barricades, but have learned to live with their ring-folders and, now, with the slim-line result of the Dearing review. They have survived five years of statutory assessment and reporting procedures, and the annual rituals of SATs (Standard Assessment Tasks). But familiarity has not bred indifference. The intense emotion generated by a controversial contribution to a conference cannot, of course, be maintained over years or even weeks; the exigencies of everyday classroom life have a calming effect on over-excited educators. But teachers still cling to their right and their responsibility to think things through for themselves, and to attend to every aspect of their professional domain, to the whole enterprise of teaching and learning in the early years, and throughout Key Stage 1.

The intellectual energy of early years educators has not been dissipated by events since 1988, as other contributors to this volume will show, notably in the accounts of the Effective Early Learning Project (Chapter 10) and the Quality in Diversity Project (Chapter 12). These two major projects convincingly demonstrate the continuing strength of educators' professional commitment to the processes of improvement, development and review: this is essential work in progress. On a much smaller scale, I will argue here, there is still important work for educators to do in thinking about play, and in communicating our thinking to interested others.

My own recent work in two local authorities (Drummond, 1995a, 1995b) suggests that while there is no shortage of provision for play, and, in many classrooms, the organization of time and space does give children worthwhile opportunities for play, there is much less evidence of a proper *value* being placed on play. The ways in which early years practitioners make a case for play, justifying its importance throughout Key Stage 1, both to themselves and to others, sometimes sound less than convincing.

And yet every teacher of young children knows the necessity of making a convincing case for play; they know it from bitter experience. Every teacher has been on the receiving end of dismissive comments about play, ranging from scepticism, through mistrust, to outright hostility. One such incident sticks in my memory, though it happened fifteen years ago. 'I suppose they play all day for the first year?' said a prospective parent, as I showed her around the infant school of which I was then headteacher. I regret to report that my reply was defensive and conciliatory, rather than courageous and campaigning. Ideally, I would have answered affirmatively . . . 'indeed they do, and as we walk around, I'll explain why . . .' My lack of courage was not due to lack of conviction but to the absence of a clearly formulated argument ready to hand. The need for such an argument is still present; happily there is a wealth of published experience and expertise to which we can turn in constructing it.

The New Zealand Approach

In recent years there has been considerable interest in this country in the early years curriculum guidelines document *Te Whariki*, published by the New Zealand Ministry of Education (1993). The Maori words of the title refer to traditional woven mats, with an infinite variety of patterns; the guidelines envisage the early childhood curriculum as such a mat, woven from the principles, aims and goals defined in the document. The *Whariki* concept represents, in a vivid and meaningful way, the diversity of early childhood education in New Zealand. Different forms of provision create different patterns of curriculum, all using the common threads of goals and principles. From common starting points, each provision creates its own distinctive pattern. But the most exciting aspect of the guidelines for the early years community in this country is the way in which the early childhood curriculum is defined by five aims, on which the whole document is based. These are:

- Well-being: the health and well-being of the child is protected and nurtured;
- Belonging: children and their families feel a sense of belonging;
- Contribution: opportunities for learning are equitable, and each child's contribution is valued;
- Communication: the languages and symbols of children's own and other cultures are promoted and protected; and
- Exploration: the child learns through active exploration of the environment.

The enthusiastic response of many teachers in this country to this approach demonstrates my belief that the New Zealand educators have much to offer us. It is both challenging and instructive for us to see how their programme is constructed: at the centre of their work are those things they consider most important for young children to be and to do. Their early years curriculum framework is not derived from the subject divisions of late twentieth-century secondary education, as is our National Curriculum; nor is it parcelled out into discrete areas of experience, loosely connected to those subjects, as in some publications here (DES, 1985a, 1990). The New Zealand approach is to prioritize those aspects of living and learning, common to all young children, that are of the greatest value to the society in which the children will grow to maturity.

Much of the *Te Whariki* document is in tune with traditional English approaches to early years education. The concept of well-being, in particular, is familiar to us through the pioneering work of Rachel and Margaret McMillan, in the slums of Deptford and Bradford in the early years of this century. Their enterprise was to bring the needy children of the deserving poor into the warm and welcoming fold of nursery education; their curriculum was based on a regime of health and hygiene, good food and fresh air. Indeed it is possible to argue that their influence is still at work in the construction of early years education as rescue, which is still deeply embedded in the work of some practitioners.

Equally, the concept of communication is a familiar one to educators in this country, though the explicitly multilingual approach of *Te Whariki* is not, and it may be a very long time before curriculum guidelines here are published in a bilingual format (other than in Wales).

The concept of exploration corresponds to what, in the professional terminology of this country, would be called the principle of active learning. It is here that the New Zealand educators make their strongest case for play, emphasizing the value of spontaneous play and firmly setting down the principle that children learn through play. Here again, English educators will find familiar ground, and will probably recall the strength and simplicity of the great one-liner from the 1985 White Paper *Better Schools*: 'The education of young children is founded in play' (DES, 1985b).

But the remaining two aims, belonging and contribution, are new to us; here the New Zealand educators are expressing their conviction that learning to belong, and learning to contribute are of the utmost importance for their children, for their families, for their society as a whole. Our own National Curriculum, we remember with a shock, as we read the sections of *Te Whariki* that develop these ideas, is constructed around a core of maths, English and science. As many critics have observed, this is an approach that is prescriptive but not principled. O'Hear and White (1993), for example, demonstrate that the structural weakness of the core and foundation subjects is that it has never been made clear what the subjects 'are supposed to be *for*'. There is no such weakness in the New Zealand document, since it is based on clearly worked-out aims, aims with an ethical dimension, embodying a coherent set of core values.

I suggested earlier that it was necessary for early years educators in this country to become more convincing in making a case for play. What the New Zealand approach teaches us is the importance of making a case rooted in values and principles. In *Te Whariki*, play is valued because it is part of the way in which children realize their educators' aims for them. Through their imaginative and investigative play, children learn to communicate and to explore the world around them. Because the New Zealand educators are clear about what they want their children *to learn*, what they want them *to be* and *to do*, they are equally clear about the place of play in their children's lives.

The Reggio Emilia Approach

The region of Emilia Romagna, in northern Italy, is world famous for its services to young children from birth to 6 (at which age children enter elementary school). Their approach to the early years curriculum has been excitingly described in a collection of essays, interviews and commentaries: *The Hundred Languages of Children* (Edwards *et al.*, 1993). The founder of the programme, Loris Malaguzzi, explains his philosophy in a long and challenging interview, transcribed and translated. For example, the interviewer asks about curricular planning:

> **Malaguzzi**: No, our schools have not had, nor do they have, a planned curriculum with units and subunits (lesson plans) as the behaviourists

would like. These would push our schools towards teaching without learning; we would humiliate the schools and the children by entrusting them
to forms, dittos, and handbooks. (Edwards *et al.*, 1993, p. 85)

And the alternative? Malaguzzi does not hesitate: 'Suffice it to say that the
school for young children has to respond to the children.' This principle is taken
up, and extended, in another interview: Carlina Rinaldi is a pedagogical coordinator
who works to support curriculum development and in-service education in a group
of preschools and nurseries. She explains:

> The cornerstone of our experience, based on practice, theory and research,
> is the image of children as rich, strong and powerful . . . They have . . . the
> desire to grow, curiosity, the ability to be amazed and the desire to relate
> to other people and to communicate . . . Children are eager to express
> themselves within the context of a plurality of symbolic languages . . .
> Children are open to exchanges and reciprocity as deeds and acts of love
> which they not only want to receive but also want to offer. (Edwards *et al.*,
> 1993, pp. 102–3)

These characteristics of children, curious, loving, creative, exploring, are the
key concepts in the 'Reggio Emilia approach'. The central ideas of reciprocity and
exchange are the basis for a curriculum derived from children's emerging and
developing powers: their powers to relate and to communicate, not just in words,
but in a whole range of symbolic languages. Children's intellectual and emotional
development is fostered through the systematic provision of many, many forms of
symbolic representation: words, movement, drawing, painting, sculpture, shadow-
play, collage and music. Children's symbolic, imaginative and exploratory play are
seen as part of what children necessarily do, as they establish reciprocal relationships of caring and understanding, with the world and the people in it.

Another key concept for the Italian educators is documentation. The work of
the preschools and nurseries is explained and publicized through the painstaking
documentation of what the children and their educators do. They use written descriptions, transcriptions of children's words in discussion sessions, photographs
and videotapes. These form

> an indispensable source of materials [for] recording, understanding, debat-
> ing among ourselves, and finally preparing appropriate documents of our
> experience. (Edwards *et al.*, 1993, p. 122)

This approach suggests some interesting possibilities for our development,
in this country, as advocates for children's play. If we could learn, as the Italian
educators have done, to document children's play in ways that show the richness,
strength and power of their learning, we would be in a very strong position indeed.

In effect we are faced with some crucial choices. After their fifth birthdays,
we are obliged, by statute, to record children's learning in terms of the National

Curriculum, its core subjects, attainment targets, and level descriptions (see Chapter 6). But we are not constrained by statute to stop there. We can, if we wish, do more. We can choose, if we really are convinced of the value of play, to document children's learning in other terms, in terms of what they *do* and *understand* and *learn* through play. Indeed, in the absence of such documentation, the sceptical parent ('I suppose they play all day . . .') is entitled to remain sceptical. The most effective antidote to scepticism is robust evidence: I am arguing that evidence of children's powers, as we see them exercised in play throughout Key Stage 1, could be the foundation of an effective and principled case for play.

Documenting Children's Play

This possibility is best explored through example, rather than exhortation.

In a class of 4-year-olds, a group of young children spent twenty-five minutes absorbed in water play. The nursery nurse had, at their request, added some blue dye to the water, and the children were intrigued by the different shades of blue they could see: paler at the shallow margin, and darker at the deepest, central part of the water-tray. One child was even more interested in another, related phenomenon. He spent nearly ten minutes of this period of water play observing his own shoes and how their colour appeared to change when he looked at them, through the water and the transparent water tray. The child seemed to be fascinated by what happened when he placed his feet in different positions; he leaned intently over the tray to see what colour his shoes appeared to be at each stage. He did not use the words 'experiment' or 'observation', but that was what he was engaged in, nonetheless. After each trial, he withdrew his feet into the natural light of day, as if to check that they retained their proper colour. Had the dye stayed in the water, where he had seen it put, or had some of it seeped out, into his shoes?

At the end of the morning session, the teacher and nursery nurse announced that it was time to tidy up. The children worked together to empty the water tray of the sieves, funnels and beakers they had been using. They took out the jugs, the teaspoons and the ladles, emptied them, and put them away. When they had nearly finished, the boy stopped and asked aloud, of no-one in particular, 'How do we get the blue out?'

What is happening here? Is this the kind of evidence we are looking for? Yes. This child is, in his play, taking strenuous intellectual exercise. In the process, his developing powers are strengthened: his powers to observe, to compare, to enquire, to test, to repeat and to vary, to generalize and to move one step forward. He has already learned so much of importance about the world, and his relationship to it. He has not, it is plain, learned all that there is to learn about colour and light, permanence and impermanence. But he *has* learned, which is more significant, that the world is accessible to his questions and his experiments; that the world is made up of puzzling and difficult possibilities that invite his interest and attention; that there are regularities and irregularities, patterns and surprises in the world, waiting to be discovered and enjoyed.

'Documentation' of this kind of play could, of course, be made in terms of targets attained or programmes of study covered. I am arguing that it will be more worthwhile for educators if the evidence of learning is presented in other terms: in terms of the child's growing intellectual powers. Further, it will be more worthwhile for all those who are interested in what educators and young children do, if they can be shown how children's powers — to think and to understand — are exercised and strengthened in play.

Children's imaginative play, too, can be documented in this way. I have described elsewhere (Drummond, 1993, p. 83) the play of a group of 4-year-olds, who came running in from the playground. Her friends told the teacher that, one of them, Shazia, had been shot by a wolf. Shazia was quickly laid down on a makeshift bed and thirty minutes of sustained, spontaneous, complex play followed this startling announcement. During this time, various children explored the roles of police officers (taking statements in invented writing from witnesses), medical staff (feeling for wounds, listening to Shazia's heart) and helpful by-standers ('I saw his bushy tail'). Later, during the whole class discussion that ended the morning session, the children considered how to make themselves safe against further attacks by the wolf. Should they send for a woodcutter? (One child looked up his telephone number in the Yellow Pages.) Or Robin Hood? Or display a 'Wanted' poster? Shazia worked on this last project during the afternoon, giving a detailed description of her assailant. 'His ears went like this . . . he was standing behind the tree . . . he was *really really* thin.'

In analysing this observation I drew on the work of Kieran Egan (1988) who argues that children's imaginative play has been woefully and mistakenly neglected by educators. He attributes this neglect to the influence of Dewey, whose emphasis on children's past experience as the starting point for learning has been interpreted in terms of the everyday world of house, street and classroom. The focus of teachers' attention has been, in Egan's words 'the mundane and practical world in which children live. What has been lost is the ability to see the world as the child sees it, transfigured by fantasy' (Egan, 1988, p. 20).

Egan's work helps us to understand what is happening when children are absorbed in fantasy play. They seem to find such play more engaging and more meaningful than the everyday reality of the classroom; this is because, in their play, they are investigating the ideas that are most important and have most meaning for them:

> the unrelenting conflicts between the good and the bad, the big and the little, the brave and the cowardly, the oppressor and the oppressed . . . the embodiment of struggles between security and fear, love and hate. (Egan, 1988, p. 25)

Shazia's play, then, can be seen as an exploration of crucially important concepts: life and death, safety and danger, permanence and impermanence. The doctors' diagnosis was final: 'She's dead. For ever.' 'Her heart's broken and she'll never wake up.' But on hearing these words, Shazia dramatically revived and joined in the continuing play with gusto. She was exercising, in an invisible world made real to her by her imagination, some important intellectual powers, making new connections, trying out new possibilities. She was exploring the battleground on which are waged the 'unrelenting conflicts' that Egan describes. In this imaginative realm, the world 'transfigured by fantasy', Shazia and her friends demonstrate their powers to suffer, and to survive, to despair and to hope, to endure and to offer comfort.

There is evidence, too, in this observation, of important learning about literacy. Shazia and her friends have already learned much about the ways in which literate adults lead their lives. They understand the act of translation from spoken to written word, and the use of the written words for real-life purposes. They are not yet reading and writing independently, but they do understand the vital functions that these acts can serve. They are already doing, in their play, what literate adults do. The whole observation is, I believe, impressive evidence of these children's growing powers to do, to think, to understand and to feel, in ways that are essentially human, essentially worthwhile.

In another observation, detailed notes were made of two children in a domestic play area.

A boy and a girl were playing at mothers and fathers. They had a small baby and they all three lived in a caravan. The play became unusual when the children discovered that the caravan was on fire! They represented the fire in their play in a variety of turbulent ways: utensils, clothing and furniture were simultaneously flung hither and thither, with equally dramatic sound effects. The class teacher happened by at this moment and, noticing the disorder and hoping to reduce the sound level, commented that the people who lived in the caravan would probably want to tidy it up a bit. The children gave her a pitying look, and consigned the baby — still sleeping safely in its cradle — to the heart of the flames.

This observation is interesting, not just for the children's complex use of imaginative language to create the scene, the characters and the start of the conflagration, but because of the insights it allows us into the world of these children's emotions. The great observer of children's play, the pioneering child psychotherapist Margaret Lowenfeld, was among the first to recognize the importance of this dimension of play, and she became a most determined advocate of its importance.

Without adequate opportunity for play, normal and satisfactory emotional development is not possible. (Lowenfeld, 1935, p. 232)

Lowenfeld distinguishes three different kinds of imaginative play, which she compares to 'three common attitudes in the creation of literature — Realism, Romance and Satire.' In realistic play, children represent the features of their daily lives as exactly as they can remember: this kind of play is well known to educators, who provide many materials to support such play (pots, pan, kettles, ironing boards and so on). In romantic play, children create variations of the world in which they live, embodying secret longings of their own, 'representing life not as it is, but as they would like it to be'. (Lowenfeld, 1935, p. 135) This kind of play, too, is commonly provided for — capes and crowns, fine robes and silver shoes are popular properties in the exercise of this kind of thinking and feeling. Lowenfeld's third category, satirical play, in which children satisfy their feelings by 'violent distortion of familiar themes' is less likely to be welcomed by educators; an orderly classroom (and a tidy caravan) may figure as more important priorities than the violent expression of hostile feelings. But in the caravan play episode described above, if we can tolerate, for a little while, a little disorder, we can see, following Lowenfeld, the exercise of powerful and dramatic feelings; we can see two children, through symbolic play, expressing emotions of resentment and rage, emotions common to all children, but commonly suppressed or forbidden by adults.

Lowenfeld's detailed descriptions of countless imaginative play episodes demonstrate how, in each of the three forms of play, the child

will try himself out, and in trying himself out, come gradually to a better understanding of himself and his environment. (Lowenfeld, 1935, p. 146)

This brief summary indicates the strength of Lowenfeld's conclusions; her case for play, and the emotions that are represented in play, is being made in terms of the growth of children's *understanding* of the world, of the people in it, and of themselves. Lowenfeld demonstrates how, besides providing for play, and organizing it into children's lives, we can also express a proper value for what children *do* when they play.

Conclusion: Making a Case for Play

The English language is rich in words that can be used, without modification, as both noun and verb; for example, hope, fear, fight, desire, dress, caress, kiss, love and play. The word 'play' is regularly used by educators, parents and children for both purposes, but I have come to believe that, in thinking about play, we would do well to confine ourselves to the noun form, and to leave the verb alone. The verb 'to play' too readily suggests idle pastime; whereas 'play', the noun, can confidently be used as an umbrella term for the thousands of times and places, spaces and scenarios, where children think and feel in ways of the utmost importance. In play, under a table or up a tree, alone or in small groups, expressing themselves in words, or with blocks or music or miniature world materials, children exercise their growing intellectual and emotional powers. In play, 3-year-olds, 5-year-olds and 8-year-olds learn to do, to know, to feel, to understand.

The language of the National Curriculum, its levels, descriptions and targets, may, if we wish, be added to this account, to give it more detail, more specificity. But the case to be made for play is in the value that we attach to those things that children do when they play, rather than in the precise achievements or attainments we may be able to identify.

The New Zealand educators as we have seen, value children exploring, belonging and contributing. The Italian educators value the hundred symbolic languages that children use to represent and express their understanding of the world. Whatever it is that nursery and Key Stage 1 educators in this country value most highly, whichever kinds of thinking, feeling, doing and understanding we place at the centre of an early years curriculum, it is in play that these things will happen, most intensely, most adventurously.

In this chapter I have argued that the work of early years educators does not begin, or end, with the National Curriculum. Nor is our chief concern with the 'delivered curriculum', the things that teachers and other educators do, in the name of education. The most important task is to attend to children's learning, and to those aspects of learning that we value most. This act of attention is, in part, practical; it depends on teachers providing and organizing for learning. Here the ten subjects of the National Curriculum may come into the picture, as we check out the range and variety of the opportunities and experiences we offer. But attending to learning requires more of us. It means that we must also work at the level of principle, making certain of our core values. With these certainties made clear, with our values made plain, we can justify children's play in terms of what it means for their learning, for their doing and feeling and understanding. To support our thinking and our advocacy of play, we may turn to the work of other educators. I have discussed the New Zealand early years curriculum, and the Reggio Emilia approach, and suggested that their insights may help us towards a vision of comparable clarity. Or we may use our own observations to help us see more clearly what is happening in children's play. Or, one last possibility, we may turn to one of the early pioneers of the progressive movement — the great teacher H. Caldwell Cook, whose book *The Play Way*, published in 1917, is still an inspiration — and a reproof — to present-day educators. Writing in detail of his own practice at the Perse School, Cambridge, with boys aged 8 to 11, Caldwell Cook establishes the principles of his approach through play. He makes his case, and justifies his life's work, in many of the same terms that I have been using throughout this chapter: learning, feeling and doing.

> Even today, learning is often *knowing* without much care for *feeling*, and mostly none at all for *doing*. Learning may remain detached, as a garment, unidentified with self. But by Play I mean the *doing* anything one *knows*, with one's heart in it. The final appreciation in life and in study is to put oneself into the thing studied and to live there *active*. And that is Playing. (H. Caldwell Cook, 1917, p. 17)

References

CALDWELL COOK, H. (1917) *The Play Way*, London, Heinemann.

DEPARTMENT OF EDUCATION AND SCIENCE (1985a) *Curriculum Matters 2: The Curriculum from 5 to 16*, London, HMSO.

DEPARTMENT OF EDUCATION AND SCIENCE (1985b) *Better Schools*, London, HMSO.

DEPARTMENT OF EDUCATION AND SCIENCE (1990) *Starting with Quality*, The Report of the Committee of Inquiry into the Quality of the Educational Experience offered to 3- and 4-year-olds, London, HMSO.

DRUMMOND, M.J. (1993) *Assessing Children's Learning*, London, David Fulton.

DRUMMOND, M.J. (1995a) *In School at Four*, Hampshire's Earlier Admissions Programme Final evaluation report, Hampshire County Council Education Department.

DRUMMOND, M.J. (1995b) *New Places*, Summary Report of the Hertfordshire Nursery Evaluation Project, Cambridge, University of Cambridge Institute of Education.

EDWARDS, C., GANDINI, L. and FORMAN, G. (Eds) (1993) *The Hundred Languages of Children: The Reggio Emilia Approach to Early Childhood Education*, Norwood, New Jersey, Ablex Publishing Corporation.

EGAN, K. (1988) *Primary Understanding*, London, Routledge.

LOWENFELD, M. (1935) *Play in Childhood*, London, Gollancz.

MINISTRY OF EDUCATION (New Zealand) (1993) *Te Whariki Draft Guidelines for Developmentally Appropriate Programmes in Early Childhood Services*, Wellington New Zealand, Learning Media.

O'HEAR, P. and WHITE, J. (Eds) (1993) *Assessing the National Curriculum*, London, Paul Chapman Publishing.

10   The Effective Early Learning Project and the National Curriculum

Christine Pascal

In the scope of this chapter I shall ask some basic questions about how we might define the concept of curriculum in the early years, and ask whether a curriculum is necessary for these children. I shall examine current initiatives to develop an appropriate curriculum for children from 3 to 5 years of age and raise issues of continuity and progression with the National Curriculum in relation to these initiatives. The aims and scope of the EEL project will then be described, and the model of curriculum evaluation employed in the project will be outlined. Finally, I shall raise the question of what kind of approach to the curriculum for under-5s is required.

Introduction

The development of high quality early learning experiences for all young children from 3 to 5 years of age is an aim which now seems to unite parents, practitioners, providers, policy makers and politicians of all persuasions. This unanimity is testimony to the overwhelming evidence which shows that high quality early childhood education can have a significant and long-term effect on children's learning, can lead to gains in educational achievement throughout schooling, and can lead to better social behaviour and more productive citizenship (Sylva and Wiltshire, 1993; Ball, 1994). There are also economic and equal opportunities issues which are embedded in the pressure to expand early childhood services (National Commission on Education, 1993; Ball, 1994). Yet, despite the growing will to enhance the quality of children's early educational experiences, the UK has no national policy for the education of under-5s, and current government policy continues to emphasize the shared responsibility of parents, businesses and local communities and to argue for diversity and choice within any expansion. In this context, educational provision for the under-5s in the UK remains patchy, diverse and, in comparison with other European countries, at a low level (DES, 1990; National Commission, 1993; Ball, 1994; Moss and Pence, 1996). In fact, it has been called 'a national scandal' (Ball, 1994).

The result of this diversity is that children under the age of 5 years in the UK are learning in a vast array of different settings, from local authority nurseries, primary schools and day nurseries, to private kindergartens and workplace creches and nurseries, through to voluntary drop in groups and playgroups. Each of these settings operates with different aims, funding, resources, staffing and quality control procedures and therefore, the quality and effectiveness of the early learning experiences they offer is variable. In addition, there is no uniformity or coherence in the kind of early learning experiences they offer to young children. The National Curriculum, which aimed to offer children from 5 to 16 years of age a 'common entitlement' to learning, has impacted differentially on these early learning providers. Many providers have expressed frustration with this situation and identified the need for guidance on how to put in place an appropriate curriculum for the children in their care (Pascal *et al.*, 1994). In the absence of this guidance, many young children in the UK are currently receiving neither the high quality, nor the range of appropriate early learning experiences they need in order to ensure a sound basis for later life. In response to this situation, the Effective Early Learning Project (or EEL Project), based at Worcester College of Higher Education but working nationally, has attempted to address these issues directly, by developing a national strategy for evaluating and improving the quality of early learning experiences offered to young children.

Some Basic Questions

Developing a high quality curriculum for young children is a project fraught with difficulty as it necessarily involves facing issues of value and belief. In one sense any curriculum may be viewed as embodying a view of culture and learning which is necessarily partial and subject to the influences of the dominant power bases which exist within a society at that particular point in time. Given this difficulty, in this chapter I shall not get embroiled in wranglings over curriculum definition and content, although I do believe that these difficult discussions need to go on, (and indeed are going on in some quarters). Rather, I shall aim to identify some key questions facing those concerned in developing a curriculum for the under-5s and try to outline some of the options and choices which we are faced with in trying to answer them.

Any consideration of a curriculum for the under-5s should be set against what exists in the diverse range of settings in which young children are currently learning. For the 0–3s there is no clearly defined or developed curriculum. For the 3 and 4s, a nursery curriculum has been defined, but there is limited access to it. For the 4s we have the recent SCAA 'Desirable Outcomes' guidelines for children entering compulsory education (DFEE, 1996) and various guidance from SCAA on Yr R classes. For the 5s we have the Year 1 regulations of the National Curriculum.

We need to ask:

• Are we happy with this?
• Do we want to change the situation or leave it to evolve dynamically?
• Do we want all children to have access to high quality learning experiences?

- Should these early learning experiences be uniform for all children or diverse, flexible and individually geared?
- What might these early learning experiences look like?
- How might they be made available to all children?

Issues of equity and social justice inevitably emerge. Developing and implementing curricula is a highly political activity — it opens doors of opportunity to children or shuts them down, it provides them with the means to gain access to social processes or denies them this privilege. Any discussion of the above issues needs to respond to a number of questions.

What Do We Mean by Curriculum?

Our first task is to be clear about what we mean by the term curriculum. The very use of this term in relation to the under-5s often causes worry and uncertainty because it carries with it emotive connotations of formality, schooling and rigidity. However, I would argue that as soon as children begin to explore the world and those around them begin to respond to this exploration, a curriculum is in existence, be it formal or informal, explicit or implicit, articulated or just experienced, going on in the home, or outside of it.

However, the term curriculum may be interpreted very narrowly:

- as relating solely to the content or subject matter (syllabus) transmitted to pupils by teachers;

rather less narrowly:

- as including all those learning experiences planned for children with an intentional and deliberated direction

or very broadly:

- as embracing everything which the child learns through exploration, language, the attitudes and values of others, and the context in which it occurs, including all life experiences and interactions which a child experiences, planned and unplanned, both within the home and outside it.

Our responses to these definitions will provide the parameters within which any discussion about the curriculum will be contained.

Do We Want a Curriculum for Under-5s and Why?

We need also to consider the question of whether a curriculum for the under-5s is necessary and/or desired. Inevitably, our responses to this question will again be based in the value positions we take on the issue of childhood and parenting. Yet, we also have to inform these decisions with reference to the research evidence which now exists about children's early learning.

We now have unequivocal evidence that good quality early learning leads to lasting social and educational benefits for all children — and especially those from less advantaged backgrounds. Research has shown clearly that it is only those early childhood programmes which provide high quality, developmentally appropriate and carefully planned learning experiences with certain characteristics that appear to have long-term educational and social benefits (Sylva and Wiltshire, 1993; Ball, 1994). Thus, this evidence would indicate that the development of a curriculum for under-5s should be a central concern for those who are developing policy and practice for this age phase.

We also have evidence that this is a critical time for children's learning. Some 60 per cent of intellectual growth occurs before the age of 6 (Trevarthen, 1995). We need to consider whether we are happy to leave this growth to the vicissitudes of fortune and family circumstance or to take Ball's position in the Royal Society of Arts (RSA) Report (Ball, 1994) and argue that it is too important to leave it to chance and that the state should take action to ensure all children's learning potential is maximized. Ball argued strongly that nursery education was so important it should be made compulsory.

One of the great problems for the 3–5s in recent years has been the downward pressure of National Curriculum. Those in the early years world have argued that this pressure has been sharply felt due to the absence of a clearly articulated curriculum for this age phase which might have acted as a buffer to this pressure, (and maybe also protected those in the early stages of primary schooling). A number of early years groups have been trying to put one in place for some time. The current Early Childhood Education Forum Quality in Diversity Project (Hurst *et al.*, 1996) described in Chapter 12 is an example of this response to the current vacuum in curriculum policy for the under-5s, although this project spans the full early years age range (0–8).

We also need to consider whether or not we need to develop a curriculum for 0–3s for the same reasons and in the same ways as for 3–5s. Or are under-3s different?

What Would a Curriculum for Young Children Look Like?

If we agree that the development of a curriculum for the under-5s is desirable, we then need to consider what it might look like. This leads us to ask other questions:

What Are Young Children Capable of?

The first of these questions might seem to be encompassed by a thorough knowledge of child development and a detailed knowledge of each child's individual growth patterns. However, more recent knowledge has shown that children's development, although biologically driven, is very culturally influenced, for example, 3-year-old travellers' children who are very skilful with a bowie knife, Japanese 2-year-olds who perform very fine motor manipulative skills with ease. Thus, the goal of a developmentally appropriate curriculum is now viewed as inadequate in recent literature, and needs to be supplemented by what is termed a culturally appropriate curriculum (Bruner, 1996).

What Do We Want Them to Know?

This question is probably the most contentious and the one most value laden in the responses we give to it. Who says what it is important for young children to know? Are there universals that all children need? What about a common entitlement — or are we just giving children what has been termed a 'white, male, middle class' curriculum? (Weiner, 1994). It is a difficult question to respond to. If we build a curriculum around individual families and communities, it has the advantage of being relevant to them, but we might worry that this might trap them within it. Should we therefore provide them with access to the dominant knowledge base within society as a whole in order to provide them with the means to negotiate a position within it, but at the cost of distancing them from their own rich culture and its particular knowledge base? Are the two responses mutually exclusive? Bruner (1996) is arguing that our curriculum should empower children by providing them with the means to negotiate across diverse cultures and communities. We might also consider the notion of a 'global curriculum' which argues that there might be a core set of knowledge, skills and attitudes which all children throughout the world should have (Ball, 1995).

What Approach Should We Take?

Before we go on to consider what the content of such a curriculum might be, it is useful to revisit the Rumbold Report's (DES, 1990) general approach to the curriculum which aimed to inform thinking and provide a framework for action. Key points from this document state:

1 There should be no suggestion of a 'National Curriculum' for children of that age (3 and 4), what is needed is a flexible framework from which the curriculum can be developed to suit the needs of individual children in a variety of settings. (para. 64)

We believe that . . . educators should guard against pressures which might lead them to over-concentration on formal teaching and upon the attainment of a specific set of targets. (para. 66)

2 This (framework) should be based on principles which complement those underlying the construction of the curriculum for children of statutory school age. (para. 64)

3   The educator working with under fives must pay careful attention not just to the content of the child's learning, but also to the way in which that learning is offered to and experienced by the child, and the role of all those involved in the process. Children are affected by the context in which learning takes place, the people involved in it, and the values and beliefs which are embedded in it. (para. 67)

4   For the early years educator . . . the process of education — how the children are encouraged to learn — is as important as, and inseparable from, the content — what they learn. We believe that this principle must underlie all curriculum planning for the under fives. (para. 68)

What Alternative Curriculum Frameworks Are There?

Again, keeping the above principles in mind it is also useful to consider those curriculum frameworks which have been articulated and widely agreed as appropriate to the udner-5s. What constitutes a high quality curriculum for under-5s has been well documented in many government and local authority documents. There is general agreement that it should be planned to foster the all round development of individual children — emotionally, intellectually, morally, socially, physically and spiritually. To be successful it must provide children with essential knowledge, skills and attitudes and provide for continuity with what came before and what learning will follow. In the literature we can see the curriculum for young children being organized around a number of different frameworks:

- some based upon subjects, e.g., mathematics, English, music;
- some based upon resource areas, e.g., water, sand, clay, dressing up;
- some based upon schema, e.g., dynamic vertical, containing and enveloping, dynamic circular;
- some based on broad themes, e.g., homes, toys, my family;
- some based on areas of experience, e.g., language and literacy, aesthetic and creative, human and social.

All of these organizing frameworks have a validity and can be justified with reference to educational and pedagogical theory and research. I shall focus briefly on three alternatives being put forward currently as a basis for developing an appropriate curriculum for the under-5s.

1   The Rumbold Report 'Starting with Quality' (DES, 1990)
The Rumbold Report was published in 1990 and in my experience it has had a formative influence on how policy and practice has developed in local authorities and also how other major reports e.g., the RSA Report (Ball, 1994), have viewed the early years curriculum. Whilst acknowledging that the curriculum can be defined and expressed in a number of ways, the Rumbold Report preferred a framework based upon nine areas of learning and experience which was adapted from the HMI

discussion document *The Curriculum From 5 to 16* (DES, 1985). These areas included:

- linguistic: listening, speaking, reading, writing;
- aesthetic and creative: imagination, art and music;
- human and social: relationships, social interaction, living together, environment, cultures;
- mathematical: shape, number, measuring, sorting, assessing, recording;
- moral: self-awareness, right and wrong, fairness, tolerance, responsibility;
- physical: bodily and spatial awareness, physical skills, bodily knowledge, health and safety;
- scientific: life and the environment, materials and their properties, energy, force, time, space;
- technological: use of materials, design, tools, planning and construction; and
- spiritual: wonder, natural diversity, curiosity.

The richness of such a curriculum is notable, so is the complexity and the inter-dependency of its constituent parts. The Report stressed that children may not experience the curriculum in this way, and acknowledged the value of an integrated and cross-curricular approach. It also emphasized the prime importance of creating an environment which fosters the development of social relationships and positive attitudes to learning and behaviour.

2   SCAA 'Desirable Outcomes' Document (1996)

This document was published as part of an innovative Nursery Education Scheme (DFEE, 1996) based upon a system of vouchers issued to parents for the education of 4-year-olds. Parents may redeem these vouchers at those nursery education institutions in the state, voluntary and private sectors who are participating in the scheme. As a condition of initial validation for the receipt of vouchers, institutions are required to publish a statement of the framework they use for planning educational activities for the children. These activities should be shown to lead towards the identified desirable outcomes of learning in the following six areas of learning:

- personal and social development;
- language and literacy;
- mathematics;
- knowledge and understanding of the world;
- physical development; and
- creative development.

Personal and Social Development were placed first because it was felt that this was the basis for positive learning in other areas. The Secretary of State for Education and Employment, Gillian Shephard, had specifically asked SCAA to recommend outcomes *not* a curriculum, but the document also included guidance on the common features of good practice and provided tables demonstrating how the desirable outcomes lead into Key Stage 1 of the National Curriculum. The role of parents in the learning process was also emphasized in the document. Play was not included in the document as it was viewed as a method of learning rather than an outcome. This is in contrast to the Scottish and Welsh Office documents (see Chapter 1).

Response to the document by those in the early years world has been mixed, some expressing relief that the targets were not overly prescriptive, others saying they were rather narrow, bland and mediocre, underplaying the complexity and breadth of what children might be expected to be learning at this age. Concern has been expressed over the declared intention to link them into a system of Baseline Assessment on children's entry to compulsory schooling at 5 (see Chapter 7). Others have argued that to implement the targets effectively would require staff with a high level of training and expertise. The lack of sensitivity to cultural differences in the targets was also highlighted.

3   Early Childhood Education Forum Quality and Diversity Project 1994–6

The Quality and Diversity Project (or QD Project) includes representatives from all the major providers of care and education services for the under-8s who have come together under the umbrella of the Early Childhood Education Forum (Hurst *et al.*, 1996). This collaborative Project aims to establish an agreed framework for early learning in England and Wales for children from 0–8 years of age. A key aim of the project is to seek a common view of what is an appropriate curriculum for young children, and to create a continuum of learning from birth to 8. They are working in three age phase groups, 0–3, 3–5, 5–8 years.

The QD Project has developed a set of basic principles called 'The Foundations of Early Learning' which they believe should underpin the education and care of young children in all settings. These are described in Chapter 12.

Under each of these foundations the project has developed a set of goals which children from 0 to 8 years of age should be working towards. The QD Project curriculum guidelines have the strength of emerging from a consensus view of a widely representative group of early childhood organizations and providers. They offer a radically different model of curriculum to that embodied in the National Curriculum and show how the foundations can be used to extend and enhance the statutory curriculum, and provide a framework for the curriculum for under-5s. The benefits of offering a curriculum which is seamless from birth to 8 years of age are also offered.

What Other Elements Need to Be Considered in the Development of Early Years Curriculum?

The Importance of Dispositions and a Mastery Orientation to Learning

The development of self-reliance, flexibility and autonomy in learners also lies at the heart of a high quality early years curriculum. Sylva and Wiltshire (1993) talk about a curriculum for mastery. They argue that a successful curriculum must do more than impart facts or cognitive skills. It must also be explicit about the means to nurture positive beliefs about one's talents and also the belief that achievement

Christine Pascal

is not God-given but is acquired, at least in part, by effort. They stress the importance of aspiration, motivation and commitment to learning. Motivation, confidence and socialization should therefore be key concerns of the curriculum.

Katz (1995) also talks about the importance of developing children's dispositions to learning. She believes that children need to have certain dispositions in order to learn effectively. These include persistence, concentration, aspiration and motivation.

How the Curriculum Is Taught

There is a growing consensus in the literature that the traditional curriculum, which emphasizes drill, rote learning and the practice of isolated academic skills, does not reflect the current knowledge we have about human learning. What is more, it fails to produce students who possess the kind of higher order thinking and problem solving abilities that will be needed in the twenty-first century (Handy, 1995). We therefore also need to look carefully at the way in which the curriculum is to be taught and in particular, to consider how more active, experiential learning strategies can be incorporated effectively into a carefully structured and flexible curriculum framework.

Children With Special Educational Needs

All children under-5 will be at different stages of development and will have particular individual needs. If children's needs are complex and wide-ranging considerable support may be required to provide for these needs. Children under 5 need to be regularly observed and assessed by competent professionals and their parents to ensure early diagnosis of particular need is made and responded to. Any curriculum needs to be flexible and responsive therefore to children's individual needs and to provide for sensitive and appropriate intervention when it is necessary (DFE, 1994) (see Chapter 8).

How Might a Quality Curriculum Be Achieved?

Key Role of Adults

The success of any initiative is dependent upon trained, confident and competent people who can interpret any curriculum guidelines in the light of what they know about young children's learning and their knowledge of the individual children and the family community they are working with. The ratio of adults to children is also a key factor in determining the effective implementation of a high quality curriculum.

Planning and Observation Based Assessment

Successful curriculum implementation requires careful planning which includes a continuous cycle of planning, observing, recording and assessing. It is also important to involve all staff, parents and other involved parties in this process. In addition it is particularly important to involve children as a central aim should be the development of responsible, autonomous, independent and self-critical learners.

Resources
The environment (both inside and out) in which children are learning, and the resources within it, will shape the curriculum and determine its effectiveness. The architecture of the building is important, the way the learning environment is designed and organized, how the equipment is made available to the children, and the way in which the locality is used are all factors in successful early learning.

Parents
Working together with parents (and carers) in a mutual respectful and empowering way is essential if children's early learning is to maximize their potential. Time invested in working at this partnership pays dividends in ensuring the development of positive attitudes of parents and children to the learning process.

The Effective Early Learning Project

The Effective Early Learning (EEL) Research Project began work in May 1993 and grew out of the urgent need for procedures to facilitate quality evaluation and improvement in the diverse range of settings in which under-5s are being educated in the UK. It also responded to the lack of a substantial empirical database on the quality and effectiveness of early learning offered in these settings. It focuses particularly on provision for 3- and 4-year-olds as these children currently are in a wider range of provision than any other age group, but has applicability throughout the early childhood years (and even beyond). The project is operating throughout the UK and is being carried out by a team of practitioner researchers, directed by the present writer and is based at Worcester College of Higher Education.

The key aims of the project are:

1   To develop a cost-effective strategy to evaluate and improve the quality and effectiveness of early learning available to 3- and 4-year-old children in a wide range of education and care settings across Scotland and Northern Ireland, England and Wales;
2   To evaluate and compare rigorously and systematically the quality of early learning provided in a diverse range of early childhood education and care settings across the UK.

The project provides a clear and targeted strategy for change and improvement which builds upon the existing range of provision for young children and attempts to extend the skills and expertise of all those who work with them. It brings together education and care provision, and includes those in the voluntary, public and private sectors but has at its heart the development of high quality learning experiences for all young children. Given this, the evaluation and development of the curriculum offered to 3- to 5-year-olds in all early childhood settings forms a major part of its action.

In short, the EEL Project trains participating practitioners in a range of research methods, including structured observations, focused interviews, documentary analysis and environmental checklists. The practitioners use these methods to systematically gather evidence about various aspects of their provision. This allows them to evaluate the effectiveness of the learning environment they offer to young children. This evaluation is used as the basis for an Action Plan for Improvement within their setting. Further evaluation following the implementation of the action plan provides evidence of its effectiveness. A key focus of the evaluation is the quality and scope of the curriculum they offer to the child. We train the practitioners to carry out a Child Tracking procedure (Pascal *et al.*, 1995), in which they follow a number of children through the whole of their daily programme on a number of occasions. At timed intervals the practitioner records systematically the curriculum experience of the child at that point in time. This process is repeated as the child progresses through the daily programme. The information gathered on each child's curriculum experience is collated to make up an overall picture of the scope and range of the curriculum offered within that setting. This information enables the practitioners to make judgments about:

- their curriculum coverage;
- their success in meeting the needs of individual children; and
- the quality of the children's responses to the curriculum activities offered.

When planning the EEL Project we had long discussions with our participating practitioners about the curriculum framework we would use as a basis for our evaluation strategy. This discussion led us to take on a number of considerations when making our decision. It was evident:

- that many practitioners working with under-5s do not have an educational focus to their training and that the very term 'curriculum' might be off putting to them;
- that the diverse range of settings we were working in demanded from us a flexible approach to curriculum, which provided for the range of cultural and social contexts;
- that we should build upon what was already in place within these various contexts; and
- that we should ensure that continuity and progression towards the National Curriculum were enhanced in our approach.

Having consulted widely we finally made the decision to use the 'areas of experience' described in the Rumbold Report (DES, 1990) as the basis for our approach to curriculum. The majority of practitioners and providers we were in contact with were familiar with this framework and felt that it offered a comprehensive and manageable approach to developing children's learning.

This decision has been vindicated in the implementation of the EEL Evaluation and Development process. Over 600 early childhood settings nationally, have

Table 10.1: Curriculum Coverage in Early Childhood Settings

Curriculum Area	Coverage
Moral and spiritual	4.7%
Aesthetic and creative	13.8%
Human and social	21.4%
Language and literacy	19.7%
Mathematics	10.2%
Physical	17.3%
Science	6.9%
Technology	5.9%

Note: These figures were derived from observations in 110 different education and care settings for 3- and 4-year-old children across the UK. In each setting a sample of children (five or eight) were observed four times on two different days (561 children, a total of 2244 observations). Each time the children were observed the curriculum areas they were experiencing were recorded. The total number of observations for each curriculum area were collated, and expressed as a percentage of the total number of observations.

now implemented the EEL process and all have been able to use the curriculum framework based on the 'areas of experience' as a framework to evaluate the range of learning activities they offer. Within different settings practitioners have documented the curriculum experience of individual children. They have also been able to measure the quality of the response of children to the curriculum activities offered by assessing the level of 'involvement' of the children (Laevers, 1994). This information has provided them with essential diagnostic information about:

- the breadth and quality of the learning experiences of individual children;
- the quality of the various learning experiences offered at different points in the programme;
- the quality of children's responses to the curriculum offered; and
- the extent to which the curriculum provides continuity and progression with the National Curriculum.

This has directly led practitioners to develop action plans with a clear curriculum focus. Some EEL action plans have looked at language and literacy coverage, others have focused on mathematics, others have seen the need to plan more carefully for personal and social development. It is perhaps illuminative to look at the curriculum coverage that has emerged from our initial analysis of the curriculum experiences offered within some 200 early childhood settings involved in Phase 2 of the EEL Project (see Table 10.1).

This analysis raises allows us to raise some key questions about the curriculum experiences of nursery children:

- Is the level of mathematics experiences offered sufficient given that it is a core area of the National Curriculum?
- Should early childhood educators be spending more time planning for children's moral and spiritual development?

151

- Does the emphasis on human and social learning reflect the priority accorded to this by early childhood practitioners? How far can this be followed through once children enter the National Curriculum?
- Should there be more emphasis on science given that this is a core area of the National Curriculum?

Conclusion

This discussion has raised some important issues about what constitutes a high quality curriculum for young children. Providing all our young children with appropriate and well planned learning experiences is a goal most would subscribe to. Yet, it is clear that there is much to be done if we are to achieve this in the near future. Development work is going on across the early childhood field, as the Effective Early Learning Project is testimony to, but we have found many practitioners and providers confused and uncertain about the form their curriculum should take. Early childhood practitioners are responding to the challenge and working to ensure that children receive a broad and rich range of early learning experiences. There is clear evidence that developing a curriculum framework for the under-5s can help them in this work. However, it is important that those in the field hold onto the need to tailor this to the developmental and cultural needs of the group of children they have responsibility for. Curriculum guidance may be required at a national level, but flexibility in any framework is essential. The under-5s need a curriculum which is designed to fit them, rather than being forced to fit a curriculum designed to cater for the needs of older children.

References

BALL, C. (1994) *Start Right: The Importance of Early Learning* (RSA Report), London, RSA.

BALL, C. (1995) Discussion at the Start Right International Conference, Barbican, London, September 1995.

BRUNER, J. (1996) *The Culture of Education*, Cambridge, Harvard University Press.

DEPARTMENT FOR EDUCATION (DFE) (1994) *Code of Practice on the Identification and Assessment of Special Educational Needs*, London, HMSO.

DEPARTMENT FOR EDUCATION AND EMPLOYMENT (DFEE) (1966) *Nursery Education Scheme: The Next Steps*, London, DFEE.

DEPARTMENT FOR EDUCATION AND EMPLOYMENT (DFEE) SCHOOL CURRICULUM AND ASSESSMENT AUTHORITY (SCAA) (1996) *Desirable Outcomes for Children's Learning on Entering Compulsory Schooling*, London, DFEE.

DEPARTMENT OF EDUCATION AND SCIENCE (DES) (1990) *Starting with Quality: The Rumbold Report*, London, HMSO.

HANDY, C. (1995) *Beyond Certainty: The Changing Worlds of Organisations*, London, Hutchinson.

HURST, V., BURGESS-MACEY, C. and OUVREY, M. (1996) *Quality and Diversity Project Information Pamphlet*, London, Goldsmiths College.

KATZ, L. (1995) *Talks with Teachers of Young Children: A Collection*, New Jersey, Ablex Publishing Corporation.

LAEVERS, F. (Ed) (1994) *The Innovative Project 'Experiential Education' and the Definition of Quality in Education*, Leuven, Katholieke Universiteit.

MOSS, P. and PENCE, A. (Eds) (1996) *Valuing Quality in Early Childhood Services*, London, Paul Chapman.

NATIONAL COMMISSION ON EDUCATION (1993) *Learning to Succeed*, Report of the Paul Hamlyn Foundation National Commission on Education, London, Heinemann.

PASCAL, C., BERTRAM, A.D. and RAMSDEN, F. (1994) *Effective Early Learning: The Quality Evaluation and Development Process*, Worcester, Amber Publications.

PASCAL, C., BERTRAM, A.D., RAMSDEN, F., GEORGESON, J., SAUNDERS, M. and MOULD, C. (1995) *Effective Early Learning: Evaluating and Developing Quality in Early Childhood Settings*, Worcester, Amber Publications.

SYLVA, K. and WILTSHIRE, J. (1993) 'The impact of early learning on children's later development', *European Early Childhood Education Research Journal*, 1, pp. 17–41.

TREVARTHEN, C. (1995) *How Children Learn Before School*, Text of lecture to BAECE, Newcastle University, 2 November 1995.

WEINER, G. (1994) *Feminisms in Education*, Milton Keynes, Open University Press.

11 Nursery Education and the National Curriculum

Tricia David

> This chapter considers the impact of the National Curriculum for children aged 5 to 16 and other related initiatives upon provision for children under 5 years old. The issues of the purposes of early childhood education and the importance of education and training needed by adults fulfilling the role of under-5s' educators are raised, in the light of recent research evidence and the societal context at the end of the millenium.

As we approach the millenium, we seem to be at a strange juncture in our country's attitude to, and treatment of, the youngest children in our society. More than ever before politicians of all parties are beginning to take an interest in educational provision for children in their earliest years. The cynics among us might question their reasons — has edu-care (daycare which engages children in appropriate learning opportunities) become a vote-catcher? Is it because of evidence that early learning promotes children's later achievements, including those assessed by the National Curriculum tasks and tests (e.g., Ball, 1994; Shorrocks, 1992; Schweinhart and Weikart, 1993)? Or that criminal tendencies can be curbed by early intervention (Schweinhart and Weikart, 1993)? Or have politicians woken up to the fact that the UK is being overtaken in economic terms by countries which are willing to invest in young children and that perhaps, after all, there may be something in what the advocates of nursery education have been saying for most of this century?

What Counts As Nursery Education?

As a result of the neglect of under-5s' provision in this country by every successive government (David, 1990), we are currently trying to start from a place which is very different from that in some of our competitor countries and our partner countries (David, 1993). We continue with the muddle, lack of coherence and, in some areas, lack of provision never mind choice, which has been detailed by Gillian Pugh (1988, 1992).

Ten years ago, the only forms of provision which were deemed 'nursery education' were those settings overseen by a qualified teacher and inspected by HMI for Education. Thus nursery education was regarded as nursery school, nursery class and combined (Education and Social Services) provision, mainly in the public, i.e., maintained, sector. In addition, other forms of provision ranging from private nurseries, local authority daycare, and playgroups, to workplace creches and child-minders, inspected by, and accountable to, social services departments were not recognized as nursery education.

Further, although many LEAs and schools implemented policies of admitting children into primary school reception classes at the start of the year in which they would become 5, so that many 4-year-olds now attend Year R classes, these did not have equivalent staffing ratios, equipment and/or space to what was defined as nursery education. A 1989 HMI report pointed out the influences of these factors on the experiences of the children, suggesting that those in nursery education derived greater benefits from 'work that is well planned with suitable emphasis on purposeful play and exploratory behaviour' (DES, 1989, p. 5).

Although in earlier times many nursery schools and classes had been able to offer at least the equivalent of the primary school day in attendance for children, the late 1980s model of nursery education tended to offer only sessional (morning *or* afternoon) attendance, thus making it impossible for an employed parent to use this form of provision even if it existed in their part of the country, unless the child attended a series of different settings to cover the working day. This is hardly the kind of life one would expect to promote continuity of relationships and learning, and one which would be rejected out of hand for older children.

Fragmentation of services creates both logistical and perceptual problems for everyone — not just for politicians. In attempts to remedy the incoherence, some local authorities have, during these last ten years, and especially since the implementation of the Children Act 1989 and the publishing of the Rumbold Report (DES, 1990), coodinated provision by placing their early childhood services administratively under one department. Examples include Strathclyde, Sheffield and Leeds. What such coordination can mean is that, given the will and the funding, parents with different needs and interests may find appropriate provision for their children and themselves. Parents for whom the late 1980s model of nursery education may have been desirable from the point of view of their child's learning opportunities and who wished to have appropriately trained staff working with their children, might at last find that this provision could also cover their working hours. Additionally, carefully planned coordination has meant that staff with different expertise and backgrounds can be brought together to learn from each other.

However, in some areas the forms of provision are limited, so attempts at coordination and cross-fertilization of ideas can be difficult. In particular, responses to the National Curriculum by those working with children under 5 years, to whom the National Curriculum does not apply, have been varied, depending to a great extent upon the levels of confidence, training and expertise of the staff involved.

The Early Years Curriculum: An Historical Perspective

In several of our partner European Community countries a national curriculum (usually guidelines based on areas of experience) for children in early years education settings has been published, either through long discussions and deliberations including parents as well as politicians and professionals (as in the case of Spain), or after years of experience (as in Belgium) (see David, 1993).

In the UK, although in general terms there has been a play-oriented nursery curriculum (Bruce, 1987; Curtis, 1986) based on theories of child development and learning, the first formulation of any government sponsored documentation outlining a framework national curriculum for young children was the Rumbold Report (DES, 1990), which argued for a curriculum constructed of areas of experience. In advance of this, HMI (DES, 1989) had published curricular principles and illustrations of good practice based on evidence from 300 visits to maintained provision. They used the areas of experience from an earlier HMI document (*Curriculum Matters 2*, DES, 1985) as their framework, to develop the following sections in their report: personal, human and social learning and experience; language and literacy; mathematical learning and experience; scientific learning and experience; technological learning and experience; aesthetic, creative and physical learning and experience.

As the National Curriculum for children from 5–16 was being implemented at the end of the 1980s, early years teachers initially found no problem in continuing to work thematically, basing their planning on areas of experience, to provide holistic learning experiences for children aged between 3 and 7 years, while at the same time recognizing the elements attributable to the different National Curriculum subjects in those themes and experiences (David *et al.*, 1992). In some Key Stage 1 classes there has subsequently been a retreat from this way of working as a result of other measures, such as the amount of recording, the perceptions of judgments which would be made by OFSTED inspectors (see especially Chapter 5 of this book). While greater liaison between teachers of under-5s and those working in infant school reception classes is greatly to be welcomed, we need to examine the nature of those liaisons and how they have changed over time. A sharing of observations and assessments of children's learning in order that the Year R teacher can gain a full picture of the child's achievements from both parents and early educators is essential — but what are the foci of these records and what the foci of the reception class teacher's questions?

Further pressure on under-5s' educators has come from parents wanting to have 4-year-olds engage in bouts of formal writing and number work, because of parental anxieties about the assessments at the end of Key Stage 1 (David, 1992). Yet parents are not blind to ideas about learning through play, they stress their wish that their children could 'afford the time for play' but believe achievement in our education system requires serious, formal inputs even for 4-year-olds. Colleagues in early years professions in some of our European partner countries, whose children romp to achieve once they enter primary school at 6 or 7, believe we will destroy the joy of learning and teaching in early childhood. Further contributions to the debate come from the USA, where experts like Lilian Katz (1995) and Ed Zigler (1987) argue against such formalization and curricular narrowness but they do not say that early education should be unchallenging, quite the contrary.

In this context, those working in the under-5s' sector in the UK have been subjected to more intense top–down pressure than ever before and from different quarters and at the same time there are many with years of experience in early years education who have grave doubts about the long-term effects of the range of reforms impacting on the sector as we approach the next century.

Early Childhood: Perceptions and Expectations

What happens to, or is thought to be 'right' for, young children in any society or subcultural group does so because of the childhoods constructed by that society (Nunes, 1994; Tobin *et al.*, 1989). For many years babies and young children were not accorded the powers psychologists now acknowledge. For example, Deloache and Brown (1987) and Elly Singer (1992) have documented the ways in which developmental psychology, because of its underlying assumptions and methods, failed to access those powers. Now Howard Gardner (1983) has added a further dimension to this issue by proposing the idea of multiple intelligences, most of which we in the West appear unable to foster because we cannot 'see' and do not value them.

Thus, it is likely that the dominant view of very young children has been one based on limited and outdated theories, for example some of Bowlby's ideas about maternal deprivation and children's emotional needs which have been used as arguments against the provision of nursery education in the past. Further, the idea that young children are active learners capable of constructing their own view of the world and of being creative cannot possibly inform the belief that it does not matter if children in this age-group experience numerous changes of settings — whether purporting to be educational or not — after all, the purpose of nursery provision is to prepare children, to lick them into shape in a number of ways, so that 'the reception class can begin the proper process of education' (*The Times*, 1995, p. 17).

We now know, from more recent research (e.g., Bruner and Haste, 1987; Trevarthen, 1994) that babies and young children will live 'up or down' to societal and family expectations, that they will try to please the adults around them to be valued, loved and accepted. So the curriculum we decide on for young children, both its content and its teaching approaches, may have crucial long-term consequences for our society. We have to decide what kind of people we want our children to be and to become. We have to ask ourselves how they will cope with a world we will not be here to see and experience, and above all we have to remember they may be small but they are still people who are actively trying to make sense of their world. And as the poet Kahlil Gibran writes:

You may give them your love but not your thoughts,
For they have their own thoughts . . .
For life goes not backwards nor tarries with yesterday.
You are the bows from which your children as living arrows are sent forth.
(Gibran, 1926, in the 1994 edition, p. 20)

SCAA Desirable Outcomes and the National Curriculum

Following the implementation of the National Curriculum for children aged 5–16, both the Prime Minister John Major and Secretaries of State for Education John Patten and his successor Gillian Shephard have made pronouncements about nursery education for 4-year-olds. These have been followed by the introduction of a nursery voucher scheme (discussed in Chapters 7 and 10 in this book). The aim of the scheme is to encourage the creation of wider early years provision than is currently available, with, we are told, greater choice for parents. The scheme is also intended to improve the quality of provision, though we are not so far told what the parameters of this quality might be other than through the messages which can be derived from analysis of the discourse embedded in some of the documentation relating to the nursery voucher scheme.

The two main documents I will explore here are the Schools' Curriculum and Assessment Authority's (SCAA) 1995 and 1996 publications concerning the 'desirable outcomes' of preschool experience to be expected at the start of compulsory schooling (after the child's fifth birthday).

The earlier document (SCAA, 1995) contains a letter from Gillian Shephard, Secretary of State for Education, requesting that SCAA put forward proposals relating to children under 5 and she emphasizes the expectations that, on entering statutory schooling, the children should be capable of taking advantage of the benefits afforded under the National Curriculum. Thus, in her view, there is need to pay particular attention to early numeracy and literacy developments.
The documentation claims to be free of curriculum prescription:

> A number of common features of good practice are recognised, across the
> full range of pre-compulsory school provision, as being effective in sup-
> porting children's learning. These features do not prescribe a particular or
> preferred curriculum or teaching approach. Such matters are for educators
> to decide. (SCAA, 1996, p. 6)

Additionally, the document stresses children's need to feel valued, effective liaison with parents, among team members and with professionals from other agencies, learning through play and talk, the place of observation, assessment, recording and reporting (sharing assessment with parents), the environment and equipment and staff identification of their own training needs.

The areas of experience for which the desirable outcomes are described include: personal and social development; language and literacy; mathematics; knowledge and understanding of the world; physical development; and creative development. The 'examples of good practice' which appeared in the draft document have been removed from the final version of the Desirable Outcomes booklet. They were highly criticized for a number of reasons, such as the 'white, middle class' orientation, over-emphasis on literacy skills and lack of imaginative use of the local environment. Further, there were anxieties among those responding to the draft that such examples might be used as prescriptive models by staff with minimal or no training working in some settings.

Another anxiety relating to the concept of 'desirable outcomes at 5' relates to young children with learning difficulties and the possibility that they would be labelled so early in their school careers. However the OFSTED inspections of voucher redeeming settings are intended to ensure appropriate practice with children with special needs, and also those with English as a second language — or rather that the latter are enabled in their acquisition of English, not that their bilingualism should be celebrated and made a positive feature of the education of their monolingual peers (see for example, Drummond, forthcoming).

Angela Anning's (1995) thoughtful evaluation of the draft version of the 'Desirable Outcomes' publication recognizes the need for a debate about the under-5s curriculum — and unlike the SCAA (1995 and 1996) documents themselves, she acknowledges that they are about defining an appropriate curriculum. The SCAA reticence on this issue seems strange since pages of their documentation, intended to be helpful, demonstrate the links between the desirable outcomes and the National Curriculum at Key Stage 1. Perhaps there was a fear that early childhood educators would find the idea of curriculum too challenging or that defining a curriculum might give parents the idea that such a statement should carry with it an entitlement for every child.

Multi-professionalism and Young Children's Learning

What has been made more overt by the voucher scheme and the desirable outcomes is the government's recognition that nursery education is offered by more providers than nursery schools, nursery classes and combined centres. However, childminders, through the National Child Minding Association (NCMA) representatives, await a decision as to whether or not they will qualify under the voucher scheme — the argument against this apparently being that the small number of children in their care prevents them from offering children large group experience.

The field is already multi-agency and multi-professional but there are discrepancies not only in hours of work, pay and conditions, but also in levels of education and training. Despite the workforce's wish to engage in further professional development and new routes which are being constructed through and 'up' the 'climbing frame', as discussed elsewhere in this book, the government has not pledged money within the voucher scheme for this purpose, although it is argued that the funding from the scheme should enable providers to cover the cost of training for staff.

Meanwhile this is probably the most acute requirement if the improvements in the standards of educational provision for 4-year-olds (and one hopes ultimately for children from birth to 4) are to be realized. The majority of the research on the impact of the National Curriculum on the nursery curriculum demonstrates time after time that training, or lack of training rather, is the key to any problems.

Research exploring the responses of early years workers in different settings by Sylva *et al.* (1992) showed us how experienced, qualified teachers knew and felt confident about the National Curriculum requirements for children aged over 5 and recognized that the play experiences they offered their pupils were laying foundations which were entirely appropriate. However, other workers, without the grounding of the teachers, bent to pressures which they felt forced them to adopt inappropriate formal teaching methods and to use the attainment targets as goals, even though the National Curriculum Council did not intend these to apply to children under 5.

The results of this research were corroborated by that carried out by Diane Shorrocks (1992) and Cynthia Knight (1993), both working in inner city schools in different areas of the country. They found in each case that children who had attended maintained nurseries operating a play-based curriculum achieved higher results in the majority of the assessment tasks than their peers who had not attended this type of provision. Thus the question is raised, to what extent is the presence of a qualified teacher, that is, someone with a depth of knowledge about young children's learning and about subject matter/curriculum content, a necessary element in early childhood education? (see Chapter 5 for a further discussion of this question).

Other research which demonstrates the importance of training and sharing ideas about practice with colleagues is that carried out by Barbara Hull (1990) who found a teachers' support group impacted upon the development of science teaching and the use of natural materials in reception classes. Kleinberg and Menmuir (1995) found staff in settings for children under 5 lacked knowledge and skills in mathematics and wanted more training. This need is reiterated by Penny Munn (1996), who highlights the differences in interpretation of assessments of children's abilities in numeracy and argues that training is needed so that practitioners can understand and provide for children's concepts and skills. As she states, if this does not happen the result of the baseline assessment process tied to the desirable outcomes (see Chapter 7) will be that children's abilities will appear and disappear.

Sarah Tann (1990) and Julie Ollis (1990), having undertaken different research studies, both point to the losses which are occurring in the early years curriculum. For example, Ollis (1990) argues that activities and observations teachers would have noted in the past concerning motor development, movement, sensory coordination, creative imagination and self-expression are less frequent in early years classrooms. Tann (1990) claims that the '3Rs' had remained a priority during the years of the 'broader' National Curriculum, before the Dearing Review, so that now one may be sure literacy and numeracy will be dominant features in the curriculum for children aged 3 to 7. We have no evidence that spending more time focusing entirely on these actually improves children's abilities in them — in fact, what evidence we do have points in the opposite direction (e.g., DES, 1978; Tizard *et al.*, 1988).

In their study for which data were collected in 1989 in nursery and reception classes, West and Varlaam (1991) found that in order to help children from disadvantaged families gain the most from early education high levels of professional support were needed by everyone involved. The nursery school and class staff, and one reception class teacher, covered the core National Curriculum areas (maths, science and English) using cross-curricular approaches, whereas the rest of the reception class teachers tended to focus on more formal types of activity.

Writing in 1993, Jackie Eyles concludes that early years practitioners do see play as a worthwhile and important activity for children's learning in the years from birth to 7, but raises the possibility that a 'back to basic' curriculum will force its decline.

In Andrew Pollard's detailed longitudinal ethnographic study of five children passing through the education system from the age of 4 to 7, we are told that the reception class teacher was warm and caring and that the children trusted her and that she provided 'a steady routine for the children with plenty of work on basic skills' (Pollard and Filer, 1996, p. 108). One of the children, Hazel, was only 4 years 4 months old when she entered this class and by the end of that we are told the teacher was 'still trying to get Hazel to concentrate on her work . . . being firm with her' and that Hazel's attitude to maths 'was one of bored incomprehension and disinterest' (Pollard and Filer, 1996, p. 109). One wonders how much of a child's early learning time we waste because of inappropriately formalizing the learning activities.

In their carefully argued book, Anne Edwards and Peter Knight (1994) stress the complexity of early childhood education and the fact that we cannot simply preside over children's 'development' — such a statement is summed up in the moral argument that not to act is a political act. We can no longer believe that children grow and develop naturally to do or to be one thing or another, and we must accept that the decisions we take, the experiences we offer, the interactions we have with them shape their understanding and their approaches to learning. We need information and open, critical minds in order to make those decisions. Our own education as early childhood educators is therefore crucial, as Edwards and Knight argue:

> early years educators should be regarded as professionals. We believe that mastery of the relevant knowledge base is a necessary condition if an occupation is to be ranked as a profession . . . Curriculum, in the sense of content and ways of working, has to be planned . . . because classrooms (*for young children*) are so often on the edge of chaos, there has to be a place for spontaneity and intuition. Yet one feature of the edge of chaos is that it is organised . . . without denying the sheer exuberance of young children, we want to insist that to work to best effect in these conditions requires a deliberate, knowledgeable and intelligent cast of mind. It needs professionals. (Edwards and Knight, 1994, p. 156)

Thinking about the Future: Despair or Hope?

During the next few years there will be a need for the evaluation and monitoring of the effects of the voucher scheme, the SCAA desirable outcomes and developments in baseline assessment, together with the new inspection arrangements. The main effects we should look for relate to the benefits to the children themselves and to their families, and to society as a whole.

For the time being, on the evidence so far, should we despair or have hope for the future? There is a feeling that while the research indicates the need for enhanced training opportunities for staff as a key to raising children's achievements, the will and the funding to provide this may not be forthcoming. Once well-qualified, staff may expect appropriate levels of pay and, in any case, policy makers may not yet be convinced of the complexity of young children's learning and the need for properly educated staff. Already there are advertisements in Yellow Pages for private provision which hopes to attract parents by claiming to teach the National Curriculum. Who can blame them or the parents who use them?

At the same time there are many exciting and forward-looking ventures in cooperation and collaboration, such as the Kent Fora which bring together the range of different workers, parents and politicians in an area to meet, train, plan and prioritize, according to their knowledge of the children, families and the locality. Further ventures are the Effective Early Learning Project (Chapter 10) and the Quality in Diversity Project (Chapter 12). This is reminiscent of the Swedish project begun by Gunilla Dahlberg and Gunnar Asen (1994), because it is about people taking decisions into their own hands, a way from which the children will learn through their role modelling, that whatever curriculum is set in place, in the end, in order to be successful, any measures must gain the support of those for whom they are intended (whether teacher, parent or child). What many children are learning from the discussions, negotiations and struggles they are now witnessing is that they can grow into people who think and act.

References

ANNING, A. (1995) *The Key Stage Zero Curriculum: A Response to the SCAA Draft Proposals on Pre-school Education*, London, ATL.

BALL, C. (1994) *Start Right: The Importance of Early Learning*, London, RSA.

BRUCE, T. (1987) *Early Childhood Education*, London, Hodder and Stoughton.

BRUNER, J. and HASTE, H. (Eds) (1987) *Making Sense*, London, Methuen.

CURTIS, A. (1986) *A Curriculum for the Preschool Child*, Windsor, NFER/Nelson.

DAHLBERG, G. and ASEN, G. (1994) 'Evaluation and regulation: A question of empowerment', in MOSS, P. and PENCE, A. (Eds) *Valuing Quality in the Early Years*, London, Paul Chapman.

DAVID, T. (1990) *Under Five — Under-educated?*, Milton Keynes, Open University Press.

DAVID, T. (1992) 'What do parents want their children to learn in pre-school in Belgium and the UK?', *Paper presented at the XXth World Congress of OMEP*, Arizona, 1992.

DAVID, T. (Ed) (1993) *Educating our Youngest Children: European Perspectives*, London, Paul Chapman.

DAVID, T., CURTIS, A. and SIRAJ-BLATCHFORD, I. (1992) *Effective Teaching in the Early Years*, Stoke-on-Trent, Trentham Books.

DELOACHE, J.S. and BROWN, A.L. (1987) 'The early emergence of planning skills in children', in BRUNER, J. and HASTE, H. (Eds) *Making Sense*, London, Methuen.

DEPARTMENT OF EDUCATION AND SCIENCE (DES) (1978) *Primary Education in England*, London, HMSO.

DEPARTMENT OF EDUCATION AND SCIENCE (DES) (1985) *Curriculum Matters 2*, London, HMSO.

DEPARTMENT OF EDUCATION AND SCIENCE (DES) (1989) *Aspects of Primary Education: The Education of Children Under Five*, London, HMSO.

DEPARTMENT OF EDUCATION AND SCIENCE (DES) (1990) *Starting with Quality* (Rumbold Report), London, HMSO.

DRUMMOND, M.J. (forthcoming) 'An undesirable outcome', *Forum*.

EDWARDS, A. and KNIGHT, P. (1994) *Effective Early Years Education* Buckingham, Open University Press.

EYLES, J. (1993) 'Play — A trivial pursuit or meaningful experience?', *Early Years*, **13**, pp. 45–9.

GARDNER, H. (1983) *Frames of Mind: The Theory of Multiple Intelligences*, New York, Basic Books.

GIBRAN, K. (1926) *The Prophet*, London, Heinemann.

HULL, B. (1990) 'The National Curriculum: Its effect on infant teachers and their practice', *Early Years*, **11**, pp. 39–44.

KATZ, L. (1995) 'A global view: An agenda for tomorrow and the future', *Paper presented at the RSA Start Right Conference*, London, September.

KLEINBERG, S. and MENMUIR, J. (1995) 'Perceptions of maths in pre-fives settings', *Education 3–13*, **23**, pp. 29–35.

KNIGHT, C. (1993) 'Educational performance in inner city schools: An analysis of the 1991 SATs results', *OMEP UPDATES*, **59**, pp. 1–2.

MUNN, P. (1996) 'The interactive context of teaching and learning at the pre-school level', *Education 3–13*, **24**, pp. 20–7.

NUNES, T. (1994) 'The relationship between childhood and society', *Van Leer Foundation Newsletter*, Spring 1994, pp. 16–17.

OLLIS, J. (1990) 'Reconciling early years teaching with National Curriculum requirements', *Early Years*, **10**, pp. 5–8.

POLLARD, A. and FILER, A. (1996) *The Social World of Children's Learning*, London, Cassell.

PUGH, G. (1988) *Services for Under Fives: Developing a Coordinated Approach*, London, National Children's Bureau.

PUGH, G. (Ed) (1992) *Contemporary Issues in the Early Years*, London: National Children's Bureau/Paul Chapman.

SCHOOL CURRICULUM AND ASSESSMENT AUTHORITY (SCAA) (1995) *Draft Proposals for Desirable Outcomes of Preschool Learning*, London, SCAA.

SCHOOL CURRICULUM AND ASSESSMENT AUTHORITY (SCAA) (1996) *Nursery Education Desirable Outcomes for Children's Learning on Entering Compulsory Schooling*, London, SCAA.

SCHWEINHART, L.J. and WEIKART, D.P. (1993) *A Summary of Significant Benefits: The High/Scope Perry Preschool Study through Age 27*, Ypsilanti MI, High/Scope Foundation.

SHORROCKS, D. (1992) 'Evaluating Key Stage 1 Assessments: The testing time of May 1991', *Early Years*, **13**, pp. 16–20.

SINGER, E. (1992) *Child Development and Daycare*, London, Routledge.

SYLVA, K., SIRAJ-BLATCHFORD, I. and JOHNSON, S. (1992) 'The impact of the UK National Curriculum on pre-school practice: Some top–down processes at work', *International Journal of Early Childhood*, **24**, pp. 41–51.

TANN, S. (1990) 'Assessment-led schooling? Reflections on Term 1 of the National Curriculum for 5-year-olds', *Early Years*, **10**, pp. 9–13.

THE TIMES EDITORIAL (1995) 'Three kind mice', *The Times*, 12 September.

TIZARD, B., BLATCHFORD, P., BURKE, J., FARQUHAR, C. and PLEWIS, I. (1988) *Young Children at School in the Inner City*, Hove, Lawrence Erlbaum.

TOBIN, D., WU, D. and DAVIDSON, D. (1989) *Preschool in Three Cultures: Japan, China and the United States*, Yale University Press.

TREVARTHEN, C. (1994) 'The need to learn about culture', *Keynote Address at the Living and Learning, Birth to Five, NCB/NES Arnold Conference*, Nottingham University, July.

WEST, A. and VARLAAM, A. (1991) 'Educational Provision for 4-Year-Olds', *Research Papers in Education*, Vol. 6, pp. 99–131.

ZIGLER, E. (1987) 'Formal schooling for 4-year-olds? No', *American Psychologist*, **42**, pp. 254–60.

12 A New Deal for Children and Practitioners? Practitioners Working towards a High Quality Curriculum for Children under 8

Vicky Hurst

The aim of this chapter is to describe an initiative towards practitioner self-development and re-moralization in a time of radical central government reform of education. Both the process and the content of this initiative are relevant to the future of early childhood education. Indeed, the single fact that the initiative is the responsibility of the Early Childhood Education Forum characterizes it as a first step along a new path. In so divided a field, in which competition for inadequate resources has set colleague against colleague, this is a step of no little consequence in itself. However, in addition to the significance of the project as an initiative, its detailed work offers an interesting perspective on how the curriculum in early childhood may be seen in terms of the application of principles of children's entitlement to curriculum plans and practice.

Introduction: From Tension to New Growth

Earlier sections of this book have highlighted some of the tensions in early childhood education that have resulted from the interpreting of the curriculum for children under 8 in a narrow and formal way. This chapter argues that a realization of these tensions provides the opportunity for a new approach to the education of young children which enhances and extends learning opportunities. Such an approach should aim to ensure that a curriculum focus on acquiring subject knowledge, understanding and skill is informed by underpinning aims to provide young children with the full range of learning opportunities suitable for their age. This could be achieved through giving children's emotional and social experiences their due weight as powerful incentives to learning and to the formation of lifelong attitudes and behaviour. To do this, we need a new development in educational thinking which can enable practitioners to tune their provision much more sensitively to the learning needs of individuals and groups of children. We must develop new criteria of quality which relate to real children's actual experiences, so that practitioners can accurately evaluate and then improve the quality of what children receive in their settings.

The potential for improvement may be judged from the marked difference in the learning of young children who have had a well-reasoned and developmentally appropriate curriculum as compared with those who have not (Jowett and Sylva, 1986; Sylva and Nabuco, 1995). Sylva and Nabuco have also shown that the more formal kinds of curriculum produce lower levels of social acceptance and competence which lead to higher levels of anxiety, which itself in turn makes it harder for children to learn and harder for practitioners to teach. A more developmental approach to the curriculum would not only benefit children; it would also make the work of early childhood practitioners less stressful if children under 8 were agreed to require a less formal curriculum. Hence this proposal that we heed the views of practitioners, some findings about which are to be discussed below, and move towards a better-founded conceptual framework for the early years curriculum. Both the children and the practitioners deserve a new deal, one which is founded on what is known about how young children learn most effectively. A reconsideration of previously held opinions about elementary knowledge and skills and about the nature of appropriate curricula for young children is inherent in this proposal. So is an exploration of the issues surrounding the nature and importance of play in human development and learning, and those about how children can be treated as competent participants in the learning process, and what the implications of such a view are. At present, the emphasis in both curriculum and practice for young children neglects the incomparable opportunities that developmental insights offer for improving early learning, and we need to consider what the consequences of this are and what can be done about them.

Since the development from 1988 onwards of central government policies based on testing of children in Key Stage 1 (age 7) of the National Curriculum in England and Wales, children in all kinds of settings for under-8s have come under pressure as anxieties have been transmitted down the age-range. Anxious parents and anxious infant teachers feel in their different ways that it is their duty to get children started on formal learning at ever earlier stages. Now that a central government curriculum for 4-year-olds has been added (DFEE/SCAA, 1996), the pressure extends to ever younger children, their practitioners and parents. It is vital to try to reduce the pressure towards formalizing the curriculum by establishing that effective education in early childhood does not consist of merely transmitting a formal curriculum or a diluted preparation for it in terms of preschool 'basic skills'. If we do not put a positive developmental model of early childhood education in the place of the formal model we may find that we have created a generation of children among whom many have not received their entitlement to educational opportunities because what was offered was not accessible to them.

Why an Entitlement Approach Is So Important

An informal and entitlement-based approach is vital at the beginnings of children's education, since, if early education confirms disadvantage rather than seeking to reduce it, the effects are likely to extend throughout a child's education. Parents see education as their children's best hope of a fulfilling life; even where children, their families and their communities have not had to contend with the effects of poverty, disability or bias, this promise is more easily redeemed through a curriculum which is entitlement-based rather than formal in conception. Efforts must be made to ensure that children are not being unfairly deprived of opportunities for learning because of their class, disability, race or gender, or because the assumptions on which their education is founded are unsuitable for their ages and stages of development.

Early childhood practitioners represented in the Early Childhood Education Forum, an umbrella group of early childhood organisations, are concerned that an over-formal curriculum in the years before 8 can have the effect of stunting the development of learning in children who, for developmental reasons, are not yet able to make confident links between their personal experi-ences and formalized expression of thinking. The damaging impact of premature exposure to formal methods of teaching is compounded by two other factors; the unusually early age at which children start school in England and Wales and the absence of a strong and coherent view of what early childhood education should be. These two factors are interconnected, for early admission to infant school inhibits the development of appropriate under-5s' education and care provision, while the failure to describe the early years curriculum in terms which can be applied by infant teachers and headteachers has led them to accept that it is their role to 'deliver' the top–down National Curriculum in increasingly subject-based ways, although this 'delivery' demands an approach very different from the principles most would claim to be-lieve in. Although there is relatively little publicity about the problems of under-achievement and alienation in under-8s settings, it is at this stage that these problems begin, and it is at this stage that they should be tackled.

We must also bear in mind the conclusions of the Carnegie Corporation's wide review (1994) of all the available research on learning in under-2s, which found that poor provision and low levels of stimulation in some settings for the youngest children were associated with actual failure of neural pathways to develop: in effect, the starvation of children's brains can have a lasting effect, just as with their bodies. There are various ways in which children's minds can be starved. Those which concern early years practitioners come from unsuitable concepts of the cur-riculum, formal tendencies in practice, and problems caused by low levels of resourcing, training and support in the settings they attend. These problems can be dealt with, but they require urgent action on more than one front.

4-Year-Olds and Formal Learning

Consider the following scenario which incorporates two observations made in dif-ferent settings.

> Thomas and Ummayal are 4. They have recently joined a group setting for
> 4-year-olds. The children's ages range from Thomas, aged 4 years 2 months,
> upwards. The practitioner *believes* in learning through play and in plan-
> ning from observation but, like the teachers observed by Wood, *et al.*

(1996), she *knows* that her responsibility is to get them settled into school behaviour and to start them with 'the basics' before they get to Key Stage 1 work in their next setting. Today one of the activities to be completed is to do a picture and write your name on it. Parents have all been asked to make sure children can write their names, among other achievements. Thomas can't get the hang of this, it seems — the whole idea of going off to do some drawing and writing to order is beyond his capacity at present. He looks from side to side, seeking support from Ummayal and the other two children. His chest heaves anxiously; Ummayal is sympathetic, but she can't help him because she can't see his difficulty. She is enjoying herself: she has two older sisters and has been playing schools at home for ages. She likes pretending to be very strict and neat and identifies with the teacher. Her writing, which she learned at home from her sisters, is quite proficient and she is a confident writer of the words she already knows. Thomas's fingers are much less dextrous and he has never played schools, or wanted to. He likes to play outdoors, learning through physical activity and exploration, and his social relationships with other children. When his Mum asks him to practise his writing he says he can't, and becomes panicky and resentful when pressed. His Mum worries that he will turn out like his brother, who is about to go into Key Stage 2 with a reputation for being very slow and for lashing out occasionally in frustration. She can't bear to think that her family is being identified as a problem family — she doesn't think her boys are stupid or bad, just 'slow developers'. Thomas' practitioner is concerned too, and fears that he is already getting behind. Ummayal's father, who works in child health, is concerned that Ummayal is becoming a perfectionist workaholic, and that she is always concerned with saying things right rather than saying what she thinks. He worries that this may make her nervy — at her age he played all day in and around his home.

The difficulties faced by these children, their parents and the practitioner, and by many others like them, stem largely from the factors highlighted above which I summarize as follows

- a restricted formal interpretation of the curriculum from birth to 8 as being almost entirely about acquiring certain 'basic skills' and being able to demonstrate a narrow range of subject knowledge;
- the downwards thrust of the requirements of hard-pressed teachers of older children;
- the premature admission of very young children to formal schooling;
- the exclusion of understanding of child development from current concepts of the curriculum which has led to devaluing the central role of emotion in learning;
- the absence of an adequate picture of the early years curriculum as a result of which play, social interaction, communication, exploration, representation

and all the other ways children learn are seen as peripheral instead of as central to the curriculum.

Qualifications of Early Years Practitioners

To all this should be added the inappropriate training of many who work in the early years of education (Blenkin and Yue, 1994). This is a particularly damaging factor, because of the much greater dependence on adults of children under the age of 8.

For the under-8s as a whole it is the relationship with one or more adults (according to their stage of development) which is the main educational opportunity. Through their dependence on adults children learn about getting on with the people they are close to, their own natures and potential, their capacity to contribute to others, the world around them, and how to learn effectively. But it is not just any adult who can successfully maintain this demanding role. For these relationships to be educational, children need to feel a sense of closeness and identification and to be close to those who can provide a high quality education that covers the full range of learning through informal methods. For this to happen practitioners must be:

- trained to teach through playful, imaginative relationships with a group of young children (Blenkin and Whitehead, 1996);
- able to base their teaching on experiences which reflect children's home learning and to work in close partnership with parents (Little and Meighan, 1995);
- mature, sensitive and generous enough to accept their emotional commitment to children as individuals, which can involve pain as children move on (Elfer, 1996);
- confident in their understanding of how a developmental early years curriculum lays the foundation of later achievement (Early Years Curriculum Group (EYCG), 1989; Athey, 1990);
- supported with appropriate ratios of trained staff, good indoor and outdoor playspace, sufficient resources and equipment, and in-service training (EYCG, 1992).

Yet of these adults who are the key to successful learning for young children in settings across the full range of provision of care and education for the under-8s, comparatively few are trained for an early years specialism (Blenkin and Yue, 1994), while since the coming of the National Curriculum there has been an abrupt disappearance of the opportunities they need for professional development in their age-phase specialism. In-service education has a strong role to play in developing practitioners' understanding of this crucial stage of learning, and has in the past brought together participants from the maintained, voluntary and private sectors of care and education. Now, the funded courses are related to subject areas, and early childhood practitioners, many of whom work for very low pay, have to fund themselves or go without age-phase specialist courses. Indeed, even in initial teacher training, 'specialism' is almost universally seen as relating only to subject specialism. This is doubly dangerous since, in contrast to later stages of education, the ratios, qualifications, accommodation and resources available are permitted by central government to vary greatly between different forms of provision.

Changing the Early Childhood Scene

There are various ways of trying to tackle these very serious problems. Vigorous efforts must be made to convince government and policy-makers at all levels of the importance of investment in developmentally appropriate provision for young children. At the same time, if we are to improve the quality of early childhood education, it makes sense to pay attention as well to the beliefs, difficulties and felt needs of the practitioners who make the immediate decisions which affect children's educational opportunities. This route, from within the early childhood settings and the organizations which provide them, may offer avenues of change which have not been explored before.

Beginning with the Practitioners

This section describes the work and preliminary findings of the Quality in Diversity Project, a collaborative project undertaken by a large group of practitioners to improve and develop educational provision for children from birth to the age of 8 years old.[1] There are two features about this project to be emphasized.

The first distinctive feature is its practitioner-based, collaborative nature. This means that this approach is very different from attempts to improve education through centrally determined policy, as in the case of the Department for Education and Employment's initiative in the education of 4-year-olds (DFEE/SCAA, 1996). It is a process of change from within and, with all the difficulties inevitable with so large and diverse a group of practitioners, it holds out hope as a model of how practitioners may take a more active role in the future development of early childhood education through using similar processes in local networks.

The second distinctive feature is that the findings show that this representative group of practitioners agrees that education and care for children under 8 must lay equal emphasis on the emotional and personal sides of children's lives within an anti-bias approach if learning is to be successful and lasting. This contrasts with the view which would restrict the goals of learning to 'subjects' and which sees personal and social development and learning as just one extra item. Yet the idea on which the project's work is based is not to put forward a new curriculum for early childhood education but to construct a tool with which all practitioners can improve and develop their work by placing it within a framework for early learning which gives weight to children's emotional and social needs, and to their distinctive ways of learning.

In describing Quality in Diversity, I shall begin by explaining the context and intentions of the project and how we have been working towards our aims through collaboration between groups of practitioners. Second, I shall describe some perspectives from the project, and the significance of these perspectives to the current debate about how to ensure quality for learning in the early years. Thirdly, I shall end by drawing attention to some of the significant features of the nature and origins of the project, and suggest some conclusions that deserve consideration.

The Context of the Development of Quality in Diversity

The need for a united view on early childhood education and care has been broadly agreed among practitioners for some time, and has acquired growing urgency because of concern about the cumulative effects of our downwardly derived and assessment-driven approach to the curriculum on provision for the learning of the youngest children (EYCG, 1993, for instance). How such an initiative might take place has been more debatable, since the strong expressions of professional concern have had little impact upon policy so far.

The major early childhood organizations have, however, begun to collaborate and have formed the Early Childhood Education Forum (ECEF), an umbrella group which represents the voluntary, private and maintained education and care sectors concerned with the under-8s. This body has initiated a new development in the history of early childhood education in England and Wales, a collaborative project by practitioners to establish an agreed conceptual framework for care and education for young children — the Quality in Diversity Project.

The project aims to help to remedy practitioners' present problems and children's difficulties by creating a continuum of appropriate provision for learning for all children from birth to 8 which will improve practice in general and will in particular provide a greater equality of opportunity for all children. Participants believe that all provision of education and care for children under 8 should be developmentally appropriate — it should be planned and provided according to individual children's needs for learning and development. We wish to encourage practitioners to reflect on their work and move towards improving planning and practice by taking children's emotional, social, physical, communicative and intellectual needs more closely into consideration.

Our intention is to do this by:

- developing a better understanding of how best to meet children's learning needs in the early years of education;
- seeking a common view of the characteristics of appropriate curricula for young children (the *Framework for Early Learning*);
- involving practitioners from the statutory, voluntary and independent sectors in collaborating to develop the *Framework*;

- making the *Framework* accessible to practitioners and other adults working with children, parents, providers, governors, advisers and inspectors of services.

The Structure and Processes of the Project

At the earliest stages in 1993 the model for the project was the development by Margaret Carr and Helen May of the *New Zealand Government Draft Guidelines for Developmentally Appropriate Programmes in Early Childhood Services* (New Zealand Ministry of Education, 1993). On the model of this practitioner-led approach the member organizations of the ECEF nominated representatives to be working members of the project. These practitioners were from the many different groups involved in early childhood education — childminders, infant and nursery teachers, nursery nurses, nursery assistants, playgroup leaders, teachers in private schools, and after-school playworkers for 5 to 8-year-olds.

These representatives have been meeting as a whole group (approximately ninety people), and also in three age-phase working groups for those working with children 0–3, 3–5, and 5–8 (approximately thirty people in each). There are also three age-phase writing groups (variable numbers between three and eight, depending on people's availability) consisting of volunteers from each working group. The functions of the three different levels are broadly differentiated into drafting (writing groups), brainstorming and commenting on drafts (working groups) and developing and reworking the Foundations of Early Learning which are at the heart of the framework (the whole group). It will be seen that the drafting related initially to age-phase issues; the drafts contribute to the thinking which is reflected in the parts of the framework which surround and support the Foundations of Early Learning.

The Foundations of Early Learning

The Foundations, which are given below, are the value-base of the Quality in Diversity approach. They show our ideas about how children are entitled to be helped to develop a wide range of essential understandings, qualities and abilities at the same time as they develop in subject-based knowledge, understanding and skill. We hope that in future the Foundations will become agreed general principles for education and care for under-8s, and will be used, not to replace practitioners' normal curriculum and their planning processes, but to inform and illuminate the thinking behind the curriculum and the planning. We are fully committed to diversity, and wish to offer practitioners a way to examine their work and improve it, without taking from them their autonomy and responsibility in their work. This is the kind of diversity that we hope to support; on the other hand we strongly oppose any suggestion that autonomy of practitioners can be taken to mean that there are no standards of what is acceptable and what is not. Our *Framework* is a structure that can help diversity to flourish by extending practitioners' awareness of the non-negotiable areas of good practice without infringing the individuality of their settings.

- Belonging and connecting: young children are learning to make good relationships with other children and with adults, in families, communities and group settings. They are learning to be members of their linguistic and cultural groups;
- Being and becoming: young children are learning self-respect, and feelings of self-worth and identity. They are learning care of self, and to be safe and well;
- Being active and expressing: young children are learning to be mentally and physically active. They are learning to express their ideas and feelings, alone and with others;
- Thinking, imagining and understanding: young children are learning to think, to imagine, and to reflect on their experiences. They are learning to understand themselves and the world around them, and to enjoy their learning;
- Contributing and participating: young children are learning to contribute, to support each other, and when to take the initiative. They are learning to be responsible for themselves and others, and to make choices and understand how their choices affect others. (Early Childhood Education Forum, 1996)

The project is now developing the *Framework for Early Learning* which will seek to show how these statements can inform diverse views of the curriculum and help practitioners in different settings to orient their concepts of the curriculum towards more developmental approaches. The Foundations are being developed into broad entitlement goals for learning which can be applied to plans and to observed practice so that practitioners can see how successful they are being at meeting the full range of children's entitlements.

The Framework for Early Learning and the Quality of Early Education: Going Beyond Good Intentions

The Framework for Early Learning is one of many possible first steps in the search for a new approach to early education. In itself, it cannot change practice or policy. Nor is it a curriculum which can be subscribed to. In fact, it is a challenge to practitioners and providers: it states a set of principles which are the good intentions of a representative group of practitioners, but the action is all to come later, for good intentions by themselves will make little difference. The impact of the document is to be determined by its users; they — the practitioners and providers — can, if they wish, use it to inform their practice and develop their provision through training and support. At local levels, practitioners and providers can network together through discussing how the *Framework* applies to their settings. At local and national levels, the major organizations across the sectors can, if they wish, use the statement of good intentions to win from policy-makers and administrators the support and training that is most needed, showing that the quality of provision depends on their action.

How the *Framework* could operate to enhance and enrich practice can be seen in the example of its relationship to the National Curriculum and to the Desirable Outcomes for Learning. The National Curriculum is a binding legal responsibility on practitioners, and the desirable outcomes are the headings under which voucher-receiving settings are to be inspected and judged. The *Framework* has the aim of making plans and practice under these and other curricular commitments more supportive of learning according to the entitlement goals. These goals will help practitioners to meet the full range of children's needs and entitlements as well as their statutory commitments.

This may seem a modest aim. It is not. Many, though not all, early childhood practitioners have become demoralized by the pressure on them to teach to narrow and formal objectives, and have found themselves accepting what they would have challenged on professional grounds ten years ago; the admission of children of nursery age to infant school classes with no adaptation to suit their needs is a case in point. Perhaps the most important product of the *Framework* and of the whole project would be a change in the morale, professional self-confidence and collaborative action of practitioners and providers. Quality in Diversity's sponsors and participants are aware that a new and more assertive role for early childhood practitioners and providers is essential if young children are to receive their entitlement to a sound and appropriate education. The project, and the *Framework for Early Learning*, will, it is hoped, provide a first step towards a greater solidarity among practitioners and a stronger base for their advocacy of young children's needs and entitlements which is a crucial responsibility they bear. Both the children and the practitioners deserve a new deal, one which is founded on understanding about how young children learn most effectively and how it is the practitioners who have the responsibility for articulating and implementing this understanding. It is a weighty responsibility at any time and particularly so now, when pressures in early education work against the informal, personal, homelike and playful ways in which children learn best. Those who have been involved in Quality in Diversity hope that both the *Framework for Early Learning* and the processes of discussion, consultation, testing and articulation which formed it will help practitioners carry out this responsibility. If they are able to become more self-confident and articulate the results could transform their own lives as well as improving the educational opportunities of young children.

Note

1 The Quality in Diversity Project Team are Vicky Hurst, Marjorie Ouvry and Celia Burgess-Macey who are based at Goldsmiths' College, London University. The project

participants have been meeting together since November 1994 to agree processes of collaboration, establish shared principles for early childhood education and care, and to develop and elaborate the Foundations of Early Learning. The Framework for Early Learning will be published in 1997.

References

ATHEY, C. (1990) *Extending Thought in Young Children*, London, Paul Chapman.

BLENKIN, G.M. and WHITEHEAD, M. (1996) 'Creating a context for development', in BLENKIN, G.M. and KELLY, A.V. (Eds) *Early Childhood Education: A Developmental Curriculum* (2nd ed.), London, Paul Chapman.

BLENKIN, G.M. and YUE, N.Y.L.U. (1994) 'Profiling early years practitioners: Some first impressions from a national survey', *Early Years*, **15**, pp. 13–22.

CARNEGIE CORPORATION (1994) *Starting Points: Meeting the Needs of our Youngest Children*, New York, Carnegie Corporation.

DEPARTMENT FOR EDUCATION AND EMPLOYMENT (DFEE)/SCHOOL CURRICULUM AND ASSESSMENT AUTHORITY (SCAA) (1996) Desirable Outcomes for Children's Learning on Entering Compulsory Education, London, DFEE/SCAA.

EARLY CHILDHOOD EDUCATION FORUM/QUALITY IN DIVERSITY PROJECT (1996) 'Draft working party papers', Unpublished.

EARLY YEARS CURRICULUM GROUP (1989) *Early Childhood Education: The Early Years Curriculum and the National Curriculum*, Stoke on Trent, Trentham Books.

EARLY YEARS CURRICULUM GROUP (1992) *First Things First: Educating Young Children*, Oldham, Madeleine Lindley.

EARLY YEARS CURRICULUM GROUP (1993) *Early Education in Jeopardy*, Oldham, Madeleine Lindley.

ELFER, P. (1996) 'Building intimacy in relationships with young children', *Early Years*, **16**, pp. 30–4.

JOWETT, S. and SYLVA, K. (1986) 'Does kind of preschool matter?', *Educational Research*, **28**, pp. 21–31.

LITTLE, J. and MEIGHAN, J. (1995) 'Developing appropriate home–school partnerships', in GAMMAGE, P. and MEIGHAN, J. (Eds) *Early Childhood Education: The Way Forward*, Derby, Education Now.

NEW ZEALAND MINISTRY OF EDUCATION (1993) *Te Whariki: Draft Guidelines for Developmentally Appropriate Programmes in Early Childhood Services*, Wellington, Learning Media.

SYLVA, K. and NABUCO, M. (1995) 'Comparisons between ECERS ratings of individual preschool centres and the results of Target Child Observations: Do they match or do they differ?', *5th European Conference on the Quality of Early Childhood Education*, Paris, La Sorbonne, September 7–9.

WOOD, E., BENNETT, N. and ROGERS, S. (1996) *Reception Teachers' Theories of Play*, Buckingham, Open University Press.

List of Contributors

Theo Cox	Honorary Departmental Research Fellow at the University of Wales Swansea
Tricia David	Professor of Early Childhood Education at Canterbury Christ Church College, Canterbury
Mary Jane Drummond	Tutor in Primary Education at the Cambridge Institute of Education
Gill Harper Jones	Lecturer in education and Co-tutor to the Primary PGCE Course (Early Years) at the University of Wales Swansea
Vicky Hurst	Director of the Early Childhood Education Project 'Quality in Diversity' at Goldsmiths University of London
Trisha Maynard	Lecturer in Education and Co-tutor to the Primary PGCE Course (Early Years) at the University of Wales Swansea
Christine Pascal	Professor of Education and Director of the Effective Early Learning Project at the Worcester College of Higher Education
Susan E. Sanders	Lecturer in Education and Director of the Primary PGCE course at the University of Wales Swansea
Felicity Wikeley	Research Fellow at the Centre for School Improvement at the School of Education, University of Bath

Author Index

Subject Index